THERE REALLY WAS A HOLLYWOOD

THERE REALLY WAS A HOLLYWOOD

Janet Leigh

DOUBLEDAY & COMPANY, INC.
Garden City, New York
1984

DESIGNED BY LAURENCE ALEXANDER

Library of Congress Cataloging in Publication Data

Leigh, Janet.

There really was a Hollywood.

Includes index.
1. Leigh, Janet.   2. Moving-picture actors and
actresses—United States—Biography.   I. Title.
PN2287.L35A36   1984   791.43′028′0924 [B]   84–4119
ISBN 0-385-19035-2

MANUFACTURED IN THE UNITED STATES OF
AMERICA

To my adored husband, Bob, who is my foundation.

To my cherished daughters, Kelly and Jamie,
who are as beautiful internally as externally.

To my family and my friends—
all of whom have made this life worth living.

And to the countless number of talented people
who have made this profession worth loving.

ACKNOWLEDGMENTS

I am filled with wonderment and gratitude toward Laura Van Wormer of Doubleday for her caring and for sharing her brilliant expertise; to Charles Hunt and Fifi Oscard for their belief in me; to John Malone for his support and guidance; and to Ada Tesar for the endless typing of my #3 penciled pages.

CONTENTS

PREFACE

When I started my career as an actress, a member of the crew with whom I was working came up to me and reminisced as people often do about working with my mother. Besides being in love with her for many years, he said something very significant. "Your mother is one of the few people in Hollywood that no one has anything bad to say about." I had no idea how important that statement was and as I have continued my career, I have realized how right he was and what a remarkable achievement that is.

When people examine a career in acting, they look for three things: the length of the career, the diversity of the roles, and the excellence with which those roles were performed. My mother has excelled and conquered in all of those categories. But the most important element to any career is survival, and survive she did . . . she not only carved out a startling film career and family life but she remained a lady while doing so. She entered the lion's den and tamed the lions and even taught them something about kindness. She brought please and thank you into vogue. Now don't get me wrong—when she needed to she could fight with the best of them, but somehow even a right hook was delivered with grace. While so many around her bitched their way through Hollywood, her way was paved with zest, enthusiasm, and a joy that is still as abundant as when she started. She always taught me, "Do unto others as you would have them do unto you"—and she still applies that philosophy to everything she does.

She is one of the great *ladies* on the screen and off the screen. She

has my true admiration and undying respect. I am honored to be
her daughter and friend.

JAMIE LEE CURTIS
1984

INTRODUCTION

"When are you going to write your book?" had been a recurring question over the years. Usually it came at the conclusion of an interview or after an evening of conversation with relatively new acquaintances, because the thrust of the discourse would unwaveringly be riveted on my work, my experiences, my cohorts, my travels, and my family. Not that I invited this direction. Rather, it resulted from the wish of others to know more about the universal business, "show biz."

"Oh, writing an autobiography seems so presumptuous. Anyway, I'm not sure I know how. I mean, I know how to write of course, but *write* write?" was my normal answer.

Gradually, almost defensively, however, I began to respond, "Well, it has crossed my mind."

And then it kept crossing my mind.

Obviously, the seed had definitely been planted—deep enough that the idea wasn't just going to fade away into the sunset. Something was required, even if it was just the contemplation of the idea: to write or not to write.

I found myself doing a lot of reminiscing, about people, places, turning points, the new times, the not so new times, and the old times . . .

The old times . . . Sounded like my girls teasing me whenever I gave motherly or adult reactions, "What was it like in the olden days, Mommy?"

Now I began to wonder, was it just their way of saying I wasn't "with it"? Or did they really want to know? Would it be useful for them to know?

But oh boy—writing a book! *God knows, it wasn't as if I'd have to think of a plot*—the scenario had been unfolding for over fifty years. And I certainly wouldn't have to invent characters. And I wouldn't need to conjure up exciting locations. Hollywood would do for starters.

However, I reminded myself, so much had already been written about me. Was there anything that hadn't been said? Come on, Janet, ol' girl, be honest. You *bet there was*. With all the thousands of interviews, all the media coverage, the press had never gone beyond the superficial. By necessity, the writer's goal was to entertain his readers with facts, figures, latest films, marriages, divorces, brawls, babies, etc. No reporter really had the time or the space to seek the person behind the personality.

But finding the real person. Ah, there was the rub. Reliving the highs would obviously not be difficult. But would I be up to facing the lows again? Could I find the courage to do that?

I had a need to revisit family albums and allow old but not forgotten sensations to emerge; to reread notes from my treasure box of correspondence. I came across a photograph of my grandma and grandpa and their four sons. What a strong, healthy, handsome group—dear God, I thought, they were all gone. I wished I'd known them better, wished the world had known about them.

I visualized future generations looking at such a portrait of me, and I felt the compulsion for them to understand the forces that guided *this* person, who was mother, wife, daughter, friend, and actress.

Now committed on this one level, I decided to superimpose another intent. Maybe it would be interesting for other "Jeanette Helen Morrisons" to take an unvarnished journey with me through a life, having the mysterious and curious detours unfold for them as they did for me. Because this entity, this body, could have been anyone; it just happened to be me.

In December of 1982, I walked to the corner of Sutton Place and Fifty-sixth Street in Manhattan and hailed a cab, on my way to a publisher's office. I had written 130 pages of my book, and was in the process of discussing publication with several editors.

"Hello, Miss Leigh, how are ya today?" the driver greeted me.

"Wonderful, thank you, and you?"

"Fine! What brings you to New York?"

"Well, I am writing a book, and I'm here to meet the various representatives in the literary field."

"Is it about you?" I nodded to him in the rearview mirror. "That's good news, good news." He paused. "Now ya aren't gonna go and disappoint us, are ya?"

"I'm not sure I follow you."

"Well, it's like this. We got our heroes, see? And we put you all on a pedestal 'cause that's the way we like it, see? And when one of youse goes and tells us bad things—like ya beat your kids or cheat, or you're a pervert or somethin' like that—it hurts us."

"I promise you," I said, "no one intends to do that. But it is important to tell the truth in an autobiography." Not that everybody always does, I thought to myself.

"But youse spoil the mystery. It's like, I don't wanna see naked girls paradin' around on the TV. That takes away my imagination. My wife keeps me interested 'cause everythin's not all hangin' out. Know what I mean?"

"Sure do! Maybe the problem is the way certain facts are presented." I contemplated for a moment. "You know, you really just made my day. Because I have no desire to be trashy or malicious. I must deal with whatever has to be dealt with, but hopefully, in a tasteful manner. I'm really happy to hear your opinion."

"Here we are, Forty-sixth and Park. Good luck to you. I'll be waitin' for the book."

"My thanks for your help. And happy holidays!"

It is done. Wherever you are, dear man, I hope you like it. And I hope I didn't disappoint you or shatter any dreams. No one is perfect—we have good times and we have bad times, and we all make mistakes. I hope you can understand mine. I've had to.

I

Jeanette

(It Could Happen to You)

CHAPTER ONE

"It's good to be back," proclaimed Norma Shearer one February day in 1946, sweeping into the lobby of the ski lodge. Her presence electrified everyone within range. Her beauty, her vibrancy made every privileged bystander forget the icy wind howling outside the closed doors, forget anything but the exquisite fur-clad figure before them.

"Just as I remembered," she said, approaching the reception office. "Oh, this is new," referring to a photograph of a teenage girl on the clerk's desk. "And so are you," her gaze shifting to the man behind the counter.

"Yes, ma'am," answered Fred Morrison. "And that is my daughter," he added proudly.

"What a pretty face." A pause. "She should be in pictures. May I have a copy of that photo to take with me?"

Who could foresee what this chance encounter would mean to the life of one Jeanette Helen Morrison?

"T.P."

"Tyrone Power!" Jeanette Helen Morrison yelled, racing after Nadine and tagging her before she reached the designated boundary. The game was Movie Stars. The object—to give the initials of a star which the others couldn't guess.

For Jeanette, it was usually easy to outwit her playmates because she spent hours poring over movie magazines, devouring every scrap of information about the lives of her favorite stars. She loved the vicarious thrill of reading about Hollywood parties, knowing which famous stars were dating each other, marrying each other, and seeing pictures of the lavish gowns and beautiful homes. The stories made her laugh and cry and feel the anguish, the happiness —all the joy and pain that the stars themselves felt.

It wasn't as if she thought of herself, Jeanette Helen Morrison, as actually being one of "them"; it was just complete absorption in the wonder of her imagination.

When she read a book, nothing could distract her, she was lost in that world. When she saw a movie, she could see it over and over. Captivated, she believed the stories unfolding before her. She was never aware of anyone else being in the theatre—never heard whispering or a cough or sneeze or a candy wrapper being discarded.

Thankfully, in the mid-1930s, the movies were inexpensive— only ten cents before five o'clock. And on Saturdays and Sundays you could stay all day; Helen and Fred Morrison found the movie theatre to be an ideal baby-sitter for Jeanette. They would drop her off and then have a little time for themselves. God knows they could use it. They were married at nineteen, and with a baby arriving right away, the early days were hard for them. They were always trying to find a better, yet inexpensive, apartment or house that would take children. "What do you want me to do, drown her?" Fred would say to some manager when he was confronted with "We don't allow children." And they never had much privacy. In most of the places they lived they would have to sleep in a pull-down bed in the living room, with Jeanette sleeping a few feet away in the hallway leading to the kitchen.

And so, as much as Helen and Fred loved their only baby, it was nice to be alone once in a while. The weekend movies provided Helen and Fred with those few free hours; sometimes, too often perhaps, they didn't use that precious time wisely. They were young, spirited, and the proximity and pressures got to them—too much. There was drinking, arguments. Boy, how Jeanette hated that—feared it. Their fighting shook her right down to her toes. The minute they picked her up she could tell if something was wrong, and if so her stomach would tighten and she would immediately try to turn the tide of battle and create an armistice. She would tell them all about the movie—the plot, the performers, the costumes, all the details—and about what was coming next week, hoping that her enthusiasm would somehow bridge the rift between them and make her world all right again. Because even though Jeanette gave herself over so fully to the make-believe world she saw at the movies, read in a book, or heard on the radio, she knew where reality was, and accepted it for what it was.

She loved her mom and dad, her school, where she lived and how she lived—that's what she knew, and that was fine. Jeanette was aware that Helen and Fred did everything that was humanly possible to provide for her, so how could she complain or feel deprived? Sure, it would be nice if they had a real house and didn't keep moving around. Sure, it would be nice to have new clothes more often. Sure, it would be nice to go to the grocery store and buy more than ten cents' worth of eggs. Sure, it would be nice to just pay the bills instead of juggling accounts and borrowing. At school she saw examples of how it could be better, but she also saw how it could be worse. Anyway, *this* was how it *was* . . .

But something else did bother her. She missed the companionship of other children at home. Jeanette had her homework, the radio, reading, and movies. But after school, weekends, and especially on rainy days, she envied her friends with brothers and sisters. They had built-in playmates. She wondered why she was alone —both Fred and Helen had many brothers and sisters. She loved when they all gathered and she felt as though she was a "member of a family."

John B. Morrison and Kate Reeb had four sons—Edward, Lester, George, and Fred. They had settled in Hornitos, California, a goldmining town where Joaquin Marietta, the infamous bandit, once had thrived. John was tall, proud, strong, and handsome. Kate was petite, pretty, courageous, and a gifted musician. Theirs was not necessarily an easy existence, but it was a full one—love, hard work, hard play, and exciting times. And then Kate developed cataracts in her eyes.

By the time Fred was seven, Kate was totally blind. John used all of their savings on operations, but they wouldn't go down for the count. They moved to Merced, California, a little town in the middle of the San Joaquin Valley, and there they stayed for fifty years. John went to work for the Santa Fe Railroad, the boys did their share by taking jobs after school, and the family unit pulled through. Eventually, Edward, Lester, and George married and settled elsewhere, but never too far away to have frequent reunions.

Fred stayed in Merced and married Helen Lita Westergaard. Helen's parents, Lita Coffee and William Westergaard, had both left Copenhagen, Denmark, for California in their early twenties, and there had met and subsequently married. William had come from a fine, fairly well-off family and arrived in the new world wearing his customary attire—a top hat and tails. And that's what he wore digging ditches, the only job he was qualified for in the beginning. There was the language problem, of course, and then he had never really been trained in any profession except being a "gentleman." He was attractive—rather dashing—bright and enterprising, but it was a difficult adjustment.

Lita was beautiful, possessing Scandinavian warmth, openness, and acceptance. She was the personification of patience and understanding. Together they produced their children Herman, Helen Lita, Ethel, Willie, and Pearl. Their life was never free from difficulty, but it was exuberant.

Helen and Fred presented the parents with their first girl grandchild—Jeanette. That little blond beauty was loved and coddled and spoiled by all. No wonder she so looked forward to the trips to Merced. (When Jeanette was two, Fred had moved his family to Stockton, about sixty miles away, where job opportunities were hopefully better.) Jeanette always felt as if she was "going home" when they went to see Grandma and Grandpa Morrison. There was security—the same old house, the same friends. And there was comfort—like an old, safe sofa.

As she grew older, Jeanette was allowed to spend several weeks each summer with Grandma and Grandpa Morrison. Fred and Helen would put her on the train in Stockton, and an hour later Grandpa would meet her in Merced. How they all enjoyed that! Kate and John were very proud of their only granddaughter. She was pretty and bright and loving—and she adored her grandparents. She once wrote a composition for school, "The Most Unforgettable Character I've Known," and it was, quite suitably, about Grandma.

Kate may have been blind, but she still played the piano, composed some of her own music, wrote a book about her early years in Hornitos, cooked every day, cleaned, washed, and ironed, and even chopped kindling! (That used to give everyone the heebiejeebies.) And John's strength, dignity, comprehension, and bearing were inspirational. Both of these sturdy people made a deep impression on Jeanette, and she was in seventh heaven during those weeks each summer.

Jeanette also felt the ambiance of love and togetherness with the Westergaard side of the family. She relished their family gatherings, which occurred as often as possible, despite the fact that Lita and William moved about a great deal.

Jeanette was fond of all her aunts and uncles, but Pearl was always very special. She called her Pope because she couldn't pronounce Pearl, and Pope was stuck with that forevermore. Pope lived with Helen and Fred for short intervals and became more of a sister to Jeanette than an aunt.

And so, with these big, happy families, why did Helen and Fred have just one child? Jeanette later learned that her mother had had a miscarriage—but that did little to quell the loneliness she had always felt at home.

Jeanette was a good student and skipped three half grades by the end of grammar school. She was *always* the youngest in her class and it presented a new set of problems to her parents. Do we treat Jeanette as the *age* she is, or the *grade level?* It was difficult either way and their overprotective attitude just added to the conflict.

Helen would put two hats on Jeanette after she washed her hair, so she wouldn't catch a cold. That was embarrassing. And (not that they could afford a bicycle) she was not allowed to even *learn* to ride a borrowed bike for a long time. Again, embarrassing. And later, when she was in high school, they wouldn't give her permission to ride in a car with a boy. Now *that* was embarrassing!

Such restrictions were frustrating to Jeanette because she always wanted so to belong, to be one of the gang. She felt she just missed the mark—not always, but usually. She was just a little "different." There wasn't the social status or family background where her parents knew their parents to fall back on. And by continually skipping grades, she was constantly faced with new classes and new students; and her being smart and pretty made the other youngsters wary of her.

Despite these troubling areas, school was a haven for Jeanette. She enjoyed learning; she loved being surrounded by people on whatever grounds and so she looked forward to every school day. Because Helen and Fred had never had an opportunity for a proper education, they were determined to give their daughter every pos-

sible chance. It was fortunate then that God had endowed Jeanette
with the necessary equipment toward that end (not that she always
utilized it well).

She had also been blessed with a little talent. She had a pleasant
voice and an appreciation for music. Helen and Fred worked hard
so Jeanette could have a few lessons in singing and piano and even
some tap dancing lessons. In their eyes, of course, she was a budding child prodigy, but in actuality she was rather average—not
bad, but not great.

It was Fred's boss, Mr. Grover Grider of Grider's Electric Store,
who gave ten-year-old Jeanette her first taste of fame. Mr. Grider
was drum major of the Sciots marching band, and thought (rightly
so for 1937) it would be quite unique to have a little girl and a little
boy as miniature drum majors for the organization, and so he
trained Jeanette and Donny Babcock (another employee's child) to
strut their stuff and twirl that baton.

They marched in parades in Stockton and surrounding areas and
even went to Sacramento to compete in the state band competition.
They won First Prize! Jeanette worked so hard at twirling the baton
she wore right through the skin to the bone on her right hand,
almost messing her white skirt with the dripping blood. But she
didn't feel a thing. Her concentration on the routine and pleasing
Mr. Grider and the crowds on the sidewalk left no room for anything else.

Besides the trophy for first place, the Sciots wanted to reward
their mascots with a little gift as a remembrance. They were thinking in terms of a piece of jewelry, something lasting. But the increasingly pragmatic Jeanette expressed a desire for a raincoat. She
had needed and wanted one, but it was in the category of a luxury
item for her parents. Well, Jeanette got her raincoat, along with a
hat and umbrella to match—and did she use them proudly!

The next four years, until the summer of 1941, was a relatively
tranquil period. There was still the fighting between Jeanette's
mom and dad, still a lot of moving around, still the aloneness, and
still the family's battle with the pocketbook for Jeanette to contend
with. But some stability—some—had crept into her life.

After a few jobs, Fred had ended up selling cars at a Ford agency.
It wasn't very lucrative, until Stockton Airfield began training hun-

dreds of pilots, and then suddenly the parking lot there started to look like a Ford plant. Fred and Helen had fun during this period. The officers were about their age, and they soon all became friends and did a lot of partying together. Jeanette enjoyed this time too because she was their object to spoil.

The kids at school seemed to be finally, gradually accepting her. She was a class secretary, often sang at school functions, and was the unlikely editor of the school paper. The Morrisons also joined the Presbyterian Church and this gave Jeanette a little sense of belonging to the community for which she had always longed. Fred sang in the church choir; Jeanette sang in the children's choir and participated eagerly in the Young People's Christian Endeavor.

She was a member of a group. Those Sunday night meetings and the monthly Friday night "gatherings" were so important to her, being with other young people, learning about the teachings of Christ. She also met a boy who was probably one of the nicest human beings on earth and who later would prove to be a wonderful friend to her during a devastating time in her life—Richard Doane. Dear, wonderful Dick—handsome, tall, gentle, hardworking, from a solid family—they "went together" for a year and a half.

Jeanette graduated from Weber Grammar School in February 1940 and at twelve years of age entered Stockton High School in midyear as a freshman. More potential friends, but more of the "new girl in town" problems. But still, school was a refuge for Jeanette. Her little music training paid off—she tried out for Frank Thornton Smith's well-known Troubadors and was accepted. She was a member of *another* group!

But during these years, on her treasured jaunts to her grandparents' in Merced, Jeanette sensed something disturbing—Grandpa Morrison didn't seem quite like himself. She thought maybe she was just getting older and was looking at him differently, but Grandma was different too—the fun and laughter were a little forced. Jeanette still enjoyed the visits though and didn't dwell on it.

But her instincts were right. In early 1941 the family was told that Grandpa was terminally ill with cancer. The sons and their wives assembled for a meeting—someone had to help Grandma through the ordeal. Fred's job was the most expendable—the others' were established in their businesses—and so it was decided that Fred, Helen, and Jeanette would move back to Merced.

Oh really? Jeanette thought. *Where does that leave me?* Her life was just starting to take shape in her new world at Stockton High. *Now what? Another new class? School? Not belonging?* She loved her Grandma and Grandpa Morrison—but *why now?*

It wasn't her decision to make. When school closed in early June, they packed up and moved into the Morrisons' house in Merced. Fred and Helen slept in the little living room and Jeanette slept with Grandma; Grandpa was in the hospital. The tension affected everyone, and Fred and Helen were more on edge than ever. Fred found work at a nearby market and Helen cared for Grandma and Jeanette, did the chores of the house, visited Grandpa daily, and looked after every one's needs as best she could.

Jeanette, after the initial rebellion at the move and shock over Grandpa's illness, fell into the usual Merced summer routine. Each day, when she had completed her assigned tasks, her group of friends gathered on P Street; this year there was a new face: Kenneth Carlyle. Kenny was a little older, had dark hair, was handsome, was from a well-known local family, and over the summer he and Jeanette gradually paired off.

When her grandfather died, it was Kenny who comforted Jeanette most.

CHAPTER TWO

Jeanette had early discernment that life goes on and that decisions have to be made, under any circumstances. In September, she was skipped ahead another half grade and entered Merced High as a junior. It was necessary to move from the familiar old house on P Street to a duplex about four blocks away. At least it had two bedrooms, so it did offer a little more privacy. But it was hard! Grandma Morrison, after fifty years of marriage, found life without Grandpa empty, even with her many friends. Fred and Helen were really put to an extreme test.

Ironically, it was a good period for Jeanette, for death is so far away for the young. She was going through her own changes: the definite signs of womanhood and her real first love, Kenny. Her wonder and joy at this affair of the heart was all-enveloping, and rescued her from the strained atmosphere at home. Occasional twinges of guilt, however, intruded on her contentment.

Adjustment to the new school was not as difficult as she had feared—now she could be with her summer friends all the time. She soon found herself a member of the "in" group. *And,* since Merced was then such a small town, where everyone knew everyone, she was finally permitted to ride in a car—with a boy. And she was in *love.* Fred and Helen, immersed in their own problems, were not aware of the seriousness of the relationship. Even though Jeanette wasn't always as helpful at home as she could have been and her attitude was a little distant, her happy involvement and absorption in her new environment at least alleviated one of their worries.

Jeanette became enmeshed in an abundance of activities— dances, games, and clubs. She felt so much a part of her group that she once allowed herself to be caught up in its favorite pastime—

cutting school. She and her friends were caught and the punishment was an exam in every subject, counting for half of their final grade. Jeanette did extremely well, so her escapade didn't cost her anything in the end result. The real triumph was total participation with her peers.

Sunday—December 7, 1941.

Jeanette, Kenny, and a whole bunch of friends were playing baseball in the street outside the duplex. Fred ran out of the house, screaming, "The Japanese have bombed Pearl Harbor—we're at war!" The young group didn't know where Pearl Harbor was, but the word "war" sent chills down their spines. Like all Americans, they huddled around the radio that day, listening to every scrap of information. As the day wore on, the broadcasts became more detailed and they became aware of the full horror of what had happened.

The citizens of Merced mobilized with the rest of America. Well, at least they did what they could: sign up for the Red Cross, for First Aid, practice blackout drills, and be fiercely patriotic.

Weeks, months went by, and the news grew increasingly alarming. Now Fred and Helen had another crisis on their hands. Fred was only thirty-one and certainly not in a critical occupation, so what would they do if matters continued to worsen and he was drafted?

The school term ended with the customary festivities, only dampened somewhat by the war. But Jeanette was totally unprepared for the type of bomb Fred and Helen dropped.

"We're moving back to Stockton."

The reasons were carefully explained. Stockton had a huge inland port and there were many shipyards operating at full capacity with plans to expand. There were good opportunities for Fred to land a priority position. Grandma would move to Los Angeles with friends who managed a home and be close to Aunt Vi and Uncle John Morrison.

Carefully explained, yes, but absolutely unacceptable to Jeanette. *How could they do this? How could she go back again?* She had lost contact with the people in Stockton. She was so firmly established now, so much a part of the Merced community. And what about Kenny!

But the decision was irreversible. Jeanette left Merced in despair, with such a feeling of betrayal. Her world had crumbled again. Grandma, who was leaving so much of her life behind, had to be heartbroken, but she knew it was the only solution and understood. But Jeanette just couldn't follow her example of courage and trust.

The arrangements and the packing and the sorting were torture, and the day of departure was a scene of indescribable anguish for them all.

The Morrisons stayed in an inexpensive motel when they arrived in Stockton. Fred immediately went out scouting for work, while Helen and Jeanette sat in that *awful* room, with all of their belongings stacked around them in boxes, and stared at each other. Jeanette's misery mounted daily. Resentment started fermenting. The loneliness just about made her crazy. Even the movies and the radio couldn't make a dent in her depression. She just felt as if everyone and everything was working against her. Although Fred was soon hired by Colberg's Shipyards as a foreman, and they moved into a comfortable rented house in a nice neighborhood (1870 Jewel Court), Jeanette's silent hell persisted.

Then came the letter from one of Jeanette's best friends, Rusty, in Merced, inviting Jeanette to come and stay with her for two weeks. Jeanette was in ecstasy! It was drowning and having someone throw her a lifejacket—like finding a bottle with a genie to grant her wishes—like, oh, it was just *wonderful.*

Fred and Helen didn't have the heart not to let her go. They had not been callous to her feelings about the move—actually they had been terribly concerned and worried for her—but they were helpless to do anything about it. So the visit was planned for the following week. The time inched by, but finally, Jeanette was on that train to Merced.

What a blast! Kenny and Rusty and everybody met her, and she was deliriously happy. Such talking and laughing and good times went on the next few days. Somehow, somehow, it had to continue —but how?

Kenny, Jeanette, and Rusty sat on the front steps and contemplated the possibilities. There *had* to be a way to keep Jeanette here. One of them—who remembers who?—came up with an idea. Why didn't Jeanette and Kenny get married? And then they all could live in Merced happily ever after. It seemed so simple.

And in the beginning it was. Kenny's parents, who were delighted with the idea of having Jeanette as a daughter-in-law, loaned the couple their car. And off they went to Reno, where fourteen-year-old Jeanette Helen Morrison lied about her age and was married, and where her marriage was consummated.

From the moment Jeanette became aware she was a girl and that boys were, well, boys and somehow different, she, along with every other girl, thought about getting married and having children (although no one told them how this all happened as yet). Her paper dolls always had wedding dresses—beautiful, lacy, white, long— and her dolls were often "baby dolls," with which she played mother. And love! From fairy tales to magazines, from novels to motion pictures—almost all told of falling in love with "a prince" and living happily ever after. There was an idyllic fantasy about these mysterious happenings.

Sexuality, in 1942, was not the open subject it is today. Very little education about it was offered in school and few parents had the courage or sensitivity to discuss this taboo topic, except for the barest essentials. Stressed was "remain pure for your husband," or the consequence, getting pregnant and being ostracized.

There is no alarm clock that rings to indicate the *proper* time for a girl to experience sexual sensations. Everyone naturally is awakened at a different age.

Though she was only fourteen, Jeanette believed with all of her heart that she had found her "prince" and was ready for marriage. True, the circumstances were not exactly as in "the dream"—no church, no white dress, no festivities, no family—she rationalized that this was due to their emergency.

But the storybooks never went any further than the "prince" riding off with his love.

So who could be prepared for the time when the door closed in a hotel room, and a scared little girl faces her friend—her husband. There was never a description of the shyness, the awkwardness, the embarrassment, the fear of uncharted waters. Kenny's kisses were gentle, as always. And gradually, tenderly, the barriers were broken, and passion prevailed. No paragraph in those stories provided an understanding of the physical pain that accompanies the blending of bodies and souls. Or an understanding of the ultimate ecstasy. It was a night of discomfort, of wonder, of exploration, of discovery. It was a night which left Jeanette with many thoughts to ponder.

The fulfillment of their love—sharing of their intimate new secret, the daring of their action, the little shadow of intrigue—kept them in a state of perpetual exhilaration on the drive home until they turned onto Kenny's street and saw Fred and Helen's car parked in front of the Carlyles' house. Naïve, innocent, these two adolescents had believed their bubble would never burst.

Helen and Fred had called Rusty's just to say hello. Premonition? Who knows? Rusty, caught in the web of deception, had blurted out the truth.

At the Carlyles', Helen and Fred were tight-lipped, grim, silent. They had already collected Jeanette's things from Rusty's, now they took her by the arm and marched her to the car. A stunned Kenny was left on the sidewalk in Merced. Jeanette never saw him again.

What ensued in the next few hours—the next few days, the next few weeks—left a mark on Jeanette, the scars of which still live with her today.

"How could you do such a thing? How could you do this to your mother?"

"How could you do this to me?"

"Look at what you've done to us!"

By her parents' continued accusations, their censuring hurt, their lack of affinity, she was made to feel shameful. Bad. Someone capable of inflicting pain on those she loved. And Jeanette and Kenny's love, which had seemed so pure, was now viewed as unclean. It was as if she had committed a criminal act; now she was untrustworthy; sentence was passed on her—*guilt for life.*

If only Helen and Fred or Jeanette could have controlled their emotions long enough to bring some reason to their problem, to initiate an attempt to understand the others' positions, perhaps the severe damage done could have been diffused.

But the situation was too volatile. Words were fired and though they would fade with time and the wounds would heal, there would always be scars.

When you think about it (and Jeanette thought about it a lot), Helen and Fred's reaction to the elopement was fairly normal and particularly understandable in their case. Not many parents, then or now, would tolerate a fourteen-year-old's running off.

And no way could they allow Jeanette to be trapped in an early marriage, with all the confining responsibilities, as they had been. They were determined that she would at least have the chance to develop, if not fulfill, her potential.

No, it wasn't the response itself, but the unfortunate tactic of the response that caused the harm.

It was an unhealthy climate.

Annulment proceedings were started. More guilt was laid on. The cost of the lawyer . . .

Kenny made several attempts to reach Jeanette, but his efforts were thwarted, his letters confiscated, and the only result was that she was watched even more carefully. She was completely confused, not knowing where her loyalty lay, not knowing who was the enemy. Was there any enemy? Or was *she* the enemy? Kenny had to be hurt—angry—and as confused as she was, not understanding why there was no response, why she didn't return to Merced. And when the cold, impersonal notification of the annulment arrived in the mail, he must have been devastated.

When some communication resumed between the Morrisons, Fred and Helen sat Jeanette down and carefully explained, "Now, an annulment is not the same as a divorce. An annulment means it never happened. You were *never married.* So, as far as anyone is *ever* concerned, you were *never* married."

As I sit here writing this in the 1980s, I want to explain to the younger readers and remind my contemporaries that the moral attitudes of the 1940s were distinctly different from today's. First of all, divorce and annulment were nowhere near as commonplace or accepted as they are today. Even the term *divorcée* was considered risqué. Moreover, once a girl had been married—definite proof that she was no longer a virgin—she was considered easy prey.

The strict moral codes affected men as well. No self-respecting male would seduce a virgin (only a cad would do that), but once a girl had been "damaged," she was fair game.

The title of Frank Sinatra's hit song, "All or Nothing at All," reflected the attitude about women and sex. Either a girl didn't "do

it" at all, or she "did it" constantly. She either abstained entirely or
was insatiable. I know it seems ludicrous today, but that's the way it
was. And a once-married girl was assumed to be "doing it."

"No one in Stockton knows, and no one has to know, and that's
how we're going to keep it!"

And so Jeanette started living the lie.

She was at a low ebb. In isolation for the rest of the summer, she
grappled with heavy-duty thoughts for a just-turned-fifteen-year-
old: trying to define right and wrong—sorting out her newfound
emotions and how they fit in society's conventions—needing parental guidance and yet straining under parental control—wondering
where all this would lead in the days ahead.

Dick Doane to the rescue! (Although he wasn't aware of his
important role.) He had just heard that Jeanette was back in Stockton and started visiting 1870 Jewel Court.

It was a tentative Jeanette whom Dick spurred back into Stockton
social life. As her gradual realization of the consequences of her
"deed" took place, her fear of discovery mushroomed. And stayed.
Always, in the back of her mind, she would wonder when someone
was going to lower the boom and disclose her secret. She avoided
questions about Merced, except "safe" ones—about Grandma and
Grandpa, why and when the family had returned.

Haltingly, peace found its way into the Morrison household.
Fred and Helen were convinced that their prodigal daughter had
returned to the fold, and relaxed their vigilant attitude.

As for Jeanette, well, this whole incident certainly didn't do
much for her self-image or security. The shyness increased; self-
doubt emerged; the apprehensiveness of being "different" was
stronger than before.

But she survived. The easing of the tension at home and the
solidity of Dick's support and his belief in her helped push negative
thoughts, not out, but at least toward the back of her consciousness.
And she had been given a great gift: a love of life, an optimistic
heart, a "stars in her eyes" attitude that managed to persevere
through adversity.

When school started, Dick was invaluable in helping her re-es-
tablish her associations. He attributed Jeanette's uncertainty to her

absence for a year (he was right, in a way) and he wanted to make the transfer back to Stockton as easy as possible.

Jeanette rejoined her church group (a much needed haven) and the Troubadors, renewed old acquaintances and even made new ones—all on the protective arm of Dick.

She buried all illusions about an idyllic life with Kenny in Merced. She realized the error of their action. Of course she was too young to be married—she didn't even know what it meant. She had walked through an open door and hadn't been ready for what was on the other side. How could she have been so stupid? *If only she could take it back, reverse time.*

In that summer and early fall of 1942, Jeanette would not have bet on a happy senior year. But there was a silver lining in the cloud of her secret. The last year in high school was everything it should have been—all the normal events for a schoolgirl: football games, dances, friends, nicknames, and the inevitable and important senior prom.

Fred and Helen were now both working at Colberg's Shipyards, so they were able to buy Jeanette a pretty ice-blue tulle formal for $13.95 (and *that* was expensive). Dick sent her a white orchid—her first—and when she opened the door, he just stared.

"I've never seen anything so beautiful!"

She floated on her silver lining the whole evening.

World War II was drawing closer to Jeanette's world. The eighteen-year-old son of dear friends, a handsome gifted boy, was killed in Europe. Such a waste, one of so many. And numerous young men in Jeanette's graduating class were entering the service. Some were shipped out quickly—too quickly—with hardly time to learn the lessons needed in that deadly arena. After graduation, Dick joined the Marines and was sent to the University of Washington in the V-12 officer-training program.

At the Morrisons', Fred and Helen's dream for their daughter was going to come true—in September Jeanette was going to attend College of Pacific in Stockton. Jeanette had worked at the five-and-dime store on and off since she was eleven, but this summer she was employed by Bravo and McKeegan's, a chic men's store in downtown Stockton. She needed to save for school and clothes. Junior college (two years) was not as costly as senior college, but there still would be expenses and every bit helped.

Jeanette dated friends—Tommy McKeegan and Bill Bianci—but she was very careful, with Dick as well, about being a "nice" girl.

Be a nice girl. Jeanette was consumed by this! But no one said she wasn't, no one treated her as if she wasn't. No one except Jeanette. Because of her secret, she felt as though she was lying, felt dishonest and undeserving of her acceptance by others. She passed judgment on herself, and reacted the way they would, if they knew. But in this case, living a lie was easier than telling the truth.

God, the torture we inflict upon ourselves!

It was a precarious period for Jeanette. She was doing a juggling act—balancing the sociological and psychological aspects of her "past," while still trying to handle the normal uncertainties all adolescents experience about sexual exploration. Since she was living in an era when once you were no longer a virgin, there didn't seem to be any need to "save" yourself, she could have just said, "To hell with it," and abandoned herself to promiscuity. On the other hand, she was vulnerable to another undesirable possibility. By trying to deny the reality of her union with Kenny, Jeanette was indirectly confirming that there was something tainted about it. Hence the guilt—prompting the compulsion to keep her desires and passions under strict control—made her a perfect psychological candidate for future frigidity. Fortunately, the first was not in Jeanette's character, and she was luckily spared the last.

CHAPTER THREE

September 1943. College of Pacific was another beginning and another new school, but this time sixteen-year-old Jeanette was fortified with good friends from high school, so it wasn't as threatening. Her major was music, her minor was psychology, her job was at the information desk during free periods, and her joy was being accepted in Professor Russel Bodley's well-known A Capella Choir. Her anxiety was that her secret would somehow be disclosed.

In the spring semester, Jeanette's pals went out for freshman sorority rushing. She struggled with the decision whether to do the same. She desperately wanted to join them but wasn't sure if she should take the chance. How closely did they explore backgrounds? However, not participating might seem strange, difficult to explain. So, nervously, she submitted her name, but didn't entertain much hope of being accepted.

In the Music Department Jeanette was surrounded by students with major talents, and although academically she could hold her own and vocally she was adequate, she soon realized that she was not exceptionally gifted. But a performance with the A Cappella Choir at Stockton's State Mental Hospital resulted in another awareness. Jeanette thought, "I think *I* have problems—they're so inconsequential compared to theirs. Why are some so tested?" It was a moving experience to see the effect of the different songs on the patients. A quiet melody bestowed a calm she could feel. And with a rousing tune, she could sense the agitation and restlessness beginning.

The recognition that music could be used for purposes other than just performing, along with the acceptance that her voice was limited, guided Jeanette toward a new career direction—music therapy. In 1944 this was an innovative concept. There wasn't even a specific curriculum offered, but by combining her psychology and music courses she could achieve her goal of being a therapist, a teacher.

When rushing was over, a list was posted.

Nervously reading it, Jeanette found out she was pledged to the sorority of her choice—Alpha Theta Tau! What an exhilarating high; it was the personification of belonging, of being wanted.

At the sorority, the new pledges were introduced.

"This is Marie Arbios from Stockton."

"Jeanette Morrison from Stockton."

"And Mary Smith from Merced."

Merced! Jeanette's stomach lurched. This young woman was the first person from Merced she'd encountered in almost two years. Was this dream going to end before it even began? She didn't, *couldn't,* say anything, allowing Mary to make the first move. Did she know—?

But, miraculously, Mary didn't know her or anything about her. It took a while before Jeanette's pulse rate returned to normal.

During these war years, the V-12 program was initiated to train qualified servicemen to be officers. Naturally, the objective was to hurry them through, so colleges adapted a trisemester system to accommodate them. Civilian students were allowed to attend the third semester.

So, in the summer of 1944, Jeanette entered her sophomore year at C.O.P. Her motives were not entirely scholastic. Because of the light registration of girls, the sorority house had space to take in local members. Jeanette decided this was the perfect use for her carefully accumulated savings. So with Fred and Helen's blessing, she, along with Helen, Marie, and Peggy, moved into Alpha Theta Tau for the summer term. You can imagine how happy she was— the only child was now living in a big house, with some forty-odd sisters!

And it did cross the girls' minds that the school would be over-run with sailors and marines—probably a 4 to 1 ratio. Tempting— right? Right! Some of the servicemen had come directly from other universities, while some had been selected from the ranks. The studying was serious; if the boys didn't maintain a certain grade level, off they went to the real war. But even with that hanging over their heads, the campus had the atmosphere and spirit of an MGM college musical.

The summer far exceeded Jeanette's expectations. It was almost as if she, with the others, were taking their last grasp at innocence.

Jeanette saw Dick whenever he had leave from University of Washington, but there was no binding commitment. Their friendship would be everlasting, but they were pursuing their individual directions.*

That summer, Jeanette met Stanley Reames, a tall, attractive, worldly sailor from San Francisco who had been on active duty before passing the Officer Training application exams. His main interest was music (not naval history) and shortly after his arrival he organized an ambitiously sized band of about sixteen members. At first Stan had asked Jeanette to be the vocalist, but when their dating became more serious, he preferred she didn't perform.

Jeanette had been to nearby Sacramento several times to see the big-name bands. And she had danced—moon-eyed and swooning— to the music of Tommy Dorsey, Stan Kenton, Benny Goodman, and Glenn Miller. They were idols; everyone knew their records by heart, and every girl imagined herself as the heroine in the film *Orchestra Wives*.

So it was romantic and rather exciting to go with Stan. The student body was enthusiastic about having a dance band of its own and made quite a fuss about the group. Plus, he was good!

The enchanted summer ended and Jeanette moved back home. She and Stan continued to date and soon they became a steady duo. Then their parents were introduced. Early in the spring term of 1945, in the beginning of her junior year, Stan asked Jeanette to marry him.

Her mind worked overtime. Was she in love? As far as she could

* Dick was married shortly after the war, and settled in Seattle. About thirty-five years later, I was on a flight back to Los Angeles from shooting on location in Marin County, when a young stewardess approached me and asked if she could speak personally. She introduced herself as Dick Doane's daughter. He had died of leukemia soon after she was born, too soon altogether. She was aware of our friendship and wanted to know more about her dad—his early years, what he was like then. What he was like . . . I think, I hope, I was able to convey to the lovely girl how special a human being he was. How kind, how gentlemanly, how thoughtful, and how good! The flight was not long enough for either of us.

trust herself, she guessed so. He had stirred some deeply buried emotions. Was she mature enough to assume the responsibilities she now realized marriage brought? She believed so, and she knew better than most that it was more than "playing house." Would the war interfere? She couldn't answer that. Could she disclose to Stan her locked-away secret? She could not do it. He must have thought highly of her, since he had asked her to marry him—how could she muddy the waters?

Fred and Helen liked Stan, but something unarticulated, something subliminal, perhaps not even understood, led them and Jeanette to agree to the marriage. Somehow, they naïvely surmised, a *real* wedding would erase the other aborted one, and legitimatize Jeanette's status as a recognized married lady. And so the three of them worked longer and harder to make it a "proper" wedding. A budget was set up and strictly adhered to—proper, yes, pretty, yes, and modest, definitely. Stan's mother helped make a small trousseau, and the city was scoured for appropriately priced gowns. Jeanette had a wedding-procedure book, and the pattern was followed meticulously. This was going to be done "according to Hoyle."

Stan, however, was having problems. His grades were slipping. He had been warned to drop outside activities such as the band, but had refused to heed the advice. Now he was forced to, and his grades still didn't improve. At the end of the semester he was informed that his participation in the Officer Training program had been terminated. He was transferred to Treasure Island in San Francisco for further assignment.

Then there was even more devastating news. President Franklin Delano Roosevelt died on April 12, 1945.

The importance of the German surrender on May 7 to the whole world seemed doubly meaningful to the young couple. Troop movements from Treasure Island were temporarily halted.

August 6, 1945
First atomic bomb dropped on Hiroshima

August 9, 1945
Second atomic bomb dropped on Nagasaki

August 14, 1945
Japan surrenders!

No one knew or cared what a Pandora's box would be opened after the bombs fell. Not many knew or cared why an atomic bomb was different.

Everyone *did* know and *did* care that the war was over, that the killing would stop, that our boys would be coming home, that the country *did* have a leader.

Complete bedlam broke out in the city—people running in the streets, horns, whistles, screaming—and it seemed the entire populace had decided to get just plain soused. Emotions flowed and overflowed.

Jeanette and Stan shared the joy of all, and their private joy was Stan's discharge a few days later. Now there was no obstacle in the way of their march down the aisle.

The chapel of College of Pacific was quite lovely and small and exuded an aura of warmth and peacefulness and beauty.

Helen and Fred were proud of their accomplishments—giving Jeanette first an educational opportunity, and now a conventional wedding. It hadn't been easy. So when Jeanette and Stan left in the car, with the traditional rice and tin cans, the older group really cut loose and partied up a storm. Why not!

Mr. and Mrs. Stanley Reames drove down the coast toward Los Angeles for their short honeymoon. The wedding had functioned smoothly; the atmosphere was relaxed between them. There was the natural embarrassment of being identified as a honeymoon couple at the hotel. And then finally, the door to their room was closed. Jeanette faced her husband. Memories forced their way through and flooded her conscience. She desperately tried to subdue her rising panic and the guilt, the shame she felt, so their union would be unrestricted. And she succeeded to a point. Nervousness was expected. The pain was the same. There was satisfaction. But there were no stars—something she couldn't define was missing. Was she at fault because she hadn't been free enough? Or was the feeling just not there?

It didn't matter. Jeanette was determined that it was going to be *all right.*

In Los Angeles they visited Grandma Morrison, old friends of Stan's, and had fun driving around to see all the sights of the big city. At the time there was a strike at the movie studios, so when they went by they saw pickets indulging in a little shoving. Very exciting stuff. Just to see the outside walls of a movie compound was thrilling.

The days passed quickly and then the newlyweds returned to Stockton for the fall semester. Stan used the GI Bill to pay for school and received a stipend of fifty dollars a month.

With Jeanette settled, Helen and Fred decided to embark on an adventure. They gave the couple their car and furniture and took off. Neither one of them had ever seen snow, and so they made their destination the Sierra Nevada Mountains in Northern California. Their object was to travel around, perhaps alight and work somewhere, or just sort of "hang loose"—something they had never been able to do.

Jeanette tackled an arduous schedule. To make ends meet, she took in two of Stan's navy friends, who were also on the GI Bill, as boarders in the duplex they had inherited from Helen and Fred. The boys gave her their fifty-dollar-a-month allowance, and in return she fed them, kept house, and washed their clothes and linens. At the same time she was trying to finish her junior year. Rationing was still in effect, which meant stopping at the market on the way home from classes and attempting to put dinner together with a few cans or one piece of meat, and then rushing back to campus for evening classes. Weekends were spent cleaning, doing the laundry by hand, and trying to catch up on homework.

Helen and Fred settled at Sugar Bowl Ski Lodge in Soda Springs, California. Fred was a desk clerk and Helen worked in the dining room. It was a completely new atmosphere and enjoyable for a while, but they missed their daughter desperately. For Christmas they sent a little money to bring Jeanette and Stan up during the holiday break.

As an introduction to snow country, they arrived in a blinding blizzard. It was a scary ride, but well worth it. The only access to the lodge from the parking lot was by a horse-drawn sleigh, complete with bells and lap robes and Christmas carols. The couple felt as if they were part of a scene on a Christmas card, but in this case, their imagination could not compare with the beauty of the actuality.

The reunion was tearfully happy, and the week was glorious. None of them knew anything about skiing—it was too expensive to even contemplate learning—but romping in the snow and sharing time together was joy enough. They piled all the sweaters and jackets and underwear they owned, the layers making them look like inflated balloon dummies.

It was all over too soon.

A young impresario-type music major had resolved to produce Gilbert and Sullivan's *The Pirates of Penzance* for his term project. He asked Jeanette to play the second feminine lead. She hesitated, worrying about the strength of her voice and wondering if she could manage the rehearsal hours with her other duties. But it was so tempting . . . She accepted the offer.

And it was wonderful! She delighted in the work, the challenge, the nervousness, and in the satisfaction she felt while on stage.

Back to reality, however. This brief diversion didn't alter Jeanette and Stan's life or their goals. That spring semester, Jeanette started her senior year. Stan pretended to study, but his heart just wasn't in it. More and more his mind dwelt on having his own band, and in a big way. His aspiration was not to play around Stockton, but to go to Los Angeles and really break into the business. *How* was the question. But Jeanette opted for practicability; finish school and pursue a definite profession rather than daydreams. This issue caused a running argument.

During spring vacation they returned to Sugar Bowl Ski Lodge to visit her folks, and took the controversy with them. It was difficult for her parents to advise Jeanette on which course to follow. They were not sure if Stan *could* abandon his high hopes. Maybe he did have talent. What if he was right? Yet they too understood the value of playing it safe.

Before they left, still with no solution, Fred casually said to Jeanette, "Oh—Norma Shearer and her husband, Marty Arrougé, were here for a month. They are such nice people. And they liked the picture of you I had on my desk so much they took it home with them."

"Whatever for?"

"I don't really know. As a matter of fact, they asked for additional snapshots as well, so I think I'll send the ones we took on this trip."

Jeanette couldn't believe her mom and dad had actually *seen* Norma Shearer and spoken with her face to face.

"Is she absolutely beautiful? Did she bring trunks and trunks of clothes? Does she sound just like she did in the movies? She ate right in the dining room? Like real people? You have their address? Unbelievable!"

Jeanette was so impressed by all this information that she didn't think much about the picture incident. Besides, she was sure that it would soon be forgotten.

Stan made up their minds. They were going to Los Angeles. Jeanette acquiesced. College or a business career were clearly not for him. She couldn't force him into an unwanted situation without the chance to try for his dream. So they sold their car and few pieces of furniture, borrowed money from his parents, and took out a GI loan. At the end of the term, they packed up their belongings and headed south with Stan's friend and lead musician, Johnny.

Johnny was familiar with Los Angeles; he had played with an "almost name band" before the war, so he knew the ropes. *They* were babes in the woods—and what woods for the babes to be in. This time Los Angeles was not for vacationing or visiting or sightseeing—this was for all the marbles. The direction Johnny drove did provide some sight-seeing, however, because their previous excursion had not led them to this part of Hollywood and Los Angeles. No pretty homes or spacious parks here; they were in the core of industrial Los Angeles. Going east on Santa Monica Boulevard, about a block and a half before Western Avenue, Johnny pulled over and exclaimed, "Here it is!"

"Here is *what?*" they asked.

"Your new home!"

Jeanette looked with dismay at the four-story Harvey Hotel. It was run-down, sleazy. But the price was right—seven dollars a week for a room and bath on the third floor. And there was a place to rehearse in the basement. She walked into their quarters with trepidation—and justifiably. A stale, musty odor awaited her. She rushed to the window to let in some air and light. The curtains were heavy with dust and dirt, and when she finally wrestled the window open, she found the view to be a littered alley and another old building. The incoming light only emphasized the dingy carpet, the faded and torn wallpaper, the scarred and dented bureau and chair, and the rusty bathroom. It was the worst room she had ever seen. But she shrugged it off—nothing to do but plunge in and try to make it livable.

Johnny helped Stan corner some fine musicians, gather more sophisticated musical arrangements, and begin preparing for an audition with a major agency.

Jeanette tried to keep things together. She washed their clothes in the bathtub, ironed on the old nightstand, scrubbed the place with disinfectant daily, and kept the books. The guys had to be paid every week or they would wander off to another job. How she hated to make the checks out and watch their bank balance go down, down, down. They ate breakfast at a drugstore on Western and Santa Monica, usually Rice Krispies for ten cents. There was a greasy spoon next door where they could get a hot sandwich at night and sometimes Johnny took them to a drive-in where they split a hamburger and a shake.

Whenever Jeanette ventured out of their room, she noticed there were constantly new faces in the hotel, most of whom seemed to be on their way up or down from the fourth floor. She was always puzzled by it (and only years later did she figure out what went on up there).

She didn't spend much time at the band's rehearsals, but the few times she was there, the smell really bothered her. She didn't smoke or drink yet, but her mom and dad and their friends had always smoked with no ill effect on her, so it wasn't the cigarettes. No, this smoke was different—so strong that it reached her in the hallway before she even opened the door—a pungent, acrid— maybe sweet?—smell. (Another mystery she solved years later.)

Some of the band members introduced them to the Page Cavanaugh Trio (a popular jazz group of the time, and still playing), and they were invited to watch an actual recording session. Jeanette could see the longing for such a chance in Stan's face.

One night they splurged and enjoyed an evening at the renowned Casa Mañana Ballroom in Culver City, for years the home of many of the top orchestras. This was more than a little different from the Sacramento Civic Auditorium—much bigger, much darker, much wilder. Appearing were Stan Kenton and June Christy, considered innovative geniuses in the music world. Again,

Jeanette could see the yearning in Stan, and hoped the audition would go well.

And it did. The band division of MCA (one of—if not *the*—leading talent agencies) was obviously impressed by the band's performance. Good sound, good arrangements, good musicians, good presentation. Only one problem—they were a few years too late. Bookings were becoming increasingly difficult even for their established clients. The era of the "big bands" was sadly drawing to a close, so they had no reason to sign a completely unknown group.

What a blow! All the work, all the money—for nothing!

Jeanette was first devastated, then scared. It would take years and years to repay their loans. Stan still had hope and kept on rehearsing—he wouldn't face that it was all over. Even as their funds dwindled to a dangerous low, he wouldn't, couldn't, accept it.

CHAPTER FOUR

In late June, a letter arrived at the hotel. It had been forwarded from Stockton. The heading read MCA Inc. Jeanette thought maybe it was some news about the band. But why would the agency send it to Stockton? Why address it with her maiden name?

Dear Miss Morrison,

    We at MCA would very much like to meet with you to discuss possible representation. Please call at your earliest convenience.

                                  Sincerely,
                                  Levis Green

She read it again. Over and over again. Was this real? Could it be some kind of prank? But who, why?

There was only one way to find out. She called the number on the stationery.

"Mr. Levis Green, please." My God, they're ringing. There really is such a person.

"May I speak with Mr. Green, please? Who's calling? Well, uh, Jeanette Morrison." Better not confuse them with Reames. "I, uh, received a letter from him asking me to call, and I, uh, I am in town."

She made an appointment to visit the MCA Beverly Hills office the next day. She was dazed, unable to register. Then it hit her. What would she wear? What would she say? What was she going to *do?*

She ran down to the band rehearsal and told Stan and his boys the news. They had all been depressed, and so this was like a shot in the arm. The Hollywood-wise musicians took over: *Operation Jeanette.*

They didn't have much to choose from, but the band decided on a magenta crepe wraparound for Jeanette to wear. The vocalist, Margie, pulled Jeanette's hair back and anchored it with a fake white flower. They supervised as Margie applied makeup (Jeanette normally used only a little mascara and lipstick). When she was finished, they stood back and approved their creation—"You look beautiful." And off they sent her, armed with directions and bus information.

MCA's home was an imposing white building surrounded by carefully manicured lawns and groomed hedges, located on little Santa Monica Boulevard between Crescent Drive and Rexford Drive. The interior held thick carpets, marble, and exquisite antiques. Jeanette gazed in awe at this splendor. She was still staring when she was ushered into Mr. Green's plush office. Then Mr. Green did the staring.

"What did you *do* to yourself? No, no, no! You should look like this picture. I'm taking you to MGM tomorrow, but not like *that.* Don't *ever* do that again."

Poor Jeanette was close to tears. She didn't know what she had done wrong until she saw the picture Mr. Green held before her. It was from her last trip to Sugar Bowl. Her hair was loose and blowing; she wore an old open jacket and no makeup. Jeanette was naïve, but not dumb. She instantly realized that the boys' and her concept of Hollywood was wrong, and how ludicrous she must have looked to Mr. Green, who had expected the girl in the picture to walk through the door. She vowed silently, *no more phony airs.*

When the meeting was over, she walked along the shops on Hollywood Boulevard and found a simple, soft pink cotton dress, with black piping on the neck, pockets, and sleeves, for $7.95. She bought it with money her parents had sent for her upcoming birthday.

At the hotel, Jeanette didn't give a detailed account of the encounter, only that she was going back tomorrow. There was no need to discourage the guys any further with a description of Mr. Green's reaction.

When she saw Mr. Green the next day, he said, "Ah, now *there's* the picture." Levis Green was a handsome, silver-haired, gentle man who had never intended to be harsh with her but he had been shocked by her appearance.

They drove to Culver City in his big, long Lincoln Continental. On the way, they discussed the imminent meeting with Lucille Ryman, head of the talent department at MGM. Jeanette knew Mr. Green was aware of her inexperience, but she didn't know if he was aware of Stan.

"Mr. Green? Uh, Morrison is my *maiden* name. I've been married for eight months. Is that all right?" (No *way* she was going to bring up the other—the secret.)

"Well, of course. I wouldn't introduce the fact, but if you're asked, by all means answer."

That didn't exactly add any confidence to her already nervous state.

They parked the car and approached the gates of Metro-Goldwyn-Mayer. She was almost catatonic. *She was walking into MGM Studios.* A man passed and held the pedestrian gate for her. She looked—and gasped! José Iturbi! She had just seen him in *Holiday in Mexico* with Jane Powell.

An attractive, warm, and friendly Lucille Ryman greeted them in her inner office. Her kindness put Jeanette a little at ease. Miss Ryman gently probed her background. Training? Only a little, musically. Experience? Only the performance in *The Pirates of Penzance* and choral groups. Desire to be an actress? Only when fantasizing, maybe. Any difficulty remaining in Los Angeles? Only financially.

Jeanette was excused while Miss Ryman and Mr. Green talked. She fidgeted in the reception room alone until Mr. Green emerged.

"Was that okay? I mean, she didn't ask about Stan—about being married. I never thought about becoming an actress. I don't know anything—"

"You were fine! Everything is fine! You are now under contract to MGM."

She thought she was going to faint. Or be sick. Or scream.

She thought she was dreaming. Or going crazy.

Alarmed, he sat her down and calmly and carefully explained, "You have a seven-year exclusive contract, starting salary, fifty dollars a week. In three months the studio has the option to continue or to end the contract—the same conditions apply in another three months, then six months, then yearly. When an option is exercised, your salary increases. The concept is to give you enough time to learn, to make a screen test, to evaluate your potential—if there is any. Right now we have to make a date with the drama coach and then go back to MCA and sign a lot of papers.''

She was in a trance; nothing was really sinking in.

She followed Mr. Green into the quarters of the drama coach, Lillian Burns. Miss Burns's secretary, Muriel, was in the process of squeezing Jeanette into the already crowded schedule for the following week, when an inner door burst open, and a 4' 11 3/4" human dynamo surged forward. Jeanette was jolted from her stupor. Miss Burns shook her hand, suggested Muriel give her the bedroom scene from *Thirty Seconds Over Tokyo* to work on, dictated more instructions, and swept back into her office. Her energy seemed to linger in the small anteroom.

In the car Jeanette made Mr. Green repeat what he had said again and again until finally the realization of what had transpired dawned on her and the excitement spilled out. He couldn't help but be caught up in her fervor, and since he hadn't expected a contract so soon, he felt pretty happy himself.

She relished signing page after page of documents—it reaffirmed to her that it was indeed happening. She prolonged the process as long as possible, and then Mr. Green drove her back to the hotel, where they shared the miracle with Stan.

The entangled behind-the-scenes story of why Jeanette received the letter was eventually unraveled. Norma Shearer and Marty Arrougé had had 8 × 10's made of the photographs of Jeanette that Fred had sent them. They both liked one in particular. They waited for an opportune moment, and one night when they were dining at Chasen's with agent Charles Feldman and MGM executives Eddie Mannix and Benny Thau, they cunningly displayed the pictures to their captive audience. While none of them could dismiss Norma Shearer, there was much hemming and hawing. "Oh yes, she does have a fresh look. Uh, Charlie, why don't *you* look into it?'' Feldman glowered.

At that moment, Edie and Lew Wasserman (he was president of MCA and the most astute man in the industry) dropped by the table to say hello. Kicking one another under the table, the men saw a chance to discharge this little problem. "Ah! Here's the man to

handle these pictures! A much better agency. Lew, we're sure you'll
be happy to follow through on this." And so, Norma was placated
while the others chuckled to themselves at their clever escape. And
Lew Wasserman was reluctantly stuck with the envelope of pictures.

He subsequently passed the envelope and information on to
Levis Green in the agency's new talent department. When Levis
Green reported the day's events to Lew Wasserman, he whooped
with glee and picked up the telephone. "Benny, remember the
night you unloaded some pictures on me? That girl Norma was
pushing?"

"Do I? Ha! Ha! You should have seen your face."

"Well, guess what? We found her, and just signed her to a seven-
year studio contract!"

"Noo-oo, where?"

"At MGM." And Lew hung up.

"Hello, Eddie?"

"Hello, Charlie?"

When Jeanette later told the publicity department how she was
put under contract, they said, "That's a wonderful story! We
couldn't have thought of a better one ourselves. But you should tell
us how it really happened, so we can be prepared." Jeanette had no
idea what they were talking about. But then, it wasn't surprising—
she didn't know what *anyone* was talking about.

It took hours for Jeanette to calm down. Every time her stomach
started to relax, she would relive the day all over again, and have to
run for the bathroom. (She was destined for nerves and bathrooms
for all time.)

Fred and Helen were overjoyed, of course, as were Stan and the
boys in the band. At least *something* was going right for *someone*.
Because the band was dissolving; there was no more money, no
more hope. She felt guilty about her good fortune in the face of
their bad luck. At this time no one dwelt on the fact that it could be
all over for her as well in three months, or six months. It was too
new, a moment in life to savor, to enjoy.

Despite her contract, Jeanette and Stan had to get out of the
hotel; it was too expensive. Aunt Vi and Uncle Les Morrison lived
in Glendale in a modest, pleasant house with a large yard. There
was a small but clean and bright laundry room built onto the back

of the garage, with a bed and a tiny bathroom. They could stay there and use the kitchen and washing facilities for fifteen dollars a month. Much better. Johnny helped them move their meager belongings—everyone else in the band had already scattered, leaving the sinking ship. Aunt Vi allowed Stan to store the band equipment in a corner of the garage; an inglorious resting place for a dream.

But it was good for Jeanette to see the outdoors once more, and to breathe fresh air, be surrounded by grass and trees, be with family, and to feel clean. She rewashed every piece of clothing they owned to get rid of any hotel residue.

Miss Burns had told Jeanette to "work" on the scene, but Jeanette didn't know what that meant. Luckily, she had seen *Thirty Seconds Over Tokyo,* so she was familiar with the story and characters. It was a beautiful movie; she had cried with the characters, agonized with them, feared with them, and hoped with them. The scene chosen for her to "work" on was the one where Van Johnson, an air force pilot, says goodbye to his young wife, Phyllis Thaxter, before leaving on the mission. Jeanette remembered it well because she had been so touched by its tenderness and love and sadness and bravery. All she could think to do now was to memorize the lines and use her abundant imagination to put herself in the wife's situation.

She donned her pink dress, which she wore every time she went to the studio in the beginning (it had worked once—why change her luck?) and set out for her appointment with Miss Burns. From Glendale, she took the red car (a commuter streetcar) all the way to downtown Los Angeles, where she transferred to another red car that took her to Culver City. She got off on Jasmine Street and then walked the few blocks to the studio. In all, it was about a two-hour trip. The gateman had her name on his list, so she just breezed right in. It seemed absolutely unreal to her. *She,* Jeanette Helen Morrison Reames, was walking through MGM's gate—as if she actually *belonged* there.

Jeanette carefully retraced the path she had followed with Mr. Green—ten steps from the entrance, through a door, and to the left was Miss Burns's office. If she continued down the alleyway about forty feet and took another left, she would have been in Miss Ryman's headquarters. This was the only part of MGM she had seen. Muriel greeted her and asked her to take a seat and wait.

Jeanette was early and Miss Burns was running late. It didn't matter. She was thrilled just to be there. Beverly Tyler came bouncing in, wearing an 1860 period costume, needing to see Miss B. right away.

Muriel was a gem. English, diplomatic, she knew everyone and everything; she knew when to interrupt and when not to; and she balanced delicate egos with great aplomb. She buzzed Miss B., who came out and then went into one of the adjoining rooms with Miss Tyler. Jeanette had just seen Beverly Tyler in *The Green Years,* with Charles Coburn, Tom Drake, and Dean Stockwell, and now here she was in the same room with her, both wanting to see the same person!

People kept popping in to say hello or make an appointment—she recognized Marshall Thompson—it was an exciting atmosphere. Then it was her turn to go beyond the closed doors. She found herself in a large, softly lighted room, warmly and tastefully furnished, with a thick, deep, dark carpet. Miss Burns realized how nervous the poor creature was, and all of her vitality and strength turned into gentleness and compassion. After a little introductory chitchat, she guided Jeanette into doing the scene together.

When it was over, Miss Burns sat quietly, looking at her, wearing an expression Jeanette couldn't read.

"What did you do, Jeanette, to prepare this scene?"

"I didn't really know what to do. I learned the words and then just tried to think as if I were that girl, in that room, in that bed."

Miss Burns considered this and then said, "I have an idea. You go home now, and we'll call you when to come again."

Jeanette's heart sank! It sounded like a kiss-off. She must have been awful. And so she had no choice but to board the red car for the long ride back to Glendale, and wait for a call. She hoped it would come.

It did. Could she come in the following Monday for a meeting with Miss Burns and a director and producer? Could she? *And how* she could! She was advised to keep thinking about the scene. She couldn't think of anything else.

On Monday, Jeanette and the pink dress were ushered in and introduced to Mr. Roy Rowland and Mr. Jack Cummings. It was difficult for her to focus on them through the haze of her apprehension. Miss Burns and Jeanette did the scene, and then she was asked to step outside for a minute. She was really confused. What was happening?

When they sent for her, they explained the mystery. Mr. Cummings was the producer and Mr. Rowland the director of a picture called *The Romance of Rosy Ridge,* starring Van Johnson, Thomas Mitchell, Dean Stockwell, and Selena Royle. The setting was Missouri, post-Civil War era, and the ingenue lead called for a young, naïve mountain girl. The studio was practically set on someone else for the role, but Mr. Rowland and Mr. Cummings felt the actress came across a bit too sophisticated for it. They realized this was an extreme long shot; more than likely nothing would come of it, but they wanted to at least try—they wanted to test her for the part of Lissy Anne.

Was she hearing correctly? Her body started to tremble, she could feel tears starting to come. She hadn't acknowledged the degree of the stress she had been experiencing. It was almost too much—that this was happening—this was happening to *her.* From somewhere, while she was on this spaceship high, a sobering thought intruded.

"It's only been two weeks! I haven't had an opportunity to learn anything! I was supposed to have at least three months before being judged. I could be through in two weeks without the benefit of *some* training."

Their mouths gaped. Was this dumbbell saying *no* to a test? They couldn't believe the nonsense coming out of Jeanette's mouth. But, fortunately, it dawned on them how completely uninformed she was about the business. She obviously knew zero about procedure.

Painstakingly, they initiated her to some facts of life, à la show biz. First of all, the test had to be done now because the movie would start shooting soon. Secondly, a test made for an actual role in a picture, as opposed to a general screen test, was handled in a different manner. Mr. Rowland would direct, Selena Royle would do the test with her, and more care and time would be exercised. And last, they *guaranteed* that if this test didn't go well (and the chances of it doing so were so slim as to be almost nonexistent), she would have another screen test at a later date.

With these reassurances, Jeanette allowed the joy in her to surge forward again. They handed her a script. A real script. A real movie script. She was to go to wardrobe—Miss Burns would see her

Wednesday and Thursday—the test would be photographed Friday. She was in a daze; so much to try to comprehend, absorb. She thanked them profusely (at least she hoped she had) and made her wobbly way to wardrobe. But first, an inevitable visit to the restroom.

She made the trip out from Miss Burns's area and walked along the main street of the studio. She took the first right and halfway down that block, on the right, was ladies' wardrobe. They led her toward the back into the stockroom. It was huge—racks of clothing from all periods hung from floor to ceiling. Jeanette felt about as big as an ant. She was fitted in a coarsely woven long skirt, a cotton short-sleeved blouse, and leather sandals. They knew exactly what they were doing; she didn't open her mouth—probably nothing would have come out if she had. It didn't take long, and with the script—*her* script—clutched tightly in her hand, she was soon jolting back to Glendale on the streetcar, trying to sort out all the thoughts racing through her mind.

What was the story? What was it like to be in front of a camera? Could she do it? Would they like her? It was all an enigma and she felt lost.

Stan, Aunt Vi, Uncle Les, and their son, Jack, wanted to hear *everything.* Because of her birthday, Aunt Vi cooked dinner—a real treat. Jeanette had forgotten she was nineteen. She had forgotten she was hungry. She had forgotten everything except the name Lissy Anne. What was she like?

A Mr. Harry Friedman called from MCA that evening. He said he was Jeanette's agent. Mr. Green dealt with new talent, but Mr. Friedman covered MGM exclusively, and now he would be her contact. He knew of the impending test and wanted to assure her how advantageous it would be. He probably thought she would get cold feet. Anyway, he made arrangements to meet her and say hello at Miss Burns's office on Wednesday.

She couldn't wait to read the script—*her* script—but she had to until the dinner dishes were done.

She devoured it, line by line. And she loved it. And she loved Lissy Anne. The story: the family's older son had not yet returned to Missouri from the Civil War; neighbors were still divided between North and South sentiments. A stranger appears on the farm, endears himself to all (especially Lissy Anne), until he is forced to

reveal which side he favors. Meanwhile, villains are spreading ha-
tred and fear in the area so that landowners will leave and the land
can be bought for a price. Lissy Anne runs off with the stranger,
inadvertently they discover the evil plot, and together they set
things in order. It turns out that the stranger and the son had fought
on the same side (the North), but the son was killed, and his death
becomes a plea against prejudice.

The scene earmarked for the test was between Lissy Anne and
her mother, on the eve of the county's first social since the war.
They go to the old trunk to try on her party dress, and find she has
outgrown it—in all ways. The waist comes to the middle of her
breasts, the hem is at her knees. The mother realizes her daughter
has matured—enough, even, to be in love. A tender, touching,
sweet moment.

Jeanette was fortunate that Lissy Anne was a person she could
completely understand. She was not too unlike her—it was a different time of course, but basically they were similar souls. Miss
Burns, during a two-hour crash course, stressed simplicity. "Don't
try to *act*. Just feel. Forget the camera and people, concentrate on
the emotions happening inside this girl and with her mother. Do
what you instinctively did with *Thirty Seconds Over Tokyo*. Don't
worry about technique, you don't have any—and that's fine for
now."

She was to be at the studio at 8 A.M., which meant leaving Glendale by 6. There was no concern about awakening—Jeanette didn't
sleep a wink.

CHAPTER FIVE

Throbbing with anticipation, doubt, and fright, she arrived at MGM twenty minutes ahead of the appointed hour. The policeman gave her the route to Makeup: the main street to the second right (her farthest penetration into the studio thus far), go to the end of the street, and the building on the right is Makeup.

Testing took a back seat to actual filming, so she waited until all the other actresses were finished and on the way to their set. Her head jerked back and forth as tall and beautiful Esther Williams rushed out, and petite and adorable June Allyson rushed in. They were her favorites, her idols; she had seen every movie they had ever made. And she was so close she could have reached out and touched them!

Her turn in the big makeup chair came, and the makeup artist began. Instructions from Mr. Cummings and Mr. Rowland were, she was told almost apologetically, apply sparingly—they wanted a natural look. So she wouldn't be getting "the works." Maybe another time. (She prayed there *would* be another time.)

A thin base, light brown pencil on eyebrows, a small amount of blush, brown mascara on her lashes, and a no-color moisturizer on the lips—that was it. The hair stylist had more to do. Although her hair was long by 1946 standards, it wasn't long enough for an 1860s style. A matching fall was attached that cascaded down to her waist, using her own tresses in front and on the sides. Jeanette sat very still, fascinated by all these tricks of the trade.

When she was ready, she was directed to Stage 10 and told to ask for A.D. Backtrack to the main street, go three more blocks, turn left, walk one more block to Stage 10. The studio seemed endless; little did she know this was only the smallest lot of four. She opened the heavy stage door and found herself in a dark, gigantic building. She tentatively made her way toward some activity going on in the distance. A man passed by, and she asked where she could find a Mr. A.D. He laughed, kindly however, and said that she must mean *the* A.D.—the assistant director. She felt foolish; how was she supposed to know?

Finally, a familiar face. Mr. Rowland saw the timid soul approaching and rushed over to escort her onto the set and introduce her to everyone. She was astonished. In front of her was a small furnished room that came right out of a pictorial history book of the 1860s. Every piece, each appointment had obviously been researched and meticulously reproduced. When she had seen a period picture before, it never occurred to her what was involved in presenting a detailed image of an era; magically, she had believed it just *was*.

On her way to the unpretentious dressing room, she met Selena Royle and liked her instantly. She was a marvelous actress and a wonderful human being (one who would become a trusted friend and be oh, so helpful). Jeanette was not aware then of what an unselfish gesture it was on Selena's part to agree to do the test with her. This was not necessarily the norm, but she would discover, as time went on, that it was standard behavior for those performers who were real professionals and real people too. She was given good examples to follow, right from the start.

Dressed in her costume, with her new long hair, in the realistic setting, and rehearsing with Selena under Mr. Rowland's sensitive and gentle lead, Jeanette felt herself slipping away and Lissy Anne emerging. She felt like Lissy Anne, she was Lissy Anne. She adored her mother standing before her, and she glowed with her love for the stranger. All the foreign words and sounds—"action"—"cut" —"not good for camera"—"not good for sound"—"print"— "close-up"—"over the shoulder shot"—"master shot"—"dolly shot"—didn't break her concentration. She was lost in another world, another time.

The shooting was finished. *Already?* She didn't want it to be over; it was such fun. She liked the escape of being someone else. And there was such a group spirit on a set.

She had forgotten to be nervous—well, she soon fixed that! The doubts, the questions assailed her. How had she done? Was she all right? What happened now?

Selena and Mr. Rowland declared the day extremely productive, that Jeanette had come through with flying colors, that they were very pleased. Next step—Mr. Rowland and Mr. Cummings would see the "rushes" (viewing the previous day's filming) on Monday. Then they would "cut" it (editing by splicing the film together, combining long shots, close-ups, two shots, etc., into a smooth transitional sequence). After that, they would "dub" in "canned" music (lay over the sound tract appropriate mood music that was prerecorded and in stock). And *then*, providing they liked what they saw, they would show it to the powers that be.

Jeanette was completely flustered by all of this; all she really understood at the time was that there would be some waiting to do.

She felt an emotional and physical letdown. It was sad giving back the borrowed fall, taking off the wardrobe, saying goodbye to her newfound friends. Her energy had flowed so intensely; now she was conscious of being bone tired.

Slowly she left the studio, the big day done. Careening to Glendale on the now familiar red car, she reviewed the day's events. She knew one thing for sure. She relished whatever it was she had done this day—acting or thesping, or emoting, or whatever one called it —and she wanted to continue. The question was, would she have the opportunity to continue?

The waiting began. Thank God, the weekly check from MGM had started, because the payments on the GI loan had also started. No other income was forthcoming. Stan didn't have a job and wasn't looking for one.

"When do you think they will call?" Stan asked every day.

"I don't know!"

"Maybe with your connection now, I would have a better 'in' with the band."

"What 'connection'? I'm just barely hanging on by a shoestring. I really believe we should start checking the want ads in Aunt Vi's paper to see what is available."

Jeanette and Stan's social life was limited. Occasionally, Ty and his girlfriend, Beth, drove out to visit, and the couples would go

out for a bite to eat, dutch. And there was a nearby local movie
house.

A week passed. A week of the same conversation. A week of
hoping the telephone would ring, of dreading the telephone would
ring, of washing and cleaning and cooking, of ups and downs. She
thought she had done well because they hadn't called to say no. She
thought she hadn't done well because they hadn't called to say yes
—they hadn't called to say anything.

Jeanette had a meeting scheduled with Miss Burns the next Monday, a regular meeting; maybe she would finally start to learn what
"working on a scene" entailed. In her freshly washed and ironed
pink dress, she warily entered the office. Miss Burns saw her immediately—a good sign? A not-so-good sign? Very diplomatically and
tenderly, Miss Burns attempted to explain the state of affairs. The
rushes had been excellent; the final cut was outstanding; the test
would definitely be an asset to her future. But, although she didn't
know for sure, it didn't appear that Jeanette would be doing the
picture. She revealed that Beverly Tyler was the actress who would
probably play Lissy Anne. After all, Miss Tyler had experience and
was the protégée of a highly placed executive. (So *that* was why
Beverly Tyler had been in an 1860s costume that first day.)

Jeanette realized all was lost. Now, mind you, she logically knew
it was inconceivable that she would get the part. But, deep down
inside, she couldn't have helped harboring a sliver—just a sliver—
of hope. Even against the formidable odds.

Miss Burns tactfully suggested they reschedule the appointment
for another day. She tried to comfort the young girl; she understood only too well about that speck of hope one keeps buried
within.

Dejected, Jeanette walked down the alleyway to the bathroom,
the only place where she could safely give vent to her emotions,
indulge in a little self-pity. Then the guilt came. *I should be expressing
gratitude to all those helpful people, not moping.*

"Jeanette?"—then louder—"Jeanette? Are you in there?" Someone started pounding on the door. It sounded like Harry Friedman.
What was he doing outside the ladies' room? Oh, he probably
wanted to inform her of the decision. Well, she already knew that
answer, but it was thoughtful of him in any case.

When she opened the door, he grabbed her and yanked her back down the alleyway, through the anteroom, and into Miss Burns's study. Mr. Cummings and Mr. Rowland were there as well. Oh boy, they were making it more difficult for her.

"Sit down, Jeanette, we have some news for you."

Here it comes. Please, God, help me to be brave.

"We are pleased to tell you that you have been chosen for the role of Lissy Anne."

Oh my God. Thank you, God. She burst into tears. She wasn't alone—Miss Burns was crying, and even Mr. Cummings and Mr. Rowland and Mr. Friedman were misty. They all started hugging and crying and laughing; in his rush, Harry hadn't closed the inner door, and soon Muriel was also swept up in the commotion.

Then level heads (not hers) took command. She had to get to wardrobe immediately, if not sooner. All of her costumes had to be made and be ready to ship in two weeks. The company would locate in Santa Cruz for three months of exterior shooting and then return to the studio and complete the interiors. Hairpieces had to—

Jeanette had sunk back down in the chair and had started to sob again.

"For Pete's sake, *now* what's the matter?"

"I c-can't go. I can't d-d-do the picture."

"In heaven's name, *why?*"

"I can't afford to stay in a hotel or pay tr-train fare."

She wailed even more violently. They gazed at her in utter disbelief, completely dumbfounded. How could she be this innocent, this naïve? Her reaction on the onset about the test should have given them a clue. She really *was* Lissy Anne MacBean.

Soothingly, lovingly, they all tried to explain at once. The studio paid for transportation on location trips. The studio paid for housing when on location. She would even receive a daily allowance for food, per diem it was called. And the studio would provide a round-trip ticket for Stan as well.

Now did she think she could get her fanny over to wardrobe?

Jeanette was still crying, but from relief and happiness. She didn't know what to say. How could she ever thank them, all of them? She was floating, higher than Cloud 9. Was there a Cloud 9 trillion? On the way to wardrobe her feet didn't touch the ground—except for the rest-room stop.

The fitters were expecting her. The designs had all been approved; they just hadn't known whose body would wear them. This time she was placed in one of the front fitting rooms, but she wouldn't have noticed or cared if they had put her in a closet. In the midst of all this bustle—body measurements being taken, the hair stylist sizing her head for falls, color samples being taken—there was a knock and then a figure burst into the room. Holy cow, it was Van Johnson! Looking just like—Van Johnson! Reddish-blond hair, freckles, and sporting the famous boyish grin. Jeanette was absolutely tongue-tied; her prince, her dream man, was standing next to her.

"Saw your test—you were wonderful. Congratulations! Be seeing you soon," and he was off. She had barely stammered out a how-do-you-do.

The telephone kept ringing in wardrobe. Publicity department—had to meet with a Jeanette Morrison Reames first thing in the morning; very important. Muriel—set up appointments with Miss Burns to "work on the script" (at last she would discover what that meant). Mr. Cummings's office—don't leave before the revised script arrives. Transportation—would someone be at her house (*her* house?) at all times to receive script changes and the train tickets? Also, a studio car would pick her up on the day of departure and deliver her to the station.

There were so many departments, so many arrangements. This was no casual operation; this was a complicated business. And everything was happening so fast. She didn't want to miss one detail; she wanted this day stamped on her brain forever. And it was!

Wardrobe was done with her for the time being. Next fitting in three days; that would be Thursday. *Was this still Monday?* She stopped at Miss Burns's office and asked Muriel if she could use the phone in one of the other rooms. She was shaking; the shock had started to take effect. Stan answered and she blurted out the glad tidings. His yell almost broke her eardrums. He would meet her at the red-car exit in Glendale and walk her home.

As she waltzed out the gate, she wondered if *he* (the policeman) knew of her phenomenon. As she boarded the red car, she wondered if the passengers knew of her marvel. Naturally, no one knew, but she was so bewitched that she felt the whole world should share her blessing. She felt none of the bumps on the ride home; everything was beautiful, like a dream. *Was she dreaming?*

Was all this a fantasy? Was her mind playing cruel tricks on her? But the script in her hand was real; today *did* happen. *Thank you, thank you, thank you, dear God.*

Stan, Aunt Vi, Uncle Les, Jackie, Fred, and Helen were all thrilled. They could hardly believe her good fortune. Jeanette called Grandma Morrison, and Aunt Vi promised to drive her over to visit Grandma before she left. Aunt Vi also offered to cook dinner on the days she worked late.

What a day! She tried not to succumb to sleep and thus end it.

Van Johnson later told Jeanette how the casting decision had been reached. Mr. Cummings and Mr. Rowland, after viewing the results of the test, campaigned vigorously for the unknown Jeanette. Other factions were equally forceful for the experienced and established Beverly Tyler. Mr. Louis B. Mayer himself was prevailed upon to intervene. The preceding Saturday evening, Mr. Mayer, Van, and others gathered in Mr. Mayer's private projection room and scrutinized both tests. When the lights went on, Mr. Mayer announced: "The new one is perfect for the role. We gamble and go with her. A star is born."

Jeanette realized how much she was obligated to Miss Ryman, Miss Burns, Mr. Rowland, Mr. Cummings, Mr. Mayer—and Van Johnson. Because he was such a big star, he could have easily insisted on a "name" actress to play opposite him. It would obviously be more difficult to work with a novice, but he didn't object. A pro is a pro is a pro. And, of course, she was indebted to Miss Shearer, who was responsible for everything.

At ten the next morning, a Jeanette Morrison Reames reported to the Publicity Building (down the street from ladies' wardrobe). She was a very nervous Jeanette Morrison Reames. *Would they uncover the secret that she had so carefully concealed for four years?* Not if she could help it! She was convinced that revelation would ruin her.

She met the head of the department, Howard Strickling, a pleasant, serene, wise man. Jeanette liked him right away. He introduced her to Morgan Hudgins, who would be the unit publicist on *The Romance of Rosy Ridge.* Another winner—he was a soft-spoken Southern gentleman, in the truest sense of the word. When news had come to them who was to be Van Johnson's latest leading lady, their reaction was: Who? No one knew there was such a person under contract; they had a lot of work to do. It took hours to give the necessary information to compile a biography—names, dates, how, when, where. She told the truth; she simply neglected to mention the Merced incident.

An initial announcement would be made to the media to introduce her, followed by a well-developed advertising campaign. Their job was to take a "who" and make a "WOW." Not an easy task, even with their expertise.

On Friday, Miss Norma Shearer was graciously coming to the studio to pose for stills with Van Johnson and her "find." Jeanette caught her breath—she was going to see, to be near, this great lady. (Each time a new thing, a "first" occurred, she would think, "Now this is *it*. Nothing can top this." And then another bolt would strike. She was so full, she thought she might just burst.)

Her name had to go—too long, not enough pizzazz. Hopefully that decision would be made soon. No sense wasting publicity on an obsolete name, right? Sure, okay with her. It would be fun to have a new name.

Mr. Mayer wanted to meet his most recent roster member on Friday. The pink dress was so clean it squeaked. Jeanette brushed her hair so hard it was a wonder there was any left. She was absolutely terrified; her nerves were really working overtime. Mr. Friedman led her to the Thalberg Building, an imposing structure on the left of MGM's main entrance. They went through a spacious reception area (the desk clerk signed them in), went up in the elevator, disembarked on *his* floor, through a string of secretaries and assistants' offices, and then, the main area—a large, long, handsome room, sumptuously decorated. At the end, behind a luxurious desk, sat the legend. Mr. Mayer rose to greet them and seated them in front of his desk. He was short, balding, bespectacled, and very nice. He could see she was scared to death, so he attempted to put her at ease. He welcomed her to the MGM family, expressed his high hopes for her future, and talked about Busher. *Who in the hell is Busher?* She just nodded or shook her head (along with every other part of her body) and prayed he didn't think he had made a mistake with her. She *was* able to indicate her gratefulness for her opportunity, and her intent to work hard and learn well.

As soon as they were a safe distance from the building, she asked Mr. Friedman, *"Who is Busher?"*

"Busher is Mr. Mayer's favorite racing thoroughbred."

"He was talking about a *horse* all that time?"

She realized it was going to be a long while before she understood the ways of "show biz" people.

And now Jeanette was on her way to Mr. Strickling's office to meet Norma Shearer. Two legends in one day!

During the golden age of MGM, Norma Shearer made forty films for the studio and became queen of the MGM lot. Irving Thalberg, the "boy genius," recognized her potential and guided her career to the top. Their personal relationship culminated in marriage. After his untimely death at the age of thirty-seven, Miss Shearer continued filming until her voluntary retirement in 1942. But she maintained a strong influence at the studio—she owned a large share of company stock.

She was breathtakingly beautiful—classic patrician features, porcelain skin, and a smile that could melt stone. Her husband, Marty Arrougé, was a good-looking, dark-haired man, who was warm toward everybody, and obviously filled with adoration for his lovely wife. They were delightful to Jeanette and she was mesmerized by them. It was gratifying that their "discovery" had so quickly been recognized, that their judgment had been proven valid. *(Their* judgment, yes, but *she* still had a lot of proving to do.) Miss Shearer and Mr. Johnson kept a continual conversation going so that Jeanette's first photo session would be as relaxed and painless as possible. She was so fascinated by them and their proximity to her that she forgot about the cameraman. She thought if only she could freeze this moment forever . . . And, of course, in a way that is exactly what the camera did.

When the last shutter had clicked, Jeanette was told what her new name would be. Mr. Johnson had thought of it. She imagined how many girls in this country would have just *loved* to be named by Van Johnson, and she was the one, out of millions. He had shortened Jeanette to Janet, and because the movie dealt with the Civil War, he thought of Lee (the General), but spelling it Leigh.

"Oh no! Vivien Leigh is already a great actress."

"And Van Heflin is already a great actor." He went on, "Miss Vivien Leigh pronounces it 'Lay,' we'll pronounce it as 'Lee.' "

And so it was. And Janet Leigh was born.

I I

Janet Leigh

(Pollyanna in Hollywood)

CHAPTER SIX

Preparations for location graduated from hectic to frantic to frenetic. The studio staggered the dates of their employees' departures. First the unit manager and crew, then the director, cameraman, and first A.D., and last, the actors. Everyone connected with set design, decoration, or construction was long gone and almost finished.

I was either in wardrobe, hair styling for the falls, publicity, or with Miss Burns.

What a gargantuan assignment for Miss B. In two weeks (ten hours) she was supposed to impart to me the rudiments of the art of acting. She emphatically stated, "No one can teach someone to act, because you can't teach talent. You can give fundamental guidelines. You can teach diction, and body control. You can steer someone on how to take in and give out a living, breathing character. But you can't teach acting."

A few prescriptions:

Listen—that is a necessary key. Hear what everyone in the scene says. And let it register.

Participate—react to every sentence—not physically, but with your intellect. It will be expressed through your eyes and face. So when you speak, it comes from a natural progression of thoughts. Never just stand there waiting for your cue and then recite your lines. That has no meaning—it's empty. Only the words are written, so you must create the in-between with your imagination. (John Wayne once said, "I'm not an actor—I'm a re-actor." Succinctly stated.)

Concentration—a must. Ignore any distractions. You can't be involved in the emotions of the scene, if you are wondering about

lights, or how you look, or where the camera is located. Total
absorption is a requisite. (Van echoed this lesson while shooting
one day. I inadvertently blocked him in a shot. "Don't worry, the
camera will find me when it should—that isn't our purpose here."
I've heeded the advice to this day. I seldom am aware of camera
angles or lights; I figure I have to do my job and trust other people
to do theirs.)

Energy—very important. Not just bodily, but mental energy. The
juices have to keep flowing or you're dead weight.

Simplicity—overdoing or affectations spell phony, and only become a hindrance to a natural, honest portrayal.

Instinct—one needs to be blessed with it.

Approach—or preparing, or "working on" a script—ah ha! Everyone has their own method. I live by what was explained to me in
the beginning, hopefully enhancing some as I've matured. Learn
the entire script, so you know the continuity of the character's development (movies are not filmed in sequence). Invent a complete
background for this person, from babe forward, so you understand
the forces that guide her now. Conceptualize what occurs in the
gaps between scenes for sustainment.

Help—one needs all one can get!

On the night of August 24, 1946, the car picked me up and
drove me to the train station. Stan would follow in a week, which
would delay any employment opportunity he might have. But, what
the heck, he couldn't miss this experience. Mr. Rowland's wife,
Ruth, was my traveling companion (a lovely lady, then and now).
We had a *compartment*—Compartment F on The Lark—with two
berths and a little bath. This was quite different from the coach to
Merced. I didn't need the bed—I couldn't sleep anyway. My head
was overflowing with the script, the fear, the anticipation, the fear,
the fear, the excitement—the *fear*.

Monday, at 7 A.M., a studio car took me out to the location for
the MacBean farm. I was confronted once again with the artistry of
re-creation. The small loghouse, the barn, the shed, the interiors—
they were all perfect replicas. They even had corn and wheat growing in the field.

I met so many people. Leon (makeup), nicknamed Leonardo because he applied makeup as if he were painting a canvas. Eleanor
(hair), the sweet person who taught me how to knit. Gertie (ward-

robe), a personal lesson learned right from the start. (She was Gertrude Kirkwood, the silent picture star, once married to giant luminary Jack Kirkwood. She was penniless, down and out. She showed me her scrapbooks and she broke my heart. She wasn't a particularly adept wardrobe mistress, and I appreciated the industry's attempt to help keep one of its own afloat. *Oh boy, never me,* I hoped.) Sam Polo (Van's makeup man), who was always first in line for lunch. (Sam's son, Eddie, later became my makeup artist and friend. He never could get my mouth straight—because it isn't! We laughed a lot together.)

Thomas Mitchell, a dynamic actor, scared me at first, until I realized his gruffness was the role. Dean Stockwell, the handsome, talented little devil, was all boy. Marshall Thompson was gentle and sensitive and nice. And, of course, there was dear Selena Royle. Van was not due until Wednesday.

My opening scene was with O. Z. Whitehead, a delightful, eccentric actor from New York. He played Ninny Nat, combination mailman and gossip columnist of the territory. He was a strange sight—riding a tiny mule, his long legs dangling (almost touching the ground), garbed in a tall Lincolnesque hat and black suit. Lissy Anne is hoeing when she sees him approach, she stops and goes to the fence to greet him. "Any news, Ninny Nat?" She misinterprets his reply, and takes off across the field at full speed, yelling, "Ben's acomin home! Maw! Paw!" There was a large reflector on a broad stand in the vicinity. When I started running, and I was pretty fast, I hit the foot of the stand and did a head-over-heels spread-eagle flop. (I was a klutz then, am now, and always will be.) Mr. Rowland thought I was a goner on the very first shot. And it wasn't over yet. Later one of Lissy Anne's chores was to milk the family cow. I had never come in contact with a cow in my entire young life. (Big things, aren't they?) The cowboy in charge of the animals showed me the procedure. Bessie wasn't pleased with my hesitant hands and became restless. She then proceeded to step on my foot—all fifteen hundred pounds of her.

It seemed not to be my day. But it was! It was a glorious day! It was a perfect day! It was a never-to-be forgotten day! It was the first day of shooting on my first movie. And I loved it, every minute of it. I loved being Lissy Anne MacBean. I loved the camaraderie of everyone on the set. I loved the team effort. I even loved Bessie.

And I felt comfortable. Nervous, yes, but not the restraining kind —it was exhilarating. Unquestionably, I thought, I had found my niche. My mom and dad never were privileged to find theirs.

(I might not have been so elated if I had been aware then how easily I could have been replaced. The initial rushes were closely watched. If I had slipped or floundered or had not been right in any way, I would have been on the first train out—to oblivion. My guiding light was working overtime; I was blissfully ignorant of it all.)

About two weeks into the picture, "someone" in the Thalberg Building at MGM had second thoughts about my name—the Leigh part especially—and changed me to Jean Morrison. By this time, I had bought a three-ring school binder and had it stamped with JANET LEIGH (an investment of maybe fifty cents). I liked my new name and was disappointed with the exchange. Van, my champion, became angry and called Louis B. Mayer from location. "What's this nonsense about her name? She even has a little binder all labeled. Can't we leave it be?"

Mr. Mayer decreed, "It shall be Janet Leigh." And that was the end of that.*

Toward the end of September, Harry Friedman came to visit, two contracts in hand. With his, Van became the highest-paid actor in Hollywood at that time. And my contract had been renegotiated, the first of three such transactions during my eight years at MGM. I would now receive $150 a week, with substantial increases each year. I couldn't believe my good fortune. Verily, it *was* a fortune.

There was always a crowd gathered at the entrance of the location, watching the action, hoping to get a glimpse of the stars. Van was sweepingly popular, and unselfishly *patient* with his many fans. And he always made sure I was included. (Another valuable example for me to emulate.)

---

* About twenty years later, I had the privilege of meeting Sir Laurence Olivier. I was completely in awe of such a respected and renowned international personage. That classic profile turned my knees to jelly, and the voice that had thrilled millions —me included—was even more lyrical face-to-face. I eventually mustered enough courage to ask him if his lovely lady (Vivien Leigh) had ever voiced displeasure about the studio's choice of Leigh for my last name. To my surprise and chagrin, he replied in the affirmative. "She did believe it was presumptuous, when first notified. However, she soon rallied and recognized no one has a monopoly on a name." I was mortified.

I felt honored when asked for an autograph (I still do). It was a kick! A lot of publicity had been generated in the area's newspapers by the movie company's presence, and I was thrilled to see my name and picture in print. Press releases had begun to fly in Los Angeles and Aunt Vi sent me copies. Representatives from *Photoplay* magazine and Ideal Publications came to do stories—mostly because of Van, to be sure, but I was interviewed as well. I was convinced I would be tongue-tied with no script to follow. But on the contrary, my excitement about the overwhelming events that had occurred since June 27 exploded into a torrent of words. In fact, they couldn't shut me up.

No one, thank God, went as far back with their questions as June 1942.

Acquaintances from Stockton showed up from time to time. The papers had been full of "Jeanette Morrison Reames Becomes Janet Leigh." The guard always informed me of those arrivals so I could go out to greet them. One day he came over to say that some people I knew were there, and I said, "Oh, I'll come right away."

"No, it's not necessary," he informed me. "It seems they just want to find out from someone if you've changed."

Now what did *that* mean? Changed what? My name? They already knew that. They meant, of course, my personality. Had I become "too big for my britches," "uppity"? I felt as though I was already condemned without a trial.

They didn't even want to see me, they just expected—maybe wanted—to hear gossip about me that they could take back and tell in Stockton.

The company developed the aura of Camelot—an air of enchantment.

The cast and crew were free from tension, free from political infighting; we were a unified, happy family, working toward our mutual goal. It was due, in part, to being on location, away from studio interference. It was also, I believe, because they were pulling for me, for my innocence, my naïveté.

A few times, the crew cooked spaghetti for the whole gang in Van's suite (I rinsed the pasta in the bathtub). We went out to wonderful, charming restaurants in the surrounding area: Babbling Brook, Brookdale Lodge (which had a trout stream bubbling through), and the Chinese Tea Cup. And not too far away, there were the famous Pebble Beach Lodge, scenic Carmel and Monterey, and the breathtaking 17 Mile Drive. Wherever we went, Van was besieged by waiters, captains, owners, patrons, everyone and anyone.

One night Van donned a mustache, a wig, and glasses, hoping we could all stroll along the Santa Cruz boardwalk and enjoy the circuslike atmosphere. The disguise worked for about fifteen minutes, but there was no mistaking his walk, his manner, his build. The group was soon embroiled in a near-riot.

The only blemish, literally, was Van's encounter with poison oak during a chase scene where he had to forge his way through heavy brush. How he suffered! A few days of shooting were lost, but his was the highest price paid.

In late October, the entire company departed for Sonora, near Yosemite National Park, to complete the location work. Leaving the MacBean farm was like leaving my home. I felt a need to cling to the familiar. I didn't want to move on. But time and schedules wait for no one. While the new accommodations were quaintly rustic, the setting was stunning—wild, majestic mountain country. And the weather was glorious, crystal clear, but very cold.

The love scene between Van and myself was approaching, and I was inordinately apprehensive. I knew I was being silly, but I couldn't control my anxiety. How do you kiss in make-believe land, with fifty people watching? Do you exercise abandonment? Wouldn't that make you brazen? Or do you practice restraint? But wouldn't that make you cold and uncaring? Undeniably, the "nice girl" label still plagued me. I valued Van's opinion so much, I didn't know what to do. And then an awful thought—what if I had bad breath? And the cold! What if my teeth were chattering so hard I bit his lip? I was in a state. And my nervousness infected Van.

Perceptive Mr. Rowland halted the contagious panic. "It isn't Janet kissing Van, it's Lissy Anne kissing Henry. You know Lissy inside out. How would her first kiss be given to the man she loves?"

I had forgotten—I had lapsed into my private fears, instead of wearing the cloak of Lissy. I had allowed myself to interrupt concentration. *So much to learn.*

Mr. Rowland, of course, was right. Our contact was a pure and

TOP: left, Helen and Fred Morrison. Right, little Jeanette. BOTTOM: left, a ten-year-old Jeanette's first taste of fame as miniature drum major for the Sciots marching band. Right, Jeanette and Dick Doane — age thirteen.

OPPOSITE: the picture that started it all. ABOVE: the beginning of Janet — with Norma Shearer and Van Johnson and the pink dress.

TOP: Janet as Lissy Anne on location for *The Romance of Rosy Ridge*, 1946. BOTTOM: Esther Williams visiting the set of *The Romance of Rosy Ridge*.

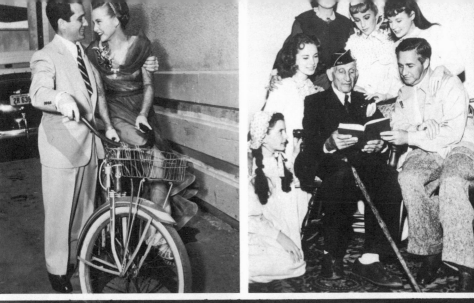

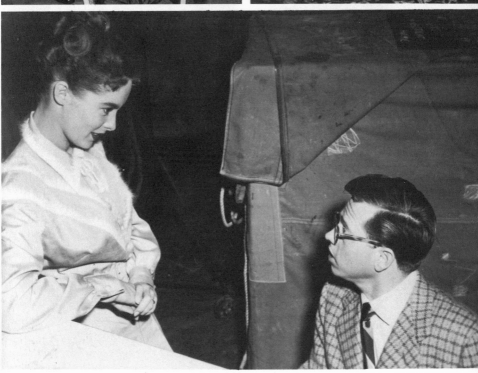

TOP: left, with Perry Como on the lot of MGM during the filming of *Words and Music,* 1947. Right, Mervyn's *Little Women* — Margaret O'Brien, Janet, Mary Astor, Elizabeth Taylor, June Allyson, Mervyn LeRoy, Civil War veteran. BOTTOM: with Mickey Rooney on the set of *Words and Music,* 1947.

Clark Gable visiting the set of *Hills of Home*, 1947.

With Errol Flynn on the set of *That Forsyte Woman*, 1948.

TOP: attending the premiere of *The Yearling*, with L.B. Mayer, Vera Ellen, and Maureen O'Hara. BOTTOM: with Arthur Loew, Jr., and a character borrowed from central casting to welcome Arthur home from filming a Western.

uncomplicated expression of simple love and shared desire. It was a
sweet, tender, touching experience. And on screen it conveyed the
proper sentiment: a young, hesitant virgin surrendering her lips to
the gentle man she adored.

When we returned from location, the studio arranged for Stan
and me to stay at the Del Mar Hotel in Santa Monica—at their
expense. It wasn't practical for them to have me make the round
trip to Glendale every day while filming. My mom and dad had
purchased a beat-up Ford and left Sugar Bowl, with the intention of
settling in Los Angeles. So we looked for a rental we could share
with them; it would be easier on all of us to split expenses. And
Stan and I had to buy a car; it was almost impossible to exist in Los
Angeles without your own means of transportation. We decided on
a used gray Chevy sedan for about two hundred dollars. I had been
able to save a little from my paycheck and per diem money. But
since the GI loan payments were still in effect (and would be for the
next two years), I had to pay the initiation fee to join the Screen
Actors Guild, and with the agency commissions, plus deductions,
there wasn't much surplus.

It was a pleasant stay at the beach. The Del Mar, a sprawling old
landmark, was quiet and staid, conducive to study and rest. And it
was a long way from the Harvey Hotel. Stan seemed lost though,
floating in a sea of indecision. I felt a job—any job—would be a
step in the right direction, but I tried not to push him too hard.

The reunion with Mom and Dad was joyful—it had been a long
time between hugs—and so much had happened to their "baby."
(Your children are always your "babies," even if they have gray
hair.) We found a little house in the San Fernando Valley that fit our
mutual pocketbooks and moved in time to have Thanksgiving dinner. We had much for which to be thankful.

Filming at the studio *was* different, but wonderful. There were
more diversions. Actors, producers, directors, publicity representatives, etc., were always coming by the set. Van introduced me to so
many people, I couldn't remember who they all were. But I did
know one was Esther Williams.

Usually I brought my lunch (one of the changes from location—
no more free food). But a few times I went to the commissary with
Marie Windsor or Jim Davis. What a sight! I could never eat, I was

too busy gawking. In that huge room—God, I was always so self-conscious walking to a table—I'd see Clark Gable in one corner, Elizabeth Taylor and her mother in another, Gene Kelly tucked against the wall, and on and on and on. My head needed a swivel. Later I discovered there were special tables, the actors' table, the writers' table, the producers' table, and so forth. They were like clubs. Such shenanigans, such jokes, such laughter, and such fun! It took me well over a year to brave the actors' table. It took *forever* for me to be comfortable entering that dining room.

I wasn't a stranger in makeup now—*I belonged.* What a good feeling. Not that I knew every one intimately, or even met everyone, but at least I wasn't an outsider. Some women, and men too, preferred being made up in their dressing rooms, so they were never seen. I always thought that was too lonely.

Old clothes were the customary attire—no need to ruin good things with stains from all that "goop." And no makeup—that, of course, was why we were there. All except beautiful Arlene Dahl. Whatever the hour, 5 A.M., 6 A.M. or 7 A.M., she would arrive impeccably groomed, coiffed, and made up, with matching shoes and bag, tailored suit, gloves. I never could see how any improvement was possible.

Every film company had a limousine, maybe two (and sometimes, each *star* had a limo), to take the performers from makeup to the stage, to lunch, to the restroom, to their dressing room. The drivers were priceless. Real characters. The stories they told were endless, and there was no doubt whom they liked and whom they didn't. (Don't get on their list!)

Without exception, their past favorites had been Jean Harlow and Carole Lombard. Glowing, the drivers would describe their realness, their humor, honesty and "one of the guys" attitude. Norma Shearer *(my* Norma Shearer) and Joan Crawford were also high on the ladder. But on the movie *The Women* (1939) the drivers faced a dilemma. The custom at that time was for *the* star to arrive last on the set, as the status symbol. The cast included Norma Shearer, Joan Crawford, Rosalind Russell, Mary Boland, Paulette Goddard, Joan Fontaine, Ruth Hussey, Marjorie Main, Hedda Hopper, and more. Imagine the billing problem on that one. Now, who was *the* star? Every lady thought *she* was. Miss Shearer would say, "No *she's* not here yet. Go around the block again." Ditto Miss

Crawford, Miss Russell, and right down the line. The studio had a film to make—what to do?—the cars could have circled all day.

The drivers solved the problem. They made a deal among themselves to alternate the days of last arrival. And that's just what they did—and the ladies were all pacified.

Why do good times have to end? I guess it's because we have to grow; we have to move forward, to learn and evolve, add to our dictionary of life. But it's always so hard. I would have been content to have *The Romance of Rosy Ridge* continue filming forever. But it couldn't. Our "family" was disbanding, each one going in a different direction. There was a great void in my life suddenly, as if a surgeon had cut out part of my insides, and the operation had been painful. (Time would show me that I would feel like this on the completion of almost every picture.)

I was convinced fate had steered me into the proper channel. How my ship was piloted from now on was up to me. I was determined to explore every inlet of my fledgling profession, because I desperately wanted it to be my permanent profession.

There were many facilities available to contract players, if one chose to utilize them. I chose. I embarked on a journey of lessons and training. Gertrude Fogler was probably the best diction and voice teacher in town. At first sight, she appeared to be a small, plumpish, white-haired, grandmother-type lady. That is, until you sat across from her and looked into the most vital, young, alert blue eyes you ever saw. And until she spoke, in a magical, full, beautiful tone. We would read classics, poems, and Shakespeare aloud, employing her exercises. Never would she invite me or anyone else to assume an unnatural quality. She strove only to enhance the actor's own instrument.

I had no idea how fast I spoke or how high the timbre of my voice was. When I "looped"† some of the outdoor scenes in *Rosy*

---

† "Looping" takes place in a sound studio. If the sound in a scene is marred for any reason—by an airplane, the wind, set noises, etc.—you synchronize the spoken words to the picture on the screen, in the controlled conditions of the studio. You wear earphones to hear the original tract and get the rhythm—it's usually done line by line—and then the earphones go silent, and you try to match the what and how of the first time. The danger is sounding parrotlike, losing the intent of the scene, reciting by rote. This is not an easy task.

Ridge, I could hardly get my mouth to move that quickly. I was surprised when I heard myself; we really aren't aware how we sound to other people.

And then there was Rosie (Arthur Rosenstein), the singing coach, who was loved by all. He had nurtured most of the musical greats at MGM. He also enlightened the not-so-greats, the neophytes, like me. Ida Mayer Cummings, Mr. Mayer's sister, always relied on Rosie to supply the talent she needed for her numerous charity functions. These appearances were helpful to her causes and provided Rosie with a showcase for his pupils. Every experience aided to make us well-rounded performers.

Miss Burns not only worked with us on an individual basis, but also conducted Friday afternoon classes where prepared scenes were presented and critiqued. It was a while before I actively participated in *that* company. Too scary to even contemplate. But I could learn just by observation.

Supplementing all of these people were specialists accessible to teach specific skills needed for a particular role, such as accents, dancing, playing a musical instrument, athletic dexterity, and so on.

Enough to keep me occupied! No idle minds or idle hands at MGM!

Christmas 1946. At nineteen, I believed I had already received my Christmas present early—on June 27 to be exact—but Santa had one more surprise up his sleeve.

Every Wednesday night CBS Radio aired a popular program called "Cresta Blanca's Hollywood Players," a company of Hollywood's greatest stars: Claudette Colbert, Bette Davis, Joan Fontaine, Paulette Goddard, Joseph Cotten, John Garfield, Gene Kelly, and Gregory Peck, who rotated weekly.

Their Christmas show, a specially written play, was to feature the four men, and to star an unknown. And that unknown was ME! Jeanette Helen Morrison Reames was going to appear on the same stage with Joseph Cotten, John Garfield, Gene Kelly, and Gregory Peck. And be paid *five hundred dollars* for the privilege. I would have paid *them!*

There are times when words are not enough to describe emotions. This was such a time.

The first read-through was a disaster. My hands were shaking so badly I could hardly hold the script. I stumbled over lines. My voice was inaudible. I felt so inadequate, being surrounded by these giant stars. I was sure everyone was rolling their eyes and thinking, *"What* have we here?" These gentlemen were paragons of patience. Perhaps they all remembered the time when they started, how the insecurity oozes from your pores.

Gradually, with their encouragement, I relaxed and allowed the play to take over. All was going well, and then, the day of the show, when an audience started filing into the theatre, it hit me. This was *live*—no second chance. We would be going over the airways to millions of listeners, direct. *Faith, don't fail me now.* I concentrated so hard, corralled all my thoughts toward the script, borrowed the strength from the four on stage—and did it. The applause at the conclusion of the performance made me feel proud and pleased. My first radio show. It's amazing what we can do if we don't put stop signs in our way.

METRO GOLDWYN MAYER

PRESENTS

VAN JOHNSON IN

"THE ROMANCE OF ROSY RIDGE"

STARRING

THOMAS MITCHELL, DEAN STOCKWELL,
SELENA ROYLE, MARSHALL THOMPSON

AND INTRODUCING

JANET LEIGH

	Excellent	Above Average	Good	Fair	Poor
1. How would you rate this picture?					
2. How would you rate performances?					
Van Johnson					
Thomas Mitchell					
Selena Royle					
Dean Stockwell					
Marshall Thompson					
Janet Leigh					

3. How would you rate subject matter?
4. How would you recommend this to
   your friends?
5. Age Group   Under 15   15 to 25   25 to 35   Over 35

This was the kind of card that was handed to audiences at the conclusion of a major studio sneak preview of a new film. These showings, usually held at a neighborhood theatre in an outlying district, whose patrons did not know which picture they would be viewing, enabled the studios to evaluate the potential of their new movie and its participants. The players were not supposed to attend, lest their presence influence the public's response. But, of course, word would leak about the location of the "sneak," and many would go, regardless of policy. The trick was to arrive when the theatre opened its doors, before the people and the studio brass showed. In my case, no one knew me anyway, and Mr. Rowland and Mr. Cummings wanted to share the experience with me. So, Stan and I, Mom and Dad, Aunt Vi and Uncle Les, Aunt Pope and Uncle Jimmy (who came all the way from Oakland) bought our tickets and went in as regular customers. (Motion pictures had never been a part of Grandma Morrison's sightless world, but after *The Romance of Rosy Ridge* officially opened, we took her so she could hear my screen voice while I, sitting next to her, quietly explained the action taking place.)

What a strange sensation! To sit there and see your name on that huge white screen. And then to see *you,* that other you, up there. How many hundreds of times had I sat in a movie house, been swept along as the magic materialized before me. But now, I was watching *me,* as a part of that wonderful illusion. I didn't think I would be able to divorce me from "me," but soon the story took precedence and I was swallowed up along with the rest of the crowd. I thoroughly enjoyed the movie, and so did everyone else. The reaction was very positive, and the smiles grew broader and broader as the preview cards were turned in. The tally registered 75 percent excellent, for picture and performers, 22 percent above average, and 3 percent good. And that ain't bad! Mr. Cummings and Mr. Rowland were proud; the studio was delighted; I was ecstatic.

There was a great deal of buzz around the lot about the results—about Van, and about a "new star" on the horizon. At my next appointment with Miss Burns, she sat me down, and offered me the sagest advice I've ever received, and would never forget.

"Janet, dear, I am happy for you. I believe you can do great things someday. But only if you continue to work, and work hard. You have a long way to go. I am aware the word 'star' has been prematurely applied. Trust me—one picture does not a star make. If, in twenty years, you are still actively in this profession, perhaps then I will call you—a *star.*"

How true! And how fortunate I was to hear it early on, before I could succumb to the lure of believing my own publicity. These thoughts of being a "star" already had never entered my head—I knew my limitations—but who can tell?—they very well might have someday. It happened to others.

As so many before us have discovered, Stan and I found that living with parents was not the healthiest arrangement for a young married couple. It was congenial, but strained. Daddy could not reconcile with the fact that Stan was not working. Naturally, they thought everything I did was fine.

When Daddy found a job, they moved to a small duplex in Inglewood, and we went into a one-room apartment on South Peck Drive in Beverly Hills. Not bad, not great, but compared to the Harvey Hotel it was the Taj Mahal. Van Johnson and Morgan Hudgins came for dinner one evening and we could barely squeeze around the kitchen table. At least I didn't have to walk far to serve; it was about two steps from stove to guests. They didn't care though; they were really good sports.

Early in 1947, Van Johnson and Evie Wynn were married, which caused quite a stir. When I was living in Stockton, I had read about Van's near-fatal motor accident and how he had recuperated in the home of his best friends, Evie and Keenan Wynn. Van had dated many Hollywood glamour queens, but had obviously fallen in love with Evie. Unfortunately, this didn't sit too well with many of his female fans and the press. If Van and June Allyson had wed, it would have been labeled "a marriage made in heaven." But human emotions can't be programmed, nor should they be. Van and Evie were entitled to their own life, even if it didn't meet with everyone's approval. *The Romance of Rosy Ridge* was the first Van Johnson picture released after the marriage, and the box-office receipts suffered. It was critically acclaimed, and it did very good business, but it wasn't the expected usual Van Johnson blockbuster.

None of this actually registered with me. Those facets of show business were way beyond me then. I was only pleased for my friends' happiness. And friends they were!

One day a telegram from Atwater Kent (the famed millionaire) arrived at the apartment, inviting me and a guest to a gala at his hilltop mansion. Movie magazines were filled with pictures of celebrities attending his soirées. *How did he know me?* Of course, he didn't know me, but I learned later that social secretaries kept a watchful eye for new faces to add to their guest lists. Stan and I immediately sought advice from Van and Evie. Their new home was off Seventh Street in Brentwood, and it was the grandest residence I'd ever beheld. Built and decorated by Cedric Gibbons (the award-winning art director), it boasted several levels, connected by a modern spiral staircase. Dining room, kitchen, servants' quarters, projection room were on the bottom floor; there was a large living and den and bar area on another; and up on yet another floor were the bedrooms and dressing rooms. Each floor had its own compact kitchen. There was a children's wing off to the side. Sprawling grounds contained a swimming pool, a playhouse, and a sunken tennis court with an overlooking cabana. Elegant—just like a movie set!

Did they think we should go? What would we do? What would we wear? Van went to a wastebasket and dug out a crumpled telegram. (They had not planned to accept the invitation.) He was jubilant. "We wouldn't miss this for anything. *Yes,* you will go. You will go with us. Stan can probably fit into one of my tuxedos—"

Evie interrupted, "And I know we can fix something of mine for Janet," and pulled me upstairs to her wardrobe. My eyes popped—it looked like a department store. She rummaged through her evening dresses. "No, this isn't right—here's one. Try this—oh, I think I like this for you. Too damn small for me anyway." She decided on a long black satin skirt and a delicate lace overblouse with a black narrow velvet ribbon and a brooch around the neck. It was very pretty. The guys voted their approval.

While getting dressed at the apartment, I wished some of Van and Stan's confidence would rub off on me. Did I really look presentable? Maybe I should have borrowed makeup from the studio or Evie. I bet Eleanor would have fixed my hair. Always the doubts! A feeling of unsuitability persistently haunted me.

At least in this case we really wouldn't be scrutinized too closely. We were sort of "with *them*" (Van and Evie), as voyeurs more than anything else.

Atwater Kent lived on top of a mountain in the Hollywood Hills, but his estate began at the bottom. As we wound our way toward the glittering summit, past terraced gardens and gushing fountains, past softly illuminated statuary, I felt like Cinderella approaching the palace. In certain ways, my fairy-tale discovery did parallel Cinderella's. I never thought to question—*did* Cinderella "live happily ever after"? And I wasn't about to ponder it now. As Scarlett O'Hara said, "I'll think about it tomorrow."

The evening proved that movie magazines didn't lie—at least about Mr. Kent's affairs. Most of those attending were "the famous," either in front of or behind the camera; the ladies were all beautiful and the gentlemen all handsome; there were elaborate gowns and expensive jewels; there were alternating orchestras and tuxedo-clad waiters carrying trays of champagne and caviar and every conceivable gourmet appetizer. Van and Evie had a ball watching our rapturous expressions as each new wonder revealed itself, introducing us to their crowd: Sonja Henie, Cole Porter, John Payne, George Cukor, Gary Cooper, Darryl Zanuck, Claudette Colbert, Joe Pasternak, Cesar Romero, and on and on, and seeing our reactions. We didn't contribute much to any conversation, and I doubt that we made a lasting impression on anyone, but we were *there.*

And so were Van's famous red socks. I knew from my movie magazine reading that Van had a superstition about always wearing bright red socks. I had peeked when we were in Santa Cruz, and sure enough, they were very much in evidence. And formal attire made no difference.

CHAPTER SEVEN

In the spring of 1947, I was cast in my second picture, *If Winter Comes,* starring Walter Pidgeon, Deborah Kerr, and Angela Lansbury.

The role was Effie, a poor English waif who gets pregnant by a local village boy before he leaves for the war. She is befriended by Walter Pidgeon, commits suicide when the lad is killed, and unwittingly sets up Mr. Pidgeon's character to be blamed for her death; but she also leaves a note, that when discovered, vindicates him. Very dramatic, and very English. The studio hired the niece of Sir C. Aubrey Smith to tutor me. I have a good ear, but accents just don't come easily. (I've always envied performers who have the knack of launching into a variety of accents at the drop of a hat— comedians especially seem to have this ability.) For me, it means a lot of studying. We read several *New Yorker* magazines from cover to cover, practicing intonations and inflections, so that the accent would become a familiar and natural part of my speech. We did not read the lines from the script, thus preventing any built-in interpretation. We must have pulled it off, since Victor Saville, the director, wasn't aware of my actual heritage until late in the shooting. The majority of my scenes were with Walter Pidgeon, and what a distinguished actor and person he proved to be! He also sponsored me for membership in the Academy of Motion Picture Arts and Sciences, and I was accepted about six months later. That was a proud moment.

Wouldn't you know, despite my struggle with accents, that my next immediate assignment was as Margit, a Scottish lass, in *Hills of Home.* This was a Lassie picture with Edmund Gwenn, Donald Crisp, and Tom Drake. I'd had a secret crush on Tom Drake and his breathy voice for years, and I blushed like a teenager when I met him in makeup. But I was no longer a teeny-bopper, I had just turned twenty.

There is an old adage in show business: Whenever possible, avoid scenes with animals and children because a "regular" performer doesn't stand a chance against them. Absolutely a truth! Who can compete with the soulful, wise eyes of Lassie gazing lovingly at her master! Or the complete vulnerability and guilelessness of a child's face! I was still innocent enough not to know this, or I would have been more frazzled. As it was, I was caught in that quagmire of the more I learned, the more I realized how little I knew.

Miss Burns took extra care with me in the preparation for this film, taking me deeper into an analysis of the character, making sure *each* line meaning was fully explored, almost assuming a directorial posture. I discovered why very soon.

We left for three weeks location in late July, again in the rugged splendor of the Sierras. Everything was more familiar to me now; there was no more panic about living and transportation problems. There were even some duplications on the crew list from *The Romance of Rosy Ridge.* But there was a big difference. Fred Wilcox, the director, was a very nice man but an extremely weak director. An actor was really left on his own. Obviously Miss B. was aware of this but didn't want to alarm me. So she provided me with as much ammunition as she could in advance, since she could not be present on the set. This was my first encounter with such a problem but not my last. Fortunately, I have usually had the advantage of being guided by the very top of the field—the masters. But there have been rare exceptions when I was faced with a limited leader. It becomes easier as one grows in one's craft to depend on one's own instincts, to create a full portrayal, to fill the conspicuous gaps. One may not give an inspired performance—may not reach the heights of which one is capable without a gifted captain, but at least, one survives on film.

But on my third time at bat!

Margit was not a complicated girl to understand; I had learned the brogue; and I was surrounded by excellent, well-seasoned, helpful thespians (including Lassie); so I managed to squeak by without making a fool of myself. All gathered data helps, inch by inch, to build a foundation on which to stand. I am grateful that I kept having opportunities to build up mine.

During the final weeks of *Hills of Home* at the studio, Stan and I moved from our one room on Peck Drive to a new one-bedroom duplex on Elenda Street in Culver City, three blocks from MGM. Stan had a commission job with a collection agency with flexible hours—"no collecting, no salary"—which still gave him a lot of free time. But he needed use of the car, and from the duplex I could walk to work. Only one problem—it was unfurnished. My Aunt Pope and Uncle Jimmy had recently moved to Los Angeles, and as much as I hated debt, I had no recourse but to ask them for a loan of $200 to purchase some essential furniture. One consolation —this time I could see how we would repay our obligation (it only took three months). A young couple, whom we had met on *The Romance of Rosy Ridge,* leased the other side of the duplex, and we shared some pleasant potluck evenings.

Miss Burns felt it was time for me to take the plunge and begin doing scenes for the Friday afternoon drama group. Not every Friday produced a session, and not every session produced a scene—a job might cause a cancellation from a participant, or the necessary rehearsal hours could be thwarted by other commitments, or Miss B. might be called "upstairs" for an emergency. But when the afternoon sessions took place, they were not treated lightly. A great deal of time and energy was poured into these presentations. And there was an abundance of talent. Sitting in the room, one might see Betty Garrett, Arlene Dahl, Ricardo Montalban, Beverly Tyler, Linda Christian, Gloria DeHaven, Edmund Purdom, Jim Davis, Marie Windsor, Don Taylor, Tom Drake, Marshall Thompson, Cyd Charisse, Barry Nelson, or Peter Lawford. Even Van Heflin visited a few times. Producers and directors were invited to attend on special occasions. It's not too difficult to appreciate my trepidation in testing the waters.

Miss Burns arranged for me to meet Barry Nelson, whom she believed to be the most gifted of all the contract players. He was filming with Ann Sothern in a *Maisie* picture, so our first encounter was in his trailer between shots. I had seen him on the screen, but not in person. His were unconventional good looks: he was rugged, of medium stature, with an ageless Scandinavian square face, and twinkling but probing blue eyes.

We engaged in introductory small talk, and then he suggested I read Clifford Odets's play *Night Music.* He thought we should consider it for our drama group project. Appointments were set up, with the understanding that actual work had priority. I really liked the play and could see why he thought it would be appropriate for us. But I also had doubts. How do we rehearse without a director, without Miss Burns? How do we make it believable without the proper sets and props?

My fears were groundless. Miss Burns was right—again. Barry was an accomplished director, especially adept in working with people, and a skilled actor as well. In the months we worked together, he taught me as much as anyone I've ever known. He was strong and demanding, but gentle. He was patient with his explanations, meticulous in his search for honesty and reality. Any false note, any line read without thought, sent him right up the wall. There was no conflict with other teachers' concepts, but there was the time to expand and explore and experiment with theories under knowledgeable tutelage.

A small example. This may seem trivial, but no segment is unimportant to the whole. I was having trouble finding the right meaning to the line "A stitch in time saves nine," referring to torn pants in an uncomfortable situation. It sounded contrived. Barry said, "Before you say the line, say to yourself, 'Well, you know what they say. . . .' " And it worked! It was no longer a non sequitur; it came from a premise. Simple, right? Wrong! Someone has to think of all those helpful hints for each line. And that someone, someday, should be the actor himself.

On the Friday designated for our scene, I kept hoping for a stay of execution. And when that didn't occur, I willed that no one would show up. And when that failed, I tried "thinking sick." But I was too damn healthy—scared, nervous, trembling, but healthy. No way out!

Barry introduced the scene; we took time to prepare inwardly, set our own stage, so to speak; and we began. Again I had that sensation of being apart from myself. I was in New York, I was Fay in love with Steve, and we were in need of a home, of something secure and dependable in a slippery and nervous world; we laughed and cried and fought our way together. And it was over. And I felt wonderful. And our reception was extremely gratifying. And even more important, I hadn't disappointed Miss Burns—or Barry.

Nineteen forty-seven proved to be a busy year. I was cast in *Words and Music* (the musical story of the collaboration between Richard Rodgers and Lorenz Hart), with Arthur Freed producing and Norman Taurog directing. I would portray Dorothy Rodgers, with Tom Drake as Dick Rodgers, Mickey Rooney as Larry Hart, and Betty Garrett playing his girlfriend. Plus—big *big* plus—musical numbers and scenes by June Allyson, Cyd Charisse, Perry Como, Vera-Ellen, Judy Garland, Gene Kelly, Lena Horne, Ann Sothern, Mel Torme, and others. I was beside myself with excitement. And *the* Helen Rose was designing the wardrobe. I was going to be in a real MGM musical extravaganza, wearing beautiful dresses and having more legends come to life.

When I was ten, I remember spending one whole Sunday in a movie house watching *Captains Courageous* over and over again. It was a classic, starring Spencer Tracy, Lionel Barrymore, Freddie Bartholomew, Melvyn Douglas, and Mickey Rooney. I also remember growing up with Andy Hardy. Now, in 1947, I was face-to-face with the Mighty Mite. Working with Mickey was like being exposed to a mental and physical tornado. He could have been wired to generate the electric power for Los Angeles County. I promise you the set was never dull. But there was a very tender quality as well.

The day came that we were to do the Judy Garland sequence, a scene which led into the numbers "Johnny One Note" and "I Wish I Were in Love Again," sung by Mickey and Judy. The prospect of the proximity of every girl's heroine, Dorothy, sent chills through me. I arrived very early; I didn't want to miss one second. Gradually, everyone else assembled for the big party scene. And we waited. And we waited. And we waited. Normally, Mickey would have boiled over, but he was only calm and patient. He knew, I guess most knew (except me), that Judy had been going through one of her rough periods and was having trouble pulling herself together. Around eleven o'clock Mr. Freed escorted Miss Garland to the stage, where she was greeted like royalty. Which she was! She was also warm and open and dear—and nervous and thin and drawn. It never occurred to me that someone as proficient in her profession as Judy Garland could be insecure or unsure. I thought that problem was reserved for me. It took a while, but the sequence was finally on film. My God, she was pure magic. I was hypnotized. When she and Mickey sang and danced they lit up that sound stage like exploding rockets.

Judy and I became quite close over the years. In time I heard from her about the forced pills, the exhaustion that prompted the drugs, the abuse from her mother, the misuse by the studio. In 1956, Judy and her husband, Sid Luft, would come for dinner. There were just the four of us, and the evenings developed into nights of deep conversation and revelation. She looked at Tony and me with pain-filled eyes, and said, "How would you feel if your boss called you a—a no-necked monster?" One would have to be a saint to deal with such pressures at that young age and not succumb to overindulgence. And once the pattern is formed . . . But what a tragic waste.

I remember another dinner a year or so before her death on June 22, 1969. Dolores Naar and I gave Pat Lawford a birthday party. Judy had divorced Sid and then Mark Herron and was with her hairdresser that evening. I hadn't seen her often (she had been in England and New York) and had read with sadness each account of collapse, hospitalization, replacement. I hardly recognized the shell of my exalted Judy. There was no brain guiding that skeletonlike frame. Her behavior was inexcusable but was completely excused. We just yearned to hold her, protect her, pat her and say, "It's okay, baby, everything is going to be okay."

She always gave 150 percent of herself to us, her audience. She never failed to bring me to my feet yelling, "Bravo!" and she tugged at every heartstring in me.

Tom Drake and I, as Dorothy and Richard Rodgers, were in a nightclub to hear the great lady Lena Horne sing two Rodgers and Hart songs: "Where or When" and "The Lady Is a Tramp." Before she appeared, I was riveted watching Robert Alton, the talented choreographer, set up the shot on the camera crane. This mechanized marvel has a base similar to a jeep, with a long extending arm, atop which is perched the camera and two suspended-in-air seats. It has the capability of reaching the rafters and then swooping down to a close position. It seemed dangerous as hell to me. And there he was, nearly at the roof of the huge stage, directing movements below with his feet (and the toes were pointed too). "You—move over *there,*" and he would give a high kick indicating where. I was sure he was going to land right on top of our table, with us underneath.

My attention was diverted, and anxiety forgotten, by the arrival of Miss Horne. Oh, was she beautiful—breathtaking! They did a few rehearsals, and then a take. I thought it was wonderful. But Mr. Alton, dangling in midair, yelled, "Come on, Lena baby, turn it *on* —give it to me!" And turn it on she did. Those eyes were so on fire they needed an extinguisher, that mouth passionately caressed each word, each syllable. She was dynamite. It wasn't in the script, but the "audience" spontaneously responded with a standing ovation.

I recently saw Lena in her show *A Lady and Her Music.* Time has not dulled that star. If anything, it shines even brighter.

At one time during the shooting, the real Dorothy and Richard Rodgers visited the studio, and the set. I had awful thoughts—what if they didn't like me, or the manner in which I depicted Mrs. Rodgers? Tom confided he had the same misgivings about meeting Mr. Rodgers. There is a tremendous responsibility when playing a live, renowned personage. But, fortunately, they couldn't have been nicer or more gracious or more complimentary.*

Between working days, Barry and I rehearsed more scenes, another from *Night Music* and one from Maxwell Anderson's *High Tor.* We spent hours together, sharing the learning process and genuinely enjoying the company.

Stan and I were stumbling along. We had some good times now and then, but we didn't seem to be growing together. It bothered

---

* When my daughter Jamie graduated from the Choate–Rosemary Hall boarding school in Connecticut, in 1976, my daughter Kelly and my husband, Bob, and I flew back for the ceremony. The senior class presented a production of *Oklahoma* by Richard Rodgers and Oscar Hammerstein II. During intermission, an attractive woman, about my age, approached and surprised me by saying, "Oh, hello! I'm sure you don't remember, but you played my mother in a movie once." I was truly astonished. How could I have been her *mother?* Unless I was a lot older than I thought, or she was a lot younger than she looked. My confusion must have been apparent, for she quickly explained, "I am Mary Rodgers." Of course—I played Dorothy Rodgers, *her* mother.

me that because his aspirations hadn't materialized, his ambition was stunted. He didn't seem to be motivated toward any action; he was content with my own small progress. I felt my respect for him slowly corroding.

Toward the end of the year, the studio asked a group of us to put on a show for military personnel on a base in Blythe, California. Barry did a comedy monologue, I sang, Jane Powell *really* sang, along with many other MGM contractees. The whole adventure was pleasurable. Before boarding the bus for the ride home, Barry and I strolled outside to look at the dazzling desert sky. The stars seemed close enough to touch. We were close enough to touch. He kissed me. And the stars came right down out of the sky and exploded inside of me. I responded wholly. *What was happening to me?* I had no wish to create complications in my life. But it was impossible to block the surge of emotion welling up, almost spilling over.

I was frightened—and guilt-ridden. Memories of what happened in Merced came flooding back. I could not surrender to this temptation.

In my penitent state, I felt compelled to make an even greater effort with Stan. We bought another used car, a little Ford, and moved to a one-bedroom apartment on Clark Drive, away from the studio. Maybe the distance would help.

And we went out more frequently. He always enjoyed the big affairs; I hoped this would be a diversion. Anything to stay afloat and keep desires in check.

The publicity department wanted us to attend the annual Society of Hollywood Press Photographers Costume Ball and arranged for costumes from the vast wardrobe storeroom. We would double-date with Elizabeth Taylor and Tom Breen. I had been introduced to Elizabeth but didn't really know her. This occasion was the launching pad for a long and rewarding friendship. We both went as Spanish señoritas—Elizabeth in white and me in black. When I recently saw some of the newspaper pictures, it looked as if we were having a "Who Can Wear the Lowest-Cut Bodice" contest. I hadn't even noticed when I looked in the mirror. But the photographers sure did—and now I know why they were standing on chairs shooting downward. Inadvertently we were exercising the old rule, "If you've got it, flaunt it."

The always resourceful wardrobe department also provided me

with a gown to wear to the premiere of MGM's newest block-buster, *The Yearling*, starring Gregory Peck, Jane Wyman, and Claude Jarman, Jr. Everyone was expected to be there. We did not regard it as a chore; our eyes were as bright as the klieg lights, and our excitement as high as the beams they projected. The bleachers, the fans, the crowds lining the streets, the red carpet leading into the theatre, the press, and the presence of so many major stars all spelled Hollywood Glamour. Everyone was so caught up in the fervor that even our arrival caused a little stir. The publicity department's work was beginning to pay off. The movie was worth all the attention—it was brilliant—and won an Oscar in almost every category.

January of 1948 brought my most demanding role to date—*Act of Violence*, the story of an ex-GI who tracks down a prison-camp informer. It had moody, melodramatic, complicated characters. Van Heflin and Robert Ryan starred, Mary Astor played opposite Robert Ryan, and I was Van Heflin's wife, mother of year-old twins. Fred Zinnemann—the extraordinary, sensitive, incredible Fred Zinnemann—directed. I was fortunate to be in the company of these talents, and I knew it, and I worked like a demon to prove worthy. It was hard; there wasn't one easy scene. The tension began in the beginning and kept mounting to a crescendo, and I constantly had to overcome the liability of actually being too young for the part. But it was heady stuff, exhilarating, stimulating.

If anything ever went wrong during a rehearsal or a shot, I automatically said, "I'm sorry," immediately assuming it was my fault. And it was many times. But not always. The cast and crew initiated an "I'm sorry" kitty. Every time I said it, I had to put a penny in the jar. It contributed three dollars toward the end of the picture party.

I was still somewhat religious. Stan's mother had introduced Christian Science to my life. Coincidently, Miss Burns also practiced Christian Science, so my interest was further strengthened. I accepted many of the principles, but not all. I never could reach that lofty plateau of utter trust by turning my body over completely to healing by faith. I believed in mind over matter up to a point, but then I balked. Something kept me from absolute conviction, so I did not join the church. But we did attend the services, and I did read Mary Baker Eddy every day.

Not even that, however, saved our marriage. I did try, maybe not hard enough. Maybe Stan didn't either. I felt such a sense of failure—I wanted it to work. But I couldn't pretend any longer, the feeling just wasn't there. Dear God, I wonder if it ever really was. We were both too young to continue our misery. There was no alternative. We divorced. Stan took the Chevy and was responsible for the loan from his parents. I kept the Ford, assumed the government debt, and moved in with Mom and Dad. Even in a weak relationship, the ending is still poignant. Two and a half years of sharing someone's life, whatever the circumstances, cannot be dismissed lightly. And with us there wasn't anger, or hate, or a bitter confrontation to make the parting easier.

I was worried that the divorce would affect my status at MGM. And naturally, I was afraid it would somehow reveal the Merced secret. I could have saved myself those anxious thoughts. No one paid much attention. It was handled quietly; there was no scandal, no other married parties involved, no boats were rocked—except ours. It was over.

CHAPTER EIGHT

Act of Violence progressed well. It was a giant step forward in my development as an actress. The unhappiness of the separation did not interfere with my performance. On the contrary, I learned how to use my ordeal within the character's turmoil. Laurence Olivier said it well: "Use your weaknesses and aspire to your strength."

Work engulfed me. George Sidney (Miss Burns's husband and a good director, especially adroit with the camera) was preparing to test me for an important historical film, *Young Bess,* the saga of the young Queen Elizabeth. Every day after shooting I had an appointment with Miss B. to rehearse the scene. Barry agreed to do the test with me.

And then Mervyn LeRoy, the famed director, stopped me on the lot and stunned me with the announcement that he had chosen me to play Meg in the remake of the classic *Little Women,* with June Allyson as Jo, Elizabeth Taylor as Amy, Margaret O'Brien as Beth, Mary Astor as Marmie, and Peter Lawford as Laurie. Maybe I wasn't lucky in love, but I sure was lucky in work!

As the end of *Act of Violence* drew closer, I was drained. I had started wardrobe for *Little Women* on my lunch hours, the publicity department was in high gear, and I was seeing Miss Burns every early evening. The last day, Fred Zinnemann knew I was out of it. He took me aside.

"I realize you are tired," he said. "This has not been an easy picture to make and I am aware of your other activities for the studio, as well as your personal problem. But you must put everything *except this film* out of your head. I cannot allow anything to obstruct your concentration. Draw upon your energy reserves."

"I am so sorry." (Three dollars and one cent in the jar.) His pep talk and admonition were the necessary stimulus. He pulled me through.

After the final shot, everyone gathered on the set for a small celebration. Miss Burns even made a rare appearance on a stage. Then a surprise. The cast and crew presented me with a leather script holder, the inside of which was signed by each person. I treasure it to this day. (It is particularly dear to me now since we have lost Van Heflin and Robert Ryan.) I didn't know what to say or do, except cry.

The *Young Bess* test was completed, and it turned out well. The studio saw another facet of my possibilities. When the time arrived for actual casting, however, the producer, Sidney Franklin, settled for a real English actress, Jean Simmons. (That was one of two times I lost out to Jean, that I know of. When I read *The Robe,* a story of the robe worn by Jesus when he was crucified, I was totally captivated. I would have given anything to play the girl. It went to Jean Simmons; I didn't even have a crack at it. But I can't lay the blame for that anywhere but on my own doorstep—I never disclosed my longing.*)

I can use persuasive powers to further another's cause, but not mine. The old nemeses—shyness and diffidence—inhibit me. Salesmanship is just not a trait of mine. A part of this attitude is due to the circumstances of my rudimentary induction to the profession. I didn't go knocking on office doors to get a break, it just happened. Everything was arranged for me, so I assumed it always would be. "They" would take care of me. It didn't enter my head that agents or producers might need prodding, and I'm sure roles I might have played have been lost or overlooked because of this. Paradoxically, I was—and am—ambitious. 'Tis a puzzlement!

Predictably, Barry and I grew closer. Not only did we work together, we played together. He had an insatiable curiosity about life, about places and people. We would drive to obscure areas in

---

* I didn't (and don't) have the faculty of promoting me. I admire the tenacity and drive of someone like Frank Sinatra. The odds were against his doing Maggio in *From Here to Eternity,* but he persisted. He practically camped in Harry Cohn's office at Columbia Studios day after day, until Mr. Cohn relented and gave Frank a chance. The rest is history—he won an Oscar and completely revitalized his career.

the county just to observe different cultures, or to sample new tastes, or to roam around museums and points of interest.

One Sunday afternoon, he took me deep in the heart of Los Angeles to a small auditorium that housed the Jewish Repertory Theatre. It was an experience never to be duplicated. Long before today's audience-participation shows, this assembly was already an integral force in the play. They knew the plot, the characters, even the lines. And they knew the emotions. The "good" son drew applause, and "Oh, what a nice boy. That's my boy; see how he behaves." The "bad" son entered and there was booing and hissing and catcalls and "Look at him—look how he treats his mama and papa. No respect for his grandma and grandpa—thief." During an argument, they would join in the fray and talk back to the performers. When an elder died, moans and sobs echoed through the hall. The poor actor who played the "bad" son had to have a strong ego, for many of the women viewers would wait for him at the stage door to continue the beratement, even to hurl things. It was wonderful!

Elizabeth Taylor's family had taken a house near Malibu that summer, and we were invited to a weekend beach party along with Roddy McDowall, Peter Lawford, Van Johnson, June Allyson, Dick Powell, Bill Shepard, and other chums. This was a day that caused me to forever fear the ocean. Two boys and another girl and I went for a ride in one of those rubber dinghies. We paddled about a mile out, where the boys dove overboard with their fins and masks to take a look at the bottom. When they surfaced, they threw something in the boat, something slimy and slithery. It was a baby octopus, complete with its saclike body and eight sucker-bearing tentacles. Yuk! And then, the dinghy started taking water; it had sprung a leak. I freaked! I was not (am not) a strong swimmer. I could never make it back to shore. I wouldn't go in the water anyway, since the mama octopus couldn't be too far from its offspring, right? I'd read how they wrapped those tentacles around their prey and squeezed it to death, not to mention death by drowning. We girls furiously attempted to bail with our hands, while the boys swam and pushed us toward land. I became more hysterical, and when we were close to the beach, I jumped out and splashed and screamed my way in. The waiting group wrapped us in blankets and poured brandy down our throats. Even then I couldn't stop shaking.

So much for beach parties.

There was no water problem on *Little Women,* however, unless
the artificial snow caused one. The exteriors of the houses and
streets were built right on big stage 30. It truly did look like winter
wonderland. More technical magic. And the ambiance of the set
cast its own spell. The four little women blended beautifully, weaving the web of sisterhood. We misbehaved, we fought, we giggled
—we drove Mervyn LeRoy right out of his mind.

One day we were lining up a four shot. We put black tape on our
teeth, and when Mervyn said "Action," four toothless lovelies
turned and smiled into the camera. We thought we were hilarious.
Each time he would begin the shot, it triggered a snicker, graduated to full-scale guffaws, until finally he called a recess so we could
collect ourselves.

The first day we worked with Sir C. Aubrey Smith was another
fiasco. As we prepared for the take, and just before "Action!" Sir
Aubrey boomed out, "Sing!" Evidently this was a practice in theatre to focus one's resonance before speaking. It startled the hell
out of us and sent us into gales of nervous laughter. It happened
every time.

I don't know why, but when any of us goofed or flubbed a line,
we went to pieces. Peter mucked up one day, and we couldn't get
past that one sentence without breaking up. Young Margaret
O'Brien took a while before she participated wholeheartedly. She
continually looked in her mother's direction for approval. But gradually she loosened up and we won her over to our foolish ways.

Elizabeth was always looking for some diversion to take her mind
off wearing that blond wig—she detested the thing. The light hair
really didn't do justice to her coloring. This daily exposure allowed
me a deeper perception of Elizabeth. I think I had anticipated a
different person, because of the early recognition of her incredible
beauty and her success. I didn't expect the warmth, the humor, the
openness, and the regard she extended to her friends.

June was our ringleader, as June and as Jo. The interaction of the
four "little women" created the glow that suffused the film, as well
as the tableaux painted by Mervyn LeRoy. Oddly, I never heard
any concern expressed among us about the fact we were doing a
remake of a classic. Undoubtedly the studio watched the develop-

ing footage with that in mind, but to my knowledge, we didn't operate under the pressure of comparison.

And then I was twenty-one! I was congratulated on the set with a surprise party. Jerry Lewis and Dean Martin and Gloria DeHaven were there as June's guests. Dean and Jerry were riding high, and deservedly so. Even at this small gathering and brief casual appearance, one could appreciate their comic talent. I had no way of knowing how close the future would bring us.

Inevitably, Barry and I loved together. The joy of exploration carried over to our personal lives. He released my trapped emotions and freed my slaves. Wisely, tenderly, he opened a fresh depth of feeling in me. I didn't experience guilt when I was with him. I even entrusted him with my dark secret about Merced. In his patient way, he tried to defuse my fears and place my problem in proper perspective. He didn't dispel my qualms about my shaky past altogether, but he was responsible for my somewhat healthier attitude.

Late summer, 1948. "Janet, there is someone who wants to meet you," said our host, Mervyn LeRoy. Barry and I were attending the wrap party for all the cast of *Little Women* at his home. Dutifully, we followed Mervyn into the library.

A tall, thin man, fortyish, stood as we entered. He had sparse dark hair and a small mustache, and he was dressed (rather oddly I thought) in white pants, open white shirt, a not new, ill-fitting sports coat, and white tennis shoes. He squinted, or frowned a little, but his dark eyes were very aware and alive.

"Janet, this is Howard Hughes. Howard, Janet Leigh and Barry Nelson."

Obviously I had heard of the legendary Howard Hughes. Who hadn't? Billionaire, womanizer, pilot, movie mogul, crusader—so I was a little unprepared for his unusual appearance—not exactly what one would imagine for such a famous personage. His voice was also a surprise—not a booming, authoritative sound associated with men of power. Instead—a high, soft quality came forth as we exchanged our perfunctory hellos. Actually, I couldn't see what all the fuss was about. The whole encounter was rather bland and brief and soon forgotten—at least by me.

I had not finished shooting *Little Women* when I was cast to play June Forsyte in *That Forsyte Woman*. Try to top this cast: Greer Garson, Robert Young, Walter Pidgeon, and Errol Flynn. When I met Errol Flynn, I actually gasped. He was as beautiful as I could possibly have imagined, and as charming, and as lovable, *and* as naughty. When I looked at him, I saw Robin Hood and Captain Blood and Essex, and I remembered the nights I had gone home from the theatre and dreamed of him. He was such a gentleman—except when he played his practical jokes.

I had misjudged Greer Garson. I thought she would be staid, even somewhat uptight, probably because of the many serious roles she had portrayed. But she soon changed that notion. She immediately changed my calling her Miss Garson to Greer, and proved her funnybone was well oiled.

In one scene, Greer was supposedly in her room, pressing her gown for her important evening, dressed in the undergarments of the period, MGM style. She goes to the closet to put it away, and that was the end of the shot. After several rehearsals, they were ready for the take. This time, when she went to open the closet door, there was Errol, dressed only in the underwear of the moment, Flynn style. He couldn't have asked for a better reaction—she screamed and almost fainted.

But he got his. Not to be outdone, Greer planned something for Mr. Flynn. She timed it perfectly, for the last day of shooting. They were in a carriage, playing a tender love scene that ended with a passionate kiss. They did several takes, but Compton Bennett, the director, wanted one more. When their lips met, Greer pressed a button, and Errol shrieked and almost went through the roof of the carriage. She had arranged to put an electrical charge under his seat.

This was another intriguing period picture, another chance for my imagination to run rampant about the life and times of these people. The wardrobe, the furniture, the reactions to a given situation, and the mores were so completely foreign. And it was another opportunity for the talent at MGM to give you all the tools with which to work. And such care was taken in casting every role! The Forsyte family portrait could have indeed been taken in the nineteenth century.

The time was approaching when Barry was to leave for the East

Coast to do Moss Hart's play *Light Up the Sky.* It was his big break, and naturally I was thrilled for him, but I dreaded his departure. I thought I would be lost. His input had been overwhelming. He had opened many doors for my mind and heart, taught me so much, coaxed some insecurity out of me, demanded I expand my awareness, and share his friends. The first time I met Mario Lanza was at Barry and his mother's apartment. Barry and Mario had been together on Broadway, and Barry had already told me about Mario's eccentricities, especially about his eating and drinking habits—twenty eggs at one sitting? Three chickens? Two bottles of vodka? But who cared then! That night we played the record from his triumphant Hollywood Bowl debut, and we knew we were listening to history.

Before Barry left, he received a very strange movie offer. RKO wanted him to sign for a picture to be shot somewhere in the wilds of South America. It seemed odd, because the character was so unlike the parts Barry normally portrayed. Neither of us attached any importance to this overture—until much later. In any case, he was already committed to the play.

Tearfully, I helped pack the trunk to send and the suitcase to take. And he was gone.

I was right, I missed him desperately. At the conclusion of *That Forsyte Woman,* I did something daring (for me, anyway). I asked for a few days off so I could fly to Boston. The play was in tryouts there. Luckily, I had an ally in Miss Burns. She was privy to our relationship; she was the one who had encouraged Barry to return to the stage; her husband, George Sidney, was directing my next film, *The Red Danube;* and her father-in-law, L. K. Sidney, was a top executive at the studio. So she helped my cause considerably. They gave me three weeks off.

Barry's mother and I could hardly contain ourselves. What excitement! Neither of us had been on a plane before (we didn't close our eyes all night), I had never even been out of California (except for *that* one night in Reno), and I was still reeling from the cost of the ticket. The takeoff was frightening—and exhilarating—and the sight of the lights of Los Angeles was breathtaking. Our enthusiasm must have been contagious, because the crew spent most of the ten hours around our seats. We were the only passengers awake when we refueled in Chicago, and we were the first to spot the outskirts of Boston. Boston, the seat of our country's heritage—where it all started. I flashed back to my history class where Jeanette had read and studied about Plymouth Rock and Sturbridge and the Minute Men and Paul Revere. I never dreamed I'd ever be there, and here I was, Janet, looking at Boston Harbor.

There had been a performance the night before, but Barry was at the airport to meet us. On the ride to town, I kept holding onto him, asking, "What's that?—What's that?" Poor Barry had two jumping jacks on his hands. The taxi pulled up to the Ritz Carlton Hotel. A white-gloved doorman took our bags while another opened the door, and a solemn-faced desk clerk welcomed us to Boston. My babble stopped—I couldn't utter one word. I looked around the lobby, sensing the ghosts of all the greats who had graced that room.

The uniformed bellman deposited us in our room. And with his mother's full blessing, I undeposited me and moved into Barry's room. My bravado ended there. Again, a hotel room, a closed door, facing my . . . lover. Not even my husband. All the demons surfaced and tried to spoil our happiness. But this time, love and time conquered. I concentrated on the real reason for being in Boston, and thus began a memorable three weeks.

That night we saw *Light Up the Sky.* It was so good, and *he* was so good. I had never seen a play bound for Broadway, and none where I knew someone on stage. We were very proud of him.

Barry's mom went on to New York so she could be with friends *and,* I have a feeling, so we could be alone.

We would go sightseeing whenever Barry wasn't needed at the theatre. I wish all young people could relive the biography of our nation by actually visiting the locations where it took place. It is so penetrating, so graphic, so involving. I remembered the impact vividly, and years later, took my children to Boston and Philadelphia and New York, making a chronological tour of the sites of historical events that occurred in each city.

Most of our time, however, was spent at the Plymouth Theatre. I wish that all young performers could experience what I did by observing the development and fine-tuning of a play and its actors. I was at every rehearsal, every performance, and I saw it begin to bloom and finally blossom just before the opening in New York. When I arrived, the cast were still experimenting with their charac-

terizations, as was Moss Hart with the writing and direction. I became aware of which changes worked and which didn't. I could see
which moves were effective and which weren't. I could tell when
the dialogue flowed or when it bogged down. I sensed when an
actor went off the track. At each show I would take notes, and
Barry and I discussed them thoroughly. Some of my observations
proved valid, and I was elated when Barry praised my insight. It
was invaluable seasoning that I could take back with me to Hollywood.

My first meeting with the illustrious Moss Hart, and his lovely
wife, Kitty Carlisle, was in the Ritz Carlton elevator. We walked out
onto our floor and there they were. Barry introduced us, and then
Moss looked at me and asked dryly, "Is your room comfortable?" I
turned all shades of crimson—our "secret" was hardly a secret. And
sharing a room, in 1948, was not exactly an accepted way of life. I
was so embarrassed, I have no idea how I answered.

From Boston, the company moved to Philadelphia for the last
out-of-town run before New York. Philadelphia, another haven for
the historian. I reveled in its antiquity. The timing was perfect too,
for we were there the night President Truman won his unexpected
victory over Dewey. It was bedlam—the city went totally bananas.
People were still milling around in the streets at four in the morning. This was my first participating election (I voted by absentee
ballot) and I couldn't imagine being in a more appropriate region
—where our Constitution was drafted and signed, and the home of
the Liberty Bell. What a night!

On a Sunday, the entire cast was invited to the Hart home in
Bucks County, a popular retreat for Eastern intellectuals. It was a
beautiful fall day, and an ideal time to see the changing colors of
the trees, a vision completely new to a native Californian. So was
the style of luxury of the old, magnificent, sprawling farmhouse.
Barry and I wandered in the woods and thoroughly enjoyed the
relaxing and splendrous surroundings. The glow lasted until after
dinner—until the contests started.

These were all extremely bright, sophisticated people and any
new word game was attacked by them with a vengeance. The latest

fad was called "charades."† Eventually I became quite proficient, but at that time there were so many things I had to have knowledge in for the studio, I just never had the time to learn recreational things—I always seemed to be playing "catch up." Barry held his own very well, but I felt like a dunce—I was mortified. No one was unkind, but that old feeling of "not belonging" reared its ugly head again.

On my last weekend, Barry took me to New York City. We walked through Central Park early in the morning (it was safer then); had eggplant steaks on Delancey Street; took the subway (it was safer then too) to see the Brooklyn Dodgers play baseball; went to the top of the Empire State Building; and on the Staten Island Ferry, I turned away from the skyline and there it was—the Statue of Liberty—in all its glory. I was so *full*.

And then I was so empty.

On the way home there was much to contemplate—all of the wondrous exposure to other worlds, other cultures—and Barry. No commitment had been asked, or given. I thought about this and realized that Barry, knowing he was the first involvement I'd had since the divorce from Stan, wanted me to have freedom, and that he desired latitude as well. I had a tendency to conveniently "settle in" with one person, homing-pigeon style, and never was a good different night/different guy sort of dater. Barry was too wise to sanction that pitfall.

I accepted an invitation from an agent at MCA to have dinner at

† I recently saw Kitty Carlisle in New York, and we reminisced about another "game" night, around 1959, in Palm Springs. Kitty and Moss had the house next to Anne and Kirk Douglas, and Natalie Wood and Robert Wagner (when they were married the first time) were staying with Tony and me. The eight of us dined at nearby Beachcombers and adjourned to the Douglas home. There we proceeded to play charades. Natalie became bored and mischievously suggested an alternate game. I don't remember its name—or if it ever had a name—but it went something like this. You sit around in a circle, choose a category (magazines, books, movies, etc.), then all together, do clap-clap-finger snap. On the snap, in progression around the circle, you name something in the category. If you repeat or fail with an answer, you are out, and on it goes until it narrows down to one person, the winner. Nat selected "dirty words" as the category—the dirtier the better. You wouldn't believe the trash that came out of those genteel mouths. All except Kitty. She was out on the first round. She confessed she had been so surprised she couldn't think.

Silently, we both sent our thoughts to the departed Moss and Natalie.

Sugie's, a Hollywood landmark. It was uneventful until a third place was suddenly set at the table, and Howard Hughes joined us.

Strange! But not unexplainable. After all, Dick was a top agent at MCA, and I was sure he must have a great many business dealings with the owner of RKO—Mr. Hughes. Still, I wondered why he hadn't mentioned it. Did he just forget?

Howard Hughes's arrival certainly caused a stir. Captains and waiters hovered over the table like hummingbirds, and most of the other patrons didn't eat—just stared. I wondered if this reaction always followed him, and if it bothered him. I found out the answer was yes to both.

The conversation was predominantly "show biz"—current pictures, future pictures, old pictures. He had seen the films in which I had appeared and was quite complimentary. It was a pleasant enough evening, not earth-shattering but not a dud—sort of middle-of-the-road—and easily dismissed.

I had plunged into rehearsals for *The Red Danube*. First, there was another accent to learn, Viennese this time. A lovely European actress, Lisa, helped me attack that problem. Second, my few tap dancing lessons did not prepare me to play a Russian ballerina. Poor Alex Romero, a fine dancer and choreographer at MGM (and an angel), had the task of getting me on pointe. Do you have any idea how difficult it is to jam your feet into those toe shoes—those damn torture chambers—let alone stand on them? And the muscle strength needed to support one's body on one's toes? There was no way I could be expected to do the whole routine—it would have taken years—but I did have to execute a few steps for close-ups, and exude the aura of a prima ballerina. Oh, the pain! One day, I was practicing turns, and I turned but the toe shoe didn't. It stuck between two boards in the rehearsal hall floor and didn't budge—my knee hasn't been right since. That was the bad news. The good news was that Maria was a beautiful role, demanding and challenging, and the cast was very impressive: Walter Pidgeon, Angela Lansbury, Peter Lawford, *and* Ethel Barrymore. I couldn't believe I was actually going to work with a Barrymore. She was the epitome of class, power, presence; one learned from her by osmosis.

Early in 1949, the Culver City studio assembled every star under contract and those shooting pictures on the lot. The purpose was to celebrate MGM's Twenty-fifth Anniversary (actual inaugural date,

April 17, 1924) and this was the site of the famous picture pub-
lished in *Life* magazine of fifty-eight members of the family. Only
the clockwork efficiency of the MGM machine could have pulled
this off without a hitch or loss of shooting time. The lunch hours
were synchronized on each set, and every chair predesignated al-
phabetically to eliminate possible ego problems. And there was
Jeanette Helen Morrison sitting next to Mario Lanza, a part of this
historical moment.

(On May 17, 1974, following the world premiere of *That's Entertainment*, again "More Stars Than There Are in Heaven" gathered
for MGM's gala Fiftieth Anniversary Reunion Ball and the follow-
up photo. I was one of thirteen who appeared in each still.)

When I had the stamina, I dated. Danny Scholl, a singer, was one
companion. (A while later, I saw Danny in a Broadway musical,
Texas Li'l Darlin'. He was singing the love song in the second act
straight to me, pouring out his heart. It was all so romantic, except
when he faced the audience—his fly was open.)

And Arthur Loew, Jr., was another beau. Danny and I had
double-dated with Arthur and Elizabeth Taylor a couple of times,
but they weren't a steady duo, so I didn't hesitate to consent to a
dinner engagement; I enjoyed his company immensely. Arthur is
the grandson of Adolph Zukor (Paramount) and Marcus Loew
(Loew's, Inc.), so our backgrounds were diametrically opposite. He
had grown up surrounded by great wealth, and received with it
both the accompanying benefits and the hindrances. He was raised
being famous and knowing the famous, but despite this (or because
of it), he was the most natural, easygoing kind of person. He was
comfortable in all situations, and blessed with a superior sense of
humor. He introduced me to a whole other view of Hollywood.
We attended most of the opening nights at Ciro's and Mocambo's
on Sunset Boulevard, where he had his regular table; he had
friends in *all* circles, so the social life with him was full.

My financial stress by this time had lessened considerably. My
contract had been renegotiated twice, and I was earning a substantial salary. But I also had been paying back the GI loan incurred
with Stan, so there wasn't much left over for luxuries—like clothes.
Naturally I needed *something* to wear, and I had bought a red cocktail dress. I wore it to almost every affair, until the press photogra-

phers approached me one night and said, "We want to take pictures of you, Janet, but we can't use any more in that dress—they all look as if they were taken on the same night." How dumb! (If you have limited funds, never buy a bright, identifiable color; buy a basic color that can be changed with accessories.)

Amelia Gray owned a dress shop, then on South Beverly Drive, now on Rodeo Drive. A new friend, Ann Strauss, who was in the publicity department and fashion-coordinated all the still photo sessions, introduced me to Amelia and thought she could advise me on how to get maximum mileage from my wardrobe selections. She suggested two skirt-and-vest outfits that interchanged, and a black dress that could take me anyplace. Ann and Amelia were invaluable. I shopped there for years, as did most of young Hollywood. Amelia was always careful to alert a customer if someone else purchased a similar garment—hoping to prevent two people from arriving at a party in the same outfit.

I might as well discuss photo sittings at this point. They are, beyond a doubt, the most difficult aspect of being an actress. At least for me. The minute the photographer says, "Hold it!" I freeze. I feel stilted, unnatural. And when I started, color flashbulbs had to be replaced after every shot and each exposure took two to three seconds—forever, it seemed. It was almost impossible to catch a spontaneous expression. Gradually, I learned to ignore the bulbs and time, and just concentrated on a thought—any thought. That helped some.

Because of the required lead time for magazines, winter layouts were shot in summer, and summer ones in winter. One year, on the hottest recorded day in July, my photographer wore bathing trunks and sat on a block of ice while I posed in fur coats. And in January, I was freezing in a swimsuit while he was all toasty warm in an overcoat. Such is the price of fame!

Arthur and I had fun! A novel kind of fun for me—a carefree whirl of gaiety—something that I had not experienced before. Not that we never discussed serious subjects and work—we did—but they were approached differently. He also had a wonderful family; his mother and sister and I are still close friends, and so is Arthur.

Barry's play, *Light Up the Sky*, had opened to smash reviews, so he would be in New York for quite some time. We spoke to each other frequently on the telephone and maintained a strong relationship. But I felt no pressure, from anyone, about making a choice—I was unpossessed.

When *The Red Danube* was over, I started filming *The Doctor and the Girl* (I was the girl), with talented co-workers Glenn Ford, Charles Coburn, and Gloria DeHaven.

In one scene of the movie, Glenn had to carry me up two flights of stairs; it was supposed to be our wedding night. We were in high spirits, with much ad-libbing and giddiness. Glenn kept whispering, "I don't think I can make it." And the more he struggled, the harder we laughed, until finally I passed the threshold of restraint and wet my pants, which only made me laugh harder—and it kept coming. (I swear I could see a spot on my skirt in the actual film.)

Mom and Dad and I had moved from their tiny duplex in Inglewood to a nice roomy apartment on Roxbury Drive and Vidor. They were in one of the happier periods of their marriage; there was more security, they were a little more relaxed with each other and were thrilled for me and my golden opportunity. Sometimes I wished Mom weren't quite so wrapped up in Daddy's and my activities, so she could explore her own potential. She seemed content, or maybe "safe," to just look after Dad's and my needs, and not to venture into the "danger" zone of finding herself. I realized even then that she always felt she was inadequate, partly because of her lack of a formal education. If only she could have acknowledged how much she had to offer. But those were fleeting thoughts of mine, because the surface was relatively calm. And so much was happening to me then, I guess it was enough to preoccupy three people.

Dick, my platonic agent friend, invited me to go sailing one Sunday, and since I had never done it before, I accepted eagerly. When I entered the car, guess who was in the back seat? Howard Hughes and a girl. I excused myself for a minute, and went back inside the house.

"I don't like it—I don't like it one bit," I complained to Mom and Dad. "Why is *he* here? Dick never mentioned anyone else was coming!"

They tried to placate me. "After all, he has a companion, he isn't *your* date. You're making a mountain out of a molehill; what harm is there?"

I really couldn't explain why I felt such apprehension, and I had no intelligent comeback to their logical assessment of the situation, so, reluctantly, I returned to the car, and we were off—off on a cockeyed adventure. I thought we were on the way to Balboa but instead we stopped at an airfield in Culver City—that's right, at Hughes Aircraft.

"Howard felt it would be more convenient to fly, instead of the long drive in traffic," Dick explained.

Oh, really, I thought. Well, nothing to do but get in the darn thing. I must confess, it *was* titillating to sit in the co-pilot's seat during takeoff but alarming also, to see the ground rushing below you with such velocity. Everyone had insisted I have this prized position next to Howard, which left Dick and Howard's "friend" back in the cabin. Hmmmmmm.

I was looking out the window, gripped by the unblemished panorama, and when I started seeing sailboats, the coastline, I said, "We're almost there. Shouldn't we be slowing down—or whatever you do—in order to land?"

Howard answered haltingly, "Well, ah, we're not exactly going to Balboa. We, ah, have another spot in mind."

I remained silent for the next hour or so, anxiously searching for more ocean and ships, and then I sensed a change in the motor's rhythm.

He turned on the "Fasten Safety Belts" sign and prepared to descend. But where? *Where in the hell were we?*

"We, my dear," Dick proudly announced, "are at the Grand Canyon."

The Grand Canyon! My God, that's in Arizona! I've been taken over the state line. I've—been—KIDNAPPED!

A limousine was waiting as we taxied to a halt. This escapade had obviously been planned. But why? Why the deception? Maybe because they knew I wouldn't have come otherwise. But did they really think I would be so dazzled that I would just pass it off lightly with an, "Oh well, what the heck?" If so, they had sure guessed wrong. I felt manipulated (I hate that), and angry, scared, and said so. There were apologies, and assurances.

Outwardly, I maintained an impassive, distant demeanor. Inwardly, however, I was mesmerized by the majesty of nature's work. I felt my anger recede as I was overcome by the magnificence of the canyon.

We soon reboarded the plane quietly, filled with our own reflections of the wonder we had just witnessed. And under this influence, I thought, maybe I did overreact; maybe it was just people being nice; so I made a small effort at being passably pleasant.

When I saw the lights of Los Angeles in the distance, I started to relax. But the nearer we came, the less Los Angeles looked like the Los Angeles I remembered. No wonder it did—we were landing in Las Vegas, Nevada!

"Surprise! Dinner in Las Vegas seemed a fitting climax to a delightful day." Dick's heartiness affected me like a fingernail on a blackboard.

Delightful day, were they serious? It dawned on me that it was beyond their comprehension to understand why I was so upset. This must have been normal procedure for them, but for me it was a nightmare. Would it ever end? Nothing seemed to penetrate their thick hides!

My outburst at the Grand Canyon had obviously had no effect, so I contained my fury, and tried another tactic.

"My parents will be frantic. I really think I should go straight home." *Please,* I added silently.

"Not to worry, we'll call from the dining room," promised Dick.

The Desert Inn was expecting us, so again, this was not an afterthought! I had no choice—and that was the core of my infuriation —but to go in the limo, to the restaurant, call Mom and Dad, move the food around on my plate, and pray that this was the last state on their agenda.

My prayer was answered. We actually landed in Culver City, *California,* and I did see my apartment again. When I finally closed the door, the long day took its toll—in hysterics. But it was over, behind me. I would never date Dick again, and thus sever the Hughes Connection.

Jane and Boyd Morse (Arthur's sister and brother-in-law) honored me by naming me godmother to their newest child, Michael. Since *The Doctor and the Girl* was "in the can" (show-biz slang for a completed picture), I was free to fly to Tucson, Arizona, where they lived, for the christening. I stayed with Arthur's mother, Mickey, who had a house around the corner from Jane. Mickey had moved to Tucson when the children were small, for the healthy dry air and for a healthier environment in general. Summers were spent with the children's father, Arthur Loew, Sr., in Glen Cove, Long Island.

At the ceremony, holding that little bundle in my arms was a revelation; the baby was endearingly fragile and soft and vulnerable. (Of course, today, Michael is about six feet four and could hold me in his arms.)

That was a special week. I enjoyed being "Aunt Janet" to Jane's children. Our bond of friendship was strengthened by the proximity; I liked what I saw. And seeing where and how and with whom Arthur spent part of his childhood drew a closer circle around the two of us.

Strange how sequences tumble together and force a conclusion— a resolution. For as soon as I returned from Tucson, Barry arrived in Los Angeles on a two-week break from the play. We went out and he was in high spirits at dinner, and brimming with an inner excitement that continued as we went for a drive to the beach. There, his words substantiated what I instinctively had surmised. He had made his decision, and the time for me to make a choice had arrived.

I was happy to be with Barry again. But I recognized I wasn't prepared to make a pledge. Why couldn't life remain simple— status quo—without complications!

Barry was too dear, too deserving for me to play games. So— painfully, tearfully, agonizingly—I explained I had grown some, had developed some, and with this I had become aware that there was more out there—more to see, more to do, more roads to travel, more people to meet, more doors to open—and I just wasn't ready for a commitment.

Barry believed I had "gone Hollywood"—that I was putting too much importance on frivolity, that I had become enmeshed with a young irresponsible group and was being led astray from my goal. He didn't totally understand my reasoning.

In just under three years, my life had done a 180-degree turn and was launched in a new orbit. It had nothing to do with a financial situation or a particular way of life, but each time a new culture pattern opened up to me, I wondered how many more there were. Each new sphere expanded my dimensions as a person; and the wider the scope, the deeper insight I could exercise as an actress. Work times, play times, happy times, sad times, even "odd" times (like my crazy sailing date) all deepened the well of emotions from which I could draw.

I didn't want to stop filling the well. Not that Barry would have stifled me—not at all, except it would have been *his* way, and I was still searching for *my* way.

I had and still have a great respect and love for Barry.

CHAPTER NINE

The burning of the mortgage! Finally, the government debt was absolved. I was free. And we had some financial stability; we wouldn't have to dread what the mailman would bring. Caution still prevailed, however. When I was at the popular milliner, Mr. Kenneth's, doing a *Photoplay* picture layout, Hedda Hopper was naturally there, supplementing her already plentiful collection of hats. I spotted a fur-trimmed sweater that I longed for, but it was definitely extravagant. Hedda gave full approval, and didn't understand my reluctance. I called my dad, who was in charge of the bankbook, to ask if I could afford it, and I jumped with joy when he said absolutely. Hedda was struck dumb! "I never saw that in my life!" she exclaimed. (Thereafter, whenever we met, she would relate the story to anyone who would listen. But the incident never did seem so strange to me.)

Bit by bit, under Amelia's surveillance, my wardrobe expanded. It was a real kick to have pretty things. But one incident clearly illustrated to me that everything is relative. Arthur and I were to pick up Elizabeth Taylor one Sunday, and watch her date, Lance (Somebody) play polo. (I had always thought polo was a coat—talk about dissimilar worlds!) She wasn't ready, so I went upstairs to help. She was in a mess. "I don't like this—too big! Too dressy—too casual—I have nothing to wear!" she wailed, throwing hanger after hanger of clothes on top of the already large mound of them on the bed. I was flabbergasted. I looked at the still-full closet and the heap, and realized that normal is different for everyone. Not better or worse, just different.

By 1948, television had arrived. Arthur owned one of the rare sets in town and it became a habit to gather at his apartment on Tuesday nights to watch "The Texaco Star Theater," starring the outlandish, but beguiling Uncle Miltie (Milton Berle). The regular viewers were Shelley Winters (already the zany and spacey and talented one), Farley Granger (dear then as today), Elizabeth Taylor, Stewart Stern (Arthur's cousin and a talented writer), and me. How quickly we were drawn to this new medium, and yet, the studios chose to ignore the "minor" intruder. How they continued to do so after the impact of the Kathy Fiscus tragedy* was beyond me—and still is now.

Jane and Boyd were visiting from Tucson when, after dinner, the group by chance turned on the television set. A drama was unfolding before us. A young girl had fallen into a deep hole and rescue efforts were under way. Television brought us into immediate participation. We were riveted and stayed so through the entire night. No one could leave. We prayed, we hoped, we despaired, we cheered when rescue seemed imminent, and we cried when the final outcome was disaster.

The power of this new instrument of communication was inescapable. And still, hardly any in the film industry gave it credence, and persisted to treat it like a second-class citizen for some time.

Strange breed, Hollywood social functions. There were the intimate, "just chums" dinners. There were the "business associates" dinners. There were the "current picture friends" dinners. Some of these often overlapped. Then there were the affairs managed by public relations firms or social secretaries, and there were the wingdings put on by studios. All of which probably accounted for the misconception that everyone was on familiar terms with everyone else in our town.

Arthur and I attended the wedding reception of Shirley Temple and John Agar. As we went through the receiving line we could see the fatigue and frustration in their eyes. It was a circus—at least a thousand people—and they probably didn't really know half of them, me for sure.

---

* An excellent movie starring Kirk Douglas, *Ace in the Hole,* was based on this dramatic real-life report.

Kathryn Grayson was given a baby shower by Ava Gardner. I was excited to be included, even though it was an MGM sororal soirée. When I received a thank-you note from Kathryn for my gift, I wrote a thank-you note for the thank-you note! (I wasn't exactly what you would call "cool.")

Arthur and I were also invited to one of Errol Flynn's parties. We were curious—rumor had it that mirrors surrounded the entire bed area. Trying to appear nonchalant, we strolled through the crowded house until we found the boudoir and surreptitiously slipped inside. Rumor had it right. The bed was on an elevated platform, like a throne, and mirrors adorned the walls and ceiling and floors. As the wolf said to Little Red Riding Hood, "The better to see you with, my dear."

Errol enjoyed Arthur's sense of humor, and asked us to some quiet dinners. He regaled us with tales of his escapades with cronies John Barrymore and Lon Chaney, Jr. (among others). We lounged in the same paneled den where John Barrymore had held court. We gaped at the window from which, so as to not interrupt his train of thought, he had relieved himself on the unsuspecting flowers below. We sat in the armchair that had held his body when "the boys" smuggled the corpse away from the funeral home. (That was a bit gruesome for me.) We were fascinated by Flynn.

Arthur's godmother was Mary Pickford. When Mickey was sojourning in Los Angeles, we had tea with Miss Pickford and Buddy Rogers at fabled Pickfair (the estate of Mary Pickford and Douglas Fairbanks, who were, at one time, the indisputable King and Queen of Hollywood). The extensive grounds were guarded by a thick stucco wall. Huge iron gates opened, and we proceeded along the seemingly endless, winding driveway, flanked by velvety grass on rolling hills. An impressive mansion loomed before us. And inside this vastness was a tiny, tiny Mary Pickford. I felt like a giant standing next to her, and I'm only five feet five. Size didn't hinder her graciousness, however, and I added another legend to my growing list.

In May 1949, MGM sent me on a three-city promotional tour for *The Red Danube* to Pittsburgh, New York, and Boston. Emily Torchia, another new friend, was my traveling companion and studio representative. Each city had its own studio branch officers and personnel, and did the actual arranging of the schedule. The accompanying publicist merely approved the calendar and acted as a buffer. Sometimes the out-of-town staff were overzealous and neglected to leave time for rest stops or hair shampooing or other little necessities. After all, we were expected to look like stars.

Tours are hard work. You give interviews to newspapers, magazines, radio or television stations close to every hour, on the hour. You make appearances at luncheons, dinners, charity functions, department stores, hospitals, and schools. And since you are the object of attention, you have to be "on" constantly. A tour is not a piece of cake, but it also has a plus side. You get to see new sections of the country under the best possible circumstances; you meet different, colorful people; and you enhance the substance of yourself, your profession, your industry. You can make a tour palatable, even tasty to yourself as well as to the public.

Pittsburgh, in 1949, was the booming steel center of the world. Standing on top of a hill, I looked down on the city of rivers—the merging of the Allegheny, Ohio, and Monongahela rivers. The variance of the topography of this continent continually staggered me.

New York held more to discover: Times Square at night, Shubert Alley, Sardi's, with all the caricatures of the celebrated (I soon joined the wall covering), "21"—the popular speakeasy that became a chic restaurant, and theatre—an unforgettable performance of *South Pacific*, starring Mary Martin and Ezio Pinza. The studio had planned for me to go backstage and be photographed with the two stars. While it was definitely an "enchanted evening," it was also not a completely altruistic gesture. Ezio Pinza and MGM had negotiated a picture commitment, effective upon the completion of his two-year play contract. The choice of the movie was *Strictly Dishonorable*, the story of a May-December romance between an opera star and a young girl (me), to be made in early 1951. So the company didn't miss many tricks—already they were laying the foundation for the publicity campaign for the movie.

I saved everything—I'm a real pack rat—menus, programs, playbills, clippings, photographs, not even a silver pepper mill with "21" engraved on it was safe. The only problem the latter presented was my embarrassment when the darn thing fell out of my bag as I left.†

Arthur's father had asked me to come to Glen Cove, Long Island, the weekend I was in New York. His car called for me at the Waldorf Towers, where Emily and I were ensconced in the MGM suite, and deposited me at a pier. Arthur Sr. was waiting in his launch; weather permitting, that was his usual method of commuting. He was head of Loew's International, had been responsible for the extraordinary Montgomery Clift movie, *The Search,* and soon would personally produce another Fred Zinnemann winner, *Teresa,* Pier Angeli's first important role. A bright man.

The view of the New York skyline was spectacular from the water. I was still absorbed by it when Arthur Sr. said, "Here we are—this is Pembroke!" As we docked, I thought he was referring to the building next to the pier, which was no little cottage. As it turned out, that was the boathouse. He pointed farther inland, where there was a four-story mansion set on fifty acres. I thought it was a hotel. A car drove us to the entrance; a butler took my bags— somewhere; I was introduced to Mrs. Loew, Arthur's stepmother; and Arthur Sr. conducted a brief expedition through the interior ground floor. Spacious halls, elegant rooms, priceless antiques. The projection room was downstairs; family and guest apartments were on the second and third floors; the fourth floor was then closed off, but had previously housed generations of children, nannies, and playrooms. The "house" had sixty-four rooms.

We were to attend a ball that evening at the home of Nicholas Schenck, another founding executive of MGM. "My" (assigned) maid showed me to my suite. She had already unpacked my suitcase and laid out my clothes. She drew my bath, helped me with my dress, fixed my hair. A person could develop a definite affinity for this kind of life. And it was just beginning.

The Schenck estate was across the Sound, so our party traveled by boat. You could see the lights and decorations and hear the music and people as we approached. Other groups had arrived by water as well. There was a string of launches along the shore like taxis in front of a hotel. The premises had the appearance of a

---

† But I've benefited from the fruits of my collecting. How else could I savor the events of the past thirty-odd years?

fairyland. It was almost unreal. Indeed, I felt like Cinderella again, and I was the belle of the ball. I danced every dance, I met many people. At one point a Mr. Shubert was presented, and I blurted out, "Oh, are you Shubert's Alley?" He was.

Arthur Sr. was relishing my obvious excitement and wanted to prolong the fun. We all motored back across the moonlit Sound and he suggested a snack before retiring. He led us to the kitchen area (which was bigger than our apartment in L.A.), where I scrambled eggs on the largest stove I've ever seen. Arthur Jr. called to see how I was faring. He asked if I could meet him in Tucson on my way home. I could. It was a wonderful night.

Saturday, after I followed instructions and rang for my breakfast tray, I explored the exterior of the mansion. One building contained an indoor swimming pool and tennis court; then, outside in the gardens, were a regular tennis court, swimming pool, and pool cabana. Stables were located toward the rear of the property. And, of course, there was the beach house, with varying sizes and types of watercraft moored in front.

It was difficult to imagine what it would be like living in this environment on a regular basis. Not that I had to worry, but it was interesting to contemplate. I could see how it would be just dandy. And I could also see how it would create extensive pressures. Who was it who said, "I've been rich, and I've been poor, and I like rich better"? I guess that's right. Money does provide a freedom, an ease—that is, as long as it doesn't prevent effort and growth. Probably the best of all worlds is, first—to be rich in spirit, and second—to be materially secure. A goal most of us keep struggling toward.

Opulence on the order of the Loew estate is not prevalent today. It exists, but the sheer logistics needed for such a lifestyle make it nearly unmanageable. I am really glad I was able to observe it then.

I've described the good part of the weekend. Now let me tell you about the worst—my demoralization. On Saturday the Loews had a quiet supper planned, to be followed by a movie. (A sit-down dinner for twenty-four is quiet?) I was not schooled in social etiquette, except for basic manners, so I carefully watched the other guests and followed their choice of utensils for each course. I was doing just fine, until the dessert. The butler presented the tray to me first—*me first!* Delicately balanced on the silver platter were two small coconut halves filled with something, and alongside was a serving spoon and fork. What to do? I had a healthy appetite and it seemed to me a proper portion would be a half for each person and that more coconuts would be forthcoming. WRONG! I picked up the spoon and fork and struggled to take the shell. And I struggled. And I struggled. Finally, at the other end of the long table (the) Mrs. Loew (at the time) said with acid sweetness, "Janet, dear, I think it would be best if you sampled what is *inside.*" Damn, damn, damn her! I've always believed she deliberately choreographed that just to humiliate me. And how she succeeded.

There were two constructive results of that humbling incident. One, I boned up on expected decorum, and two, I made sure that my children, no matter how they objected, knew the accepted way to conduct themselves in almost all situations relating to formal protocol.

Boston finished the tour. Peter Lawford had been promoting the movie in different areas and we met in Boston for the opening.

While I was there, Harvard University had asked me to be a guest on its radio station. The Ivy League campus was lovely, reminiscent of College of Pacific in appearance. During the interview, I said, "How pleased I am to be in Boston." Arms were waving frantically—what had I done? I had no idea I was in Cambridge— all we had done was cross a bridge. It must have meant a great deal to them.

Peter and a mutual friend, Joe Naar, put me on the plane for Tucson. I was weary but happy, and looked forward to the reunion with Arthur. I had missed him, and he must have missed me, because we decided to become engaged, sort of unofficially. Neither of us was pushing marriage right then. We simply enjoyed and liked each other tremendously and wanted to be together. Loving was the natural continuation of those feelings. It was my first encounter with a true friendship developing into a love. It was a fulfilling, glowing, progressive relationship. Arthur could make me laugh about something as serious to me as my first "marriage", not facetiously but in a way that compelled me to deal with it more easily. That lack of "heaviness" worked miracles. It was not disregarding a problem, it was meeting a problem head-on through humor. Perhaps that is how Arthur survived so well.

The occasion for the gathering in Tucson was Mickey's wedding to her second husband. It was held in her garden. The groom was a lawyer from New York, and all of us hoped it would be a good marriage. I felt special to be included there.

Late May, 1949. "Janet darling—come in, come in—sit right over here," exclaimed Benny Thau, his secretary ushering me into his plush office. I always felt comfortable with Mr. Thau. He was not the stereotype of the gruff, cigar-smoking movie mogul. Rather, he was a quiet, soft-spoken, sensitive, dapper gentleman. I had been asked to come for a meeting. Immediately my sensitive psyche had started working—what had I done? What was wrong?

"Janet, I have the most wonderful news."

(Sigh of relief.)

"We have just completed a deal for you to star in three very powerful films with distinguished co-stars. All of us firmly believe this will be a paramount step in further solidifying your career, and naturally we are extremely pleased, as you will be. You are officially on loan-out to RKO, Mr. Howard Hughes's studio!"

My balloon of excitement that had been inflating popped as he made his announcement.

RKO? Howard Hughes? My expression stopped Mr. Thau's enthusiasm and my tears completely baffled him. I timidly related my unsettling experiences with Mr. Hughes—I didn't want to seem ungrateful for the studio's belief in me—for this opportunity—but I was afraid—

He almost looked relieved. "My dear, is that all? Is that what troubles you? I thought it was something serious. Granted, Mr. Hughes may have idiosyncrasies in his social life, but this is *business.* We're speaking of millions of dollars. This involves stars like Robert Mitchum, John Wayne, Cary Grant. I assure you everything will be conducted in a proper manner. Working at RKO will be the same as working here at MGM. And remember, I am just a phone call away."

Mr. Thau's confident, businesslike approach allayed my fears. In fact, I felt a little foolish, schoolgirlish. Wasn't it naïve of me to really think that my personal life could have any effect on major corporate decisions? Of course he was right.

Or was he?

CHAPTER TEN

RKO Studios was situated on Gower Street between Melrose Avenue and Santa Monica Boulevard. The gate policeman welcomed me and I was guided to an assigned parking spot near my quite elaborate dressing room. I was suffering from my normal nerves—unknown territory, unknown people. Don Hartman, producer and director of the first RKO project, *Holiday Affair,* greeted his new player and put her somewhat at ease. What a fine man, attractive, witty, a sensitive leader and a responsive, conscientious friend. And we had a charming script. A young war widow with a small son learns to deal with life and love again. The setting was in New York during Christmastime. The top-notch assembly of stars to tell the story included Robert Mitchum, Wendell Corey, Henry O'Neill, and Harry Morgan.

RKO had a more simple orientation process than MGM's. It was much smaller than MGM, more informal. Don explained the ground rules. He had autonomy at the creative end, but Mr. Hughes had to approve the wardrobe, hair, and makeup tests. And he had contracted the most qualified people in each department—designer Michael Wolfe, hair stylist Larry Germaine, makeup artist Jimmy House—but what we all went through! Mr. Hughes wanted my hair longer and fuller, so Larry had to combat a fall throughout the picture; it was constantly getting caught in the collar of the fur coat. Mr. Hughes wanted to cover the scar above my right upper lip (from when I had chicken pox—but no one else had ever noticed it previously), so Jimmy had to concoct different mixtures to hide my blemish. Nothing really worked—the more goop he put on, the more the scar showed. Finally Mr. H. gave in and agreed to leave it natural. Mr. Hughes wanted the wardrobe to be glamorous, so Michael had the problem of dressing me to please him and still be realistic, within the confines of the character's budget. Certainly a lot of fuss.

My consultations with Mr. Hughes were cordial, and always in the presence of someone else from the company. So far, so good. Then one night I received a telephone call at home. The "boss man" wished me to come over to the studio to view the final tests. Aha! So Daddy and I initiated our own game plan. He would drive me to my requested meetings, wait for me, and then drive me home, always staying close at hand. That, I thought, should thwart any Casanova thoughts Mr. Hughes might have been entertaining.

Robert Mitchum was the most liberated spirit I had ever come across before. The first time I saw him, he was exiting his dressing room playing a saxophone, with his entourage in tow, and the whole group paraded around the lot. A lasting impression! He was so relaxed you thought he just might topple over. And those half-mast bedroom eyes just added to the image. But all of this was deceiving, because, once at work, he was such a professional, competent actor. How he loved to tease me! And with Wendell Corey, what a parlay! Wendell was another devotee of fun and another skilled actor. Once they realized I was rather "square" and that they had a "patsy," oh boy, did I ever get it.

The group Christmas dinner scene in the movie was typical. My "family" was seated at the table and Bob and Wendell, playing my two suitors, sat on either side of me—each slipping a hand onto my knee. I knew they weren't actually groping, that they were putting on an act, but they *sure* made me fidgety. That jumpiness worked well for the text, however. I had the same results when Mitchum kissed me in the script. I mean he *really* kissed me. But since my character was supposed to be startled and unsettled, I certainly had no difficulty showing those emotions. There was a method to their madness, but I'm not sure whether it was all done in the line of duty.

The little boy cast as my son was an adorable child. But he was having trouble, and I sensed Don was not satisfied with his performance. I tried everything within my limited experience to help him —rehearsed with him between scenes, played games, tried to establish a rapport that would diminish his block, even nudged him in a shot when he was supposed to speak. But all to no avail. He evidently just didn't come across on the screen and he was replaced. I was heartbroken. I couldn't help but identify—it might have been what happened to me after two days on *The Romance of Rosy Ridge.* How fragile our footing.

Gordon Gebert, who succeeded him, was a complete opposite in appearance and behaviour: hair going in all directions, freckles, teeth missing—and an imp and a rascal. But what a natural! Unknowingly, he taught me a big lesson.

In one scene, we were to have a breakfast discussion. In the take, besides talking, I bustled about the kitchen, and finally sat, delivering my line and his cue. No response. "Did you hear me?" And I repeated my question. No response. Again, "Did you hear me?" Again, no response. He had become so engrossed with taking one dry cornflake and seeing how much sugar he could pile on it that he was oblivious to anything else. I shrugged and looked at Don, expecting commiseration.

"Cut! Janet, that was your fault. You missed an opportunity. Why didn't you react to what he was doing—incorporate it—maybe give his hand a slap and say, 'How many times have I told you the right way to eat your cereal?' and then force him back into the conversation!"

So true! It *was* my responsibility. Hell, I fretted at the time, will I ever learn?

Something registered, though. In another scene, taking place in "my" bedroom, late at night, Gordon bounded in and jumped energetically right on top of me, when he was only supposed to creep in and snuggle. I wouldn't stop the shot for anything, despite the fact I couldn't get my breath. Don was right, it just added to the script, because it was real.

I liked that picture a lot.

Spring of 1949 brought on the debacle of *Stromboli.* I watched in horror as Ingrid Bergman—the incomparable, matchless *Ingrid Bergman*—was crucified for her personal relationship with Roberto Rossellini. It seemed as though the whole world was suddenly focused on that stormy island. Ferocious indignation, outrage, combustive debates, all targeted on Ingrid Bergman because of her pregnancy without marriage. I didn't and wouldn't presume to judge, but my heart ached for her in her torment.

And in the very recesses of my innards, I shivered. Could my secret—my fourteen-year-old blunder—cause me to lose what gains had been made in my life? In no way did I equate my status with Miss Bergman's, but the damage would be as devastating to me. *Thank God* it hadn't surfaced, I thought. And all I could hope was that time would be on my side.

Arthur was cast in a movie and went on location. Many people had urged him to try his hand at acting, based on his acute wit and penetrating insight. Jane was in Los Angeles for a time during his absence, and we frequently joined friends for a dinner or movie. Soon after she left and just prior to Arthur's return, I received a summons for a meeting with Mr. H. *Holiday Affair* was nearly finished, and I presumed it was about the next project. Daddy and I drove to the studio.

"Janet, I have some disturbing information. This was brought to my attention through channels I cannot disclose, and done so because of their knowledge of my interest in your welfare."

He placed a mass of papers before me, and I read a detailed, chronicled report of my every move for the past two weeks.

Thursday, 7:15 P.M., Subject departed apartment, 9400 Vidor Drive, accompanied by dark-haired woman (approximately late 20's) with white flower in hair. Vehicle, yellow 1948 Buick Convertible.

7:30 P.M., Subject arrived La Rue Restaurant, Sunset Boulevard and Sunset Plaza Drive. Sat at table with three males (approximately 30, mid 30's, mid 40's) and two females (approximately 30, early 40's).

10:00 P.M., Subject departed restaurant with first companion.

10:15 P.M., Subject arrived at Vidor apartment. Dark-haired woman drove away in same Buick.

No activity remainder of night.

I was so stupefied I couldn't speak. Someone had hired a detective to follow me? *Why?* What did it mean? Who? And I was frightened. Was there a veiled threat in this craziness?

He broke the silence and my speculations. "I am sorry to be the bearer of bad news. Evidently that boyfriend of yours, Arthur Loew, Jr., doesn't trust you, and wanted to be informed of your activities while he was gone."

The pieces of this puzzle suddenly went together. If I hadn't been so shaken and incensed, it could almost have been funny. But it wasn't!

"Mr. Hughes, your sources didn't do a thorough job. For your edification, the dark-haired woman *happens* to be Arthur's sister, Jane Loew Morse. The yellow Buick convertible *happens* to be Arthur's car. Most of the people mentioned *happen* to be Arthur's relatives or our friends. In the future, please make sure any meeting deals with business, not nonsense. Or I intend to speak with Mr. Thau about negating whatever arrangement you made with MGM."

And with that I stomped out. And then my boldness ended. I'm not comfortable with confrontations, my stomach churns so I could make butter. I'm not innately a fighter—usually I cry from frustration, which weakens my effectiveness. At least I lasted until I reached the car.

Dad attempted to make some sense from all this. "He obviously is trying to discredit Arthur in your eyes. I can't find any dangerous motive behind his actions. It's really childish. Of course it's disquieting for you." We decided to wait to see the effects, if any, of my speech.

Cary Grant or John Wayne were Mr. Hughes's choices, for the second RKO picture, *Jet Pilot.* Not too bad! Cary's schedule conflicted with the starting date, November 1, but I did get to meet him. My God, he was good-looking, *and* suave, *and* he really does talk that way. Quite a man!

Fortunately, John Wayne could fit the film into his crowded calendar. Another hunk of man! And *he* really talked that way, and walked that way. He was the consummate model of virility.

And his real name was Marion Morrison! We wondered if, way, way, way back, there was any connection. We never found the answer to that one.

Jet Pilot was Howard Hughes's baby, because it had to do with airplanes. He wanted this to be greater than his classic *Hell's Angels* (which he had produced *and* directed back in 1930, with the one and only Jean Harlow). Consequently, no expense was spared—in any department. A unique experiment was one result of this extravagance. Duke (John Wayne's nickname) and I actually tried out directors. We made costly tests with various directors, so Howard could select the one most qualified to helm his pet project. He had brought Josef von Sternberg out of retirement (Marlene Dietrich's mentor—*The Blue Angel* was one of their collaborations). Alas, he won the competition. I say alas, because, although the trial scene was brilliantly conceived, he gradually developed into an unbearable dictator. As a matter of fact, the whole picture eventually unfolded into a giant dud. How were we to know Mr. H. would fiddle with the footage and miniatures and special effects for *seven* years? All of the extensive cooperation afforded the company by the U.S. Air Force—being allowed to photograph heretofore unseen aircraft, broad use of facilities and personnel, on-set counselling—was for naught. Because, by the time the picture was released, everything was obsolete. Not just the equipment, but the situations, even the dialogue. It was an inexcusable waste of talent: Winton Hoch, cinematographer, Bronislau Kaper, music, plus the incredible and countless technical advisers. What could have been a coup for all involved wound up a turkey. I have been told it still did make money, but certainly not what it should have. (Could-da! Would-da! Should-da!)

But it *was* an experience. Annabel Levy (hair stylist), Mary Tate (set wardrobe and what a wardrobe it was. Michael Wolfe had been given carte blanche to indulge his imagination), Jimmy House (again my makeup artist), and I formed an alliance. There were numerous locations, and we stuck together like glue. Protection—and enjoyment!

There were quite a few firsts for me on this epic. I played a Russian pilot who deliberately strays into an American-zone base to gather information on the newest inventions and maneuvers. Duke was the American officer assigned to watch the intruder and act as the counterspy. Much double dealing, many misunderstood intentions, but, of course, love transcends ideology and the girl converts to democracy. It was an unadulterated, romantic-adventure-action picture.

I was, and still am, completely unmechanical. It was an uphill task for the instructor to have me appear adept in the cockpit. All those instruments and dials sent me into a panic. Even the jargon of aviation was difficult to handle with ease. Somehow he managed the impossible and made me look and sound at least passable. In one shot I actually had to taxi the jet, as if I were about to take off. He was jammed in with me, out of sight naturally, manipulating the controls so I wouldn't kill us all. We became quite chummy.

I used my first *bad* four-letter words on the set. (It became easier with practice.) I wasn't proud of this new vocabulary, but Von Sternberg was so vexing, so increasingly tyrannical, I just couldn't help myself. Some peoples' attitudes inevitably invite the negative responses of others.

Now Duke, on the other hand, was surprisingly mild, a Superman in the disguise of Clark Kent. I knew he could be, shall we say, boisterous. On a few occasions the company held dinners for the military brass, and the boys sometimes had a mite too much to drink, and raised a little hell. So I was aware of his potential explosiveness.

Von Sternberg was a tiny man, and he staged scenes as if Duke were *his* size. I asked Duke why he didn't object, how he could be so complaisant.

"Janet, if I ever let loose, if I ever started on him, I'd kill the S.O.B." Enough said!

The worst "first": In the plot, a cigarette case was an important prop—messages were hidden inside. Everyone agreed it would look ridiculous for me to carry this case and never use it for cigarettes. That's right, I had to learn to smoke. In the beginning I tried to hold the smoke in my mouth and blow it out slowly. But progressively, I inhaled. I distinctly remember the dizziness at nine o'clock in the morning when I took the first puff. For all the years of school and the three and a half years of Hollywood, I had managed to avoid this temptation. Not that anyone knew for sure about the danger then; I just hadn't been interested, even though smoking was "the" thing to do. Well, I still have that habit, and I curse the circumstances that were responsible, and me for not stopping the addiction sooner.

Jules Furthman was the producer of *Jet Pilot.* He also was a writer and a trusted friend of Howard Hughes, a harmless, funny man, who always wore a turned-up porkpie hat and was completely involved in growing orchids. He was associated with the picture for the entire seven years. When the actors were called back for added scenes or retakes after the conclusion of the actual shooting (which occurred over a two-year period), he would direct. It was almost a lifetime occupation. Indeed, I am under the impression there was an honored contract between them until Mr. Furthman retired and Mr. Hughes sold the studio.

Quite a while later, Eddy Lasker, an attorney for many Hollywood luminaries, revealed to me one of the conditions of their arrangement. Mr. Furthman was under oath not to disclose the fact that Mr. Hughes had asked Mr. Furthman, at an opportune time, to ask Janet Leigh to marry Mr. Hughes. How is that for weird? I guess the "opportune time" didn't present itself, because Jules never posed the question. I'm sure my attitude dissuaded him from pursuing the subject. Whenever he extolled the virtues of Howard Hughes, I would automatically tune out. In my wildest fantasies, I wouldn't have put me as Priscilla Mullins to Jules Furthman's John Alden to Howard Hughes's Miles Standish.

In January 1950, two absolutely wonderful things happened. I made the down payment on a house for Mom and Dad and me. It was the first time in our lives we weren't going to rent. The house was not large—two bedrooms and a den with a comfortable backyard and patio—but it was new and clean and it would be *ours*. It was located on Medio Drive in Brentwood, a quiet residential area west of Beverly Hills, and was between Sunset Boulevard and San Vicente. This was a landmark event for the Morrison clan.

And on January 15, 1950, Stockton held "Janet Leigh and Eddie LeBaron Day." Eddie was a College of Pacific alumnus who had been successful in pro football. Do you have any idea how proud Mom and Dad and I were? I felt very grateful that I could bring a little glory to my parents, especially since their only daughter had brought a myriad of somber moments to their lives. I know we were all reflecting how different the climate could have been. I know we were all sending prayers of thankfulness to the One accountable.

Our reunions with friends were rewarding. I was amazed at the number of changes, of divorces in particular, that paralleled Hollywood, the difference being that these didn't make national headlines. The days preceding Sunday, and the big day itself, were filled with lunches, teas, dinners, parades. College of Pacific bestowed honors, as did my sorority, Alpha Theta Tau. The final touch at the testimonial dinner was the mayor's presentation of the key to the city, accompanied by a standing ovation. I could have burst, I was so happy.

I doubt if the people of Stockton, even our intimates, were fully aware of the significance of this and subsequent laurels. How could they be? Unknowingly they gave to Mom and Dad, and to me, a gift that had no price tag. *Respectability.*

Arthur and I were petering out. We remained comrades, but we were not prepared to make the ultimate pledge. It's interesting, in retrospect, to see the different attributes that bring love to us. Security, intellect, humor, respect, friendship, adjacency—each naturally interwoven with passion.

A fitting accolade to Arthur: When he eventually married his Regina, many of his ex-girlfriends were in attendance: Elizabeth Taylor (before me), me, Joan Collins (followed me), Natalie Wood (after Joan), plus a few more. We were all his friends.

So once again I was unattached, which led to a bizarre situation. Over a period of weeks I had been receiving bouquets of flowers alternated with Billy Eckstein records, almost daily, accompanied by a card simply signed "Johnny." I was in the dark as to the identity of "Johnny." A telephone call didn't do much toward explaining this enigma.

"May I speak to Janet Leigh?" a deep masculine voice asked.

"This is she."

"Hi! This is Johnny."

"Oh-uh-uh-hello! Are you the Johnny of the flowers and records?"

"That's me!"

"Well, uh, thank you very much. I'm a little confused. Do I know you? Forgive me, if we have met—I just don't seem to recall."

"No—you don't know me. But I know and admire you and would like to take you out."

"That's very flattering, but I couldn't possibly date a total stranger. I mean—that just isn't *done.*" (At least it wasn't in 1950.)

"May I *see* you then?"

"I live with my folks. If you want to come by and visit with all of us, that's okay." I thought those tidings would end the discussion pronto.

"Fine! How is tonight about six o'clock?"

I hung up the phone, still bewildered, but I must confess, intrigued.

At six sharp, the door bell rang, and I opened the door to face a tall, powerfully built, dark-haired, extremely handsome man. I noted a black Cadillac in the driveway.

"I'm Johnny!" he announced as he entered and met Mom and Dad. I don't know how he managed it, but we never heard his last name. The conversation was pleasant, and we covered a variety of topics. When Dad asked about his profession, he merely said, "I'm a businessman," and meandered to other subjects, mostly geared to us.

When he left he asked permission to come again. Permission granted. This routine occurred several times during the ensuing few weeks. One evening he inquired if he might take me for a ride and a cup of coffee. Mom and Dad felt comfortable with this and consented. We drove north along Pacific Coast Highway, and just south of Malibu, he turned right onto a steep driveway. At the top there was a gate with two men on guard who passed us through. I assumed this was some sort of private club. I was right, in a way.

Over coffee, he tendered a proposal.

"Janet, I am going to tell you something now—something about me—that is highly confidential. I must trust you with this, because I want you to be 'my girl.' "

Visions flared in my head, imagination working overtime again, he was a detective, he was FBI, a government agent, he was a spy, he was—

"I am a syndicate man, a member of the mob. This lounge is frequented only by those on the inside who are in the know and in good standing. When one of us takes a girl, he has to be sure of her loyalty. Not that she would necessarily be involved in our business, but unpreventably, she would be privy to our movements and some classified information. My name is Johnny Stompanato."

Oh Dear God in Heaven! Help me! Help me to get out of here—preferably in one piece. Please!

The adrenaline was pumping so fast through my system, I almost choked. Surely he could hear my heart pounding. I tried to take a

sip of coffee, but I couldn't hold the cup. How could I answer—
what I must answer without upsetting him?

I blundered ahead. "Johnny—I—had no idea. I appreciate your
—faith in me—and I promise—I swear—I will say nothing of this
conversation. You seem to be a—an agreeable man—certainly an
attractive one. But—but this just isn't for me. I couldn't handle
your—profession. Please—please understand."

"I'll take you home."

My knees almost buckled as he helped me into the car. The ride
back was in silence. He walked me to the door, turned me around,
and said, "You won't hear from me again. I am disappointed, but I
will live with your decision. Goodbye, Janet."

I never did see him again. His name appeared briefly in the
newspapers from time to time, but the tragedy that ended his life
about thirteen years later was on every front page in the country.
Ironically, his demise occurred in Hollywood, the result of a do-
mestic situation, not the gangland slaying one might have expected.
His appeal apparently had penetrated one part of the movie community. There is no need to dredge up the particulars for review—
innocent people might still be hurt by recollection.

And I didn't discuss "the Johnny caper," except with Mom and
Dad, who were benumbed by the whole incident.

The publicity campaign at RKO was in drive and constantly ac-
celerating. Photographic sittings, layouts, and set stills all concentrated on little ol' me. The department had their orders—all sys-
tems go. This included appearing at press cocktail parties, given by
all the studios for their current projects. One such coterie is indeli-
bly etched in my mind. At the end of a day's shooting on the lot,
Perry Lieber (chief of operations of RKO's public relations) escorted me across the street to Lucy's. This restaurant, on Gower
Street and Melrose Avenue, was the designated watering hole for
all V.I.P.s from close-by Columbia Studios, Paramount, and RKO.
Most interviews were held there, countless deals were consummated there, and many of the infamous three-hour lunches took
place there. I understand that it was put off limits, at least for lunch,
to some performers who had such a good time they didn't want to
spoil their fun by returning to work. The clientele was always a
Who's Who list.

The gathering was in full swing when we arrived, shoulder-to-shoulder people, photographers jostling for position. At one point I was introduced to a devastatingly handsome young man—beautiful really—with black unruly hair, large sensitive eyes fringed by long dark lashes, a full sensuous mouth—and an irresistible personality. His name was Tony Curtis. During our brief encounter I found out he was under contract to Universal Pictures, came from New York, had done a couple of minor roles and was about to start a picture that he hoped would be his big break. We were soon pulled in different directions by our respective representatives. But I didn't forget him.

A fresh new couple was setting Hollywood on its ear. Marge and Gower Champion had achieved national acclaim as a dance team, by their innovative dramatic approach to this art form. When they appeared at the Mocambo, all records were broken and the studio talent scouts were climbing all over themselves to be first in line. The Champions signed with MGM. However, never underestimate Howard Hughes.

Since my next and final picture for RKO was to be a musical, *Two Tickets to Broadway,* I had mentioned to Mr. H. in a meeting how talented these two were and how exciting it would be if they could choreograph *Two Tickets.* This was before I read about the contract with MGM.

The Champions' agent, Al Melnick, called and asked if I would attend their closing-night performance as his guest. There was a business matter to be discussed as well. No problem; if I'd had the stamina, I could have watched them every night. At the beginning of the show, Mr. Hughes joined the table. Something was up—for sure. We met backstage afterward. The unhoped-for became a reality. Mr. H. had somehow wangled a loan-out from MGM for the Champions' services. As soon as they finished their nightclub tour, rehearsals would commence. I was rapturous.

"Janet, why are you so distant? Why don't you go out with me?" Mr. Hughes had questioned during one of our appointments.

"Well, for starters, I don't appreciate the way you operate," was my reply. "You don't do things out in the open. Everything has to

be arranged clandestinely. You don't give me an option to accept or
decline an invitation, it's already been predetermined—"

"All right!" he interrupted. "I am asking you now, in a normal
fashion, *will you have dinner with me?*"

"*No!*" I retorted instantly. His frustration and fear of rejection
were evident. Then I thought of Dad in the car and a possible
solution, and, in a manner, relented.

"I will have dinner with you on one condition—that my mother
and father are included."

Which is how the three of us ended up in Howard's old Chevy
on our way to dinner. Mom was funny—she was positive he would
have horns. He took us to the well-known tourist attraction, The
Sportman's Lodge at Ventura Boulevard and Coldwater Canyon in
the San Fernando Valley. The interesting gimmick at this restaurant
was that you caught your own trout. Even if you didn't particularly
care for fish, the idea stimulated a great deal of action.

The evening was pleasant. Mom and Dad and Howard got along
well. A little business was even generated—Dad had an entree to
the Hughes Company for insurance purposes. A truce was called
between Howard and me. But it could lead nowhere. I had absolutely no romantic inclination toward Howard—none—not even a
flicker. In my eyes, he belonged more with my parents than he did
with me. I don't believe he would have been too pleased with that
disclosure.

At any rate, I felt I had dispatched any obligation.

Singing lessons were set for nine o'clock every morning with
Harriet Lee, an established vocal coach in Hollywood. Then onward to RKO to rehearse with Marge and Gower Champion. I was
quite apprehensive, wondering if they were fully aware of the raw
material they were to mold. The first two hours were dedicated to
exercises, at the ballet bar and on the floor. The remainder of the
day's schedule went to dance steps that might be utilized in a number, or the formation of numbers.

Marge was a strict disciplinarian. Her father still directed his
ballet schools, and she believed in his devotion to training. He
couldn't have had a more exemplary representative. Her technique
was flawless, and she had the inner fervor to bring life to style.
Gower didn't have the extensive formal instructive background,

but he had the gift of flair and imagination. His concepts were of broad scope. The two balanced each other beautifully. She served invaluably as an editor, as an objective force, applying her taste and judgment to what he created.

They were quick to spot my limited ability (not too difficult), but once they realized my willingness to work and learn, they plunged zealously into their task. My respect for them, as individuals and artists, grew daily, and our bond of friendship was firmly established for a lifetime.

We had a full stage at our disposal, access to any needed prop or set, dressing rooms, their pianist (Dick), a dance-in for me (Betty Scott), a dance-in for whoever the male lead would be (Robert Scheerer), and an assigned assistant director to handle our requirements (and who, we discovered later, had a direct line to Mr. H., to whom he reported all my phone calls and activities).

Musicals are an entire entity unto themselves. Because of the prolonged rehearsal time and the sustained proximity, the unit becomes a family, a fraternity. This was the beginning of my love affair with "gypsies,"—an honorific title bestowed upon dancers, chorus lines, and backups—those talented benevolent girls and boys who work so tirelessly, and who do most of the complicated acrobatics to make the "star" look agile. (Unless, of course, the star happens to be a Gene Kelly or Fred Astaire or Cyd Charisse or Leslie Caron.) But those of us who began as actors and only later attempted these backbreaking, muscle-killing dance movements can attest to their priceless contribution.

I felt I was in the promised land. A gratifying profession coupled now with my first attachment, music. My background at college, Rosie's schooling at MGM, Alex Romero's tutoring for *The Red Danube,* all proved helpful. I had an aptitude and the desire. I could never make twenty-two-year-old muscles do what five-year-old muscles did, but that could be circumvented. And I had no fear. Every choreographer with whom I've worked made similar observations. It was easier for them to ask me to perform certain stunts than an experienced dancer, because I didn't know enough to be afraid or say no. *Now* they tell me!

I had to share my good news with Kay Thompson (who was involved with so many of the MGM musicals and their stars, also a performer in *Funny Face,* the creator and performer of the nightclub act Kay Thompson and the Williams Brothers, and author of *Eloise*). At MGM, I would always walk around the lot singing, I was so damn *happy*. And one day I was in my favorite restroom near Miss Burns's office, warbling away, when the door burst open and a whirlwind blew in (scaring the hell out of me), yelling, "You ought to do a musical!" and whirled out again. Kay Thompson!

Bobby Scheerer and I began to date. He was good-looking, charming, fun, and skilled. Eventually, he went on to choreograph, direct, and produce. Through him I met an actor named Bob Quarry and saw him as well. Peter Lawford and Lex Barker rounded out my occasional escorts, but my concentration was mostly on work.

We rehearsed—and rehearsed—and rehearsed. And we began to wonder if that was all we were going to do. (I honestly believe we would have rehearsed for the next ten years, if Hughes had had his way.) Granted, I needed much preparation, but no production plans were even in progress. Our questions of who and when were evaded. Finally, Marge and Gower asked Mr. H. to come to their house for dinner, using me as bait, hoping to corner him and ferret out some information. I agreed to participate, only with their promise that I wouldn't be left alone and I would spend the night in their guest room, so there could be no chance of having him drive me home.

Our scheme worked to some extent. He hemmed and hawed—this actor wasn't available, that actor hadn't answered as yet—but he assured us something definite would be forthcoming.

He did assign a director, James Kern, who was one of the original Rhythm Boys with Bing Crosby. At least we had a beginning.

The telephone rang in my bedroom.

"Hello, Janet?" inquired the unmistakable voice of Cary Grant.

"Yes—hi!" Why on earth was he calling me?

As we chatted, my ear told me something was amiss. Then I recalled reading in the trades *(Hollywood Reporter* and *Variety,* our industry publications) that a certain Mr. Tony Curtis had fooled quite a few people with his imitation of Cary Grant.

"I've had a difficult time locating your number, Janet. I wonder if you would do me the honor of having dinner with me next Saturday?"

"Oh I'd be delighted, but unfortunately I have a previous engagement—with Tony Curtis."

Our rendezvous was a typical evening. It only became special because I was with Tony. Conversation revealed more of his background. He had brought his mother and father and brother, Bobby, out from New York when he signed his Universal contract. They all lived in a small apartment in the Valley, and he was the main source of support. Another brother, Julie, had been killed, run over by a truck. (I perceived that a thick veil surrounded that tragedy.) Joyce Selznick had discovered him at the Actors Studio in New York. Bernie Schwartz was his real name. And he had learned the Cary Grant accent on a submarine during the war, from watching *Gunga Din* (the only film on board) over and over again. He had a captivating boyish charm, yet there was an inner depth behind those penetrating eyes. Definitely someone worth investigating.

Progress on *Two Tickets* was still at a minimum. To ease the strain, I suppose, Jimmy Kern decided to have a get-together on a yacht with everyone involved in the picture at this point. I smelled a rat, so Marge and Gower and Bobby (Scheerer) were my shield of armor. Sure enough, when we all congregated, we were guided to Hughes Airfield. He was going to fly us in a seaplane to the ship, anchored at Catalina, and then we would cruise back. Oh well, I was getting used to his little games by now, and with my group always near, I relaxed and enjoyed another new venture. Landing on water, especially if the swells are heavy, is frightening. The spray rises above the windows, so you have the feeling of being submerged. And when the engines are cut, you bob around at the mercy of the waves. Those with queasy stomachs were anxious to disembark and stand on a more solid base. The vessel was quite large and absorbed the rolling sea. It was a lovely day, the repast was delicious, and the sun felt good on our stage-white bodies. In the evening we saw flying fish, fascinating little creatures. And every time Mr. Hughes came my way, Bobby or Marge or Gower were there.

The following week Tony Martin signed as the male lead. And Bobby was immediately dispatched to Las Vegas, where Tony was appearing, to prep him in some routines. Not too unusual. *Yet.*

Perry Lieber wanted me to participate in a RKO press junket. (This is a trip, financed by a studio, for invited journalists from all media to view a new product, and thus ensure abundant coverage. Entertainment is the key word—wining and dining and celebrities galore.) The location was Las Vegas. I jumped at the offer. Bobby was there and it would be a diversion from the rehearsal grind.

As I was winging my way toward the expected fun, little did I know that Bobby was on his way back to Los Angeles. We must have crossed in the air. I looked for him futilely. By and by I was paged to the telephone.

"You won't believe this," panted Bobby. "First of all, Tony didn't feel like working with me—two shows a night were enough for him—so it was a waste of time anyway. But three hours ago, I was told to pack up and be on the next plane out. I asked to stay because I knew you were coming, and they said, 'That is why you're leaving.' What goes?"

I was furious! I pranced over to poor Perry Lieber and demanded an explanation. "Janet, I was in hot water because I brought you on this excursion, and somebody named Bob Scheerer was here. My orders were to get him out before you arrived. I'm sorry!"

It wasn't Perry's fault, he had his job to protect. But damn Howard Hughes! There he was again, juggling my life. I remembered that odd request for a picture in South America before Barry left for the play in New York—just after we had first met Howard Hughes at Mervyn LeRoy's. Of course, that had to be his doing too. A pox on him!

Events were coming to a head. Since there was no starting date as yet, MGM called me back to do a segment in *It's a Big Country,* a film of seven individual stories depicting the diversity of the United States and the glory of being one of its citizens. It took only a week to shoot. I was Gene Kelly's leading lady, with S. Z. (Cuddles) Sakall playing my father. Ironic that I was working with Gene Kelly in a straight role; if only it could have been in the musical. Can't have everything. It was an honor just to be with him. Good man! He applied the same dedication, the same perfection, to scenes as to dance. (One time at a dinner, I actually danced with him and was so flustered I tripped over my own feet.)

I was happy to be home again, in a "normal atmosphere." And to see Miss Burns. She had not been pleased about the loan-outs, but the decision had not been in her jurisdiction. She felt the Hughes directive for publicity emphasis on the sex symbol was misleading; the main focus should be stressing the actress. She was right, but neither of us could change the course then. *Holiday Affair* was progress, she liked that, but when I told her about *Jet Pilot* she was aghast. *Two Tickets* was still an unknown commodity. Despite the popular appeal, she believed I would have an uphill struggle to regain recognition as a quality performer.

A dejected would-be dancer returned to the RKO stage, only to be hit by the biggest blow of all. Marge and Gower's time was up. They were to report to MGM to prepare for *Showboat.* Our family was breaking up. What now? Who could follow them? And when?

The incongruity of the whole mess was that everyone had benefited from this episode: Marge and Gower had made enough money to buy their home in the Hollywood Hills, Harriet Lee was able to build a soundproof studio off her house, Dick and Bobby and Betty had enjoyed higher pay scale for a longer than normal period. And me, well, I was close to a nervous breakdown. Yes, I was on salary. But the work, the harassment, the frustration had taken its toll. The menacing intrusion on my life and career had reached the point of no return. Hughes repelled me. Any intimation of physical contact induced lightning bolts of disgust. I called Dad; told the assistant director-stooge I wanted a meeting with Mr. Hughes *now;* and packed my belongings in the dressing room. Dad drove me to his bungalow at the Beverly Hills Hotel.

"Mr. Hughes, I am leaving—for—New York! I will not return until this picture has a starting date, a choreographer, a full cast, and a finished script. I don't give a pig's eye what your agreement states with MGM. You can put me on suspension, cancel the picture, I don't care! I *Cannot go on in this limbo.*" And in my irrational state I picked up the closest object, which happened to be the telephone, and threw it, missing him by a small margin, and hitting the wall behind him with a loud crash. The door burst open, and there was Dad—ready to do battle—sure that Mr. "H" had made his move. What he found was a confounded Howard Hughes and an irate daughter storming out of the room.

I had no preconceived idea of my destination, but since New York spilled out of my mouth, New York it would be.

Tony and I had plans for that evening. He was disappointed

about my intended trip, but understood the need as I unfolded my tale of woe. The convolution was somewhat baffling to him. It was to me too! All I desired was to do my job as an actress, but an actress has to act. It's all well and good to enhance the versatility of one's talent, and true, there was perpetual room for improvement in my terpsichoring, but I felt I was not furthering my predominate craft. The extracurricular aberrations were intolerable. I had heard about Jane Russell and Jack Beutel. After the gluttonous publicity campaign and monetary success of *The Outlaw*, Mr. H. had kept them under contract, with generous compensation, but also withering on the vine. Always dangling the "right" picture before them, only it never came to fruition. Some strange quirk made it uppermost for Mr. Hughes to have control and domination over the people he collected, or was it just the act of collecting? Somehow it satisfied him to have a simile of work going on, ignoring the goal of a finished product, as long as his satellites were in *his* orbit. I didn't understand any of it. How could a recently turned twenty-three-year-old brain understand the complexities of a mind like his?

Tony was full of news too. Ever since he had cut in on Yvonne De Carlo in *Crisscross* and danced a few frames with her, fan mail had begun funneling into the coffers. Successive appearances in *Winchester '73, Sierra, I Was a Shop Lifter,* and *Kansas Raiders* brought increased response, and the studio sat up and took notice. The producer Leonard Goldstein was the first to take a chance. He was going to star Tony in the picture *The Prince Who Was a Thief.* It wasn't a classic by any means, nor was it meant to be. It was intended to be, and was, a swashbuckler, a romantic adventure, a platform to launch two new faces—Tony Curtis and Piper Laurie.

He was euphoric, of course, and so pleased not to be in another Western. He had lied about his equestrian prowess in order to get parts:

"Can you ride?"

"Very well!" Like all struggling performers, he would have said he could fly if it meant a job. But he confessed he was nearly killed; New York hadn't offered much opportunity for experience in that department.

I was curious how his name had been chosen, since mine had been changed too. The shadowy "they" had said, "Bernard Schwartz has to go!" (It seemed I was listening to a playback.) After they had engaged in much discussion, he was called in to hear their decision. "We think Anthony Adverse would be interesting." He was wordless. "But—but—" didn't they know? "Uh, that's nice— but there was a film, and a novel—maybe it would be, confusing?" "So there was, so there was, good point." Somehow out of that came the name Curtis and the shortening of Anthony to Tony.

Liza Minnelli sings a song called "Ring Them Bells." I wasn't familiar with it then, but it does fit the feelings I experienced when Tony and I kissed goodnight. My bells were definitely ringing. My built-in Geiger counter was activated. I promised to return to California soon.

CHAPTER ELEVEN

Both RKO and MGM took advantage of my presence in New York. And good does come from trying experiences, for from this rebellious and revengeful trip, I met a lifelong friend. The RKO press rep was to pick me up at the hotel at twelve noon for a luncheon interview. At noon sharp I was in the lobby, waiting. And I waited. At last a harried man approached me. "You are Miss Leigh. Oh my God, I thought I had lost you. I've been ringing your room for twenty minutes. I had no idea you were in here—no one ever comes down first—I mean, I didn't even think to look—oh my goodness—I'm sorry—" And thus I met John Springer, who is now a recognized author and historian about the show business world and its inhabitants and who also has his own public relations firm. We were sympatico from the beginning. Later he confided that he had felt like a rotter. His instructions were to keep me very busy and under close scrutiny. But once we had established our fellowship, he felt himself a traitor. The busy part was okay—that was his job—but he couldn't follow through as the spy.

John initiated me that day to the "happening" of Danny's Hideaway. Danny Stradella was a Purple Heart veteran, soft-spoken, gentle, who persevered through all sorts of obstacles to establish a successful restaurant. And whose heart was bigger than he was. Then, gradually, finally, his place caught on and from there on in was usually bursting at the seams with the exalted from the sports and entertainment fields. Any friend who might be temporarily unemployed was always welcome as his guest. Even if all was well with your profession, you had to make a fuss to get a check. A good businessman, maybe not, but a special human being, definitely yes.

So, the time was filled, with publicity, plays, visiting Mickey
(Loew), and dating a little, but John was by choice my usual escort.

At last, word came back East—*Two Tickets to Broadway* was finally
under way for real and I could come home. I had begun to think
that my brave stand might have been in vain, that I might have
become a permanent refugee, or that I would be forced to renege
on my vow. But I'd won! *What* I'd won was still a question. But we
would now be propelled toward a target. Tony Martin, Eddie
Bracken, Ann Miller, Gloria DeHaven, Barbara Lawrence, and the
vaudeville team of Smith and Dale were set for the cast. Sid Silvers
and Hal Kanter had delivered a script. And Busby Berkeley had
been lured out of retirement to choreograph. Busby Berkeley was
the endorsed forerunner of the overluxuriant musical extravaganzas
of the thirties. He used more people, more cameras, more larger-
than-life angles than had heretofore been employed. His effectiveness had diminished somewhat with the advent of the more realistic
approach to musicals. Hughes, it seems, had a penchant for bringing careers out of mothballs. Another quirk, a form of ego maybe.
He either wanted to fashion a talent or be the party responsible for
reestablishing one. His was an opaque soul.

Jerry Wald arrived to head RKO during rehearsals for *Two Tickets,* and his acumen aided in pulling the floundering project together. He was sorely needed.

But in spite of all the preliminary hassle, we did enjoy the film
itself. Jack Baker was assistant choreographer and actually set the
steps, within the range of B.B.'s ever watchful camera eye. And the
gals and guys were good sports, and wacky, and kooky, and spirited. It was never dull. Annie Miller was (and still is) a case in
particular. No one knows what might pop out of her mouth, she
least of all.*

* And she has absolutely no idea how funny she really is. Years later, on Merv
Griffin's show, I was interviewed first; then Lilli Palmer came on (a bewitching
woman; she was discussing her autobiography, *Change Lobsters and Dance*); and then
Ann Miller. She had just returned from India and was prattling on about the-
Maharaja-this-and-the-Maharaja-that-and-those-poor-people-lying-in-the-streets-and-
isn't-this-silk-exquisite-and-the-peasants-are-starving . . . The camera was focused
on the interviewee, of course. And she was being so, so *Annie,* it sent me off into
convulsions. I literally fell off my chair in spasms of silent laughter. What I didn't
know until the show aired was that one operator had swung his camera over to cover
my antics. In the beginning I was distressed. In no way did I want it to appear

The darlings of the cast and crew were Smith and Dale. These two senior citizens had spanned an era in entertainment unknown to most of us. We were a fresh audience for their routines, and they played us to the hilt. Some delicious pair! And Eddie Bracken was no slouch in the comedy department either. He spent hours trying to coach me in the art of the double take, even the triple take. His pupil didn't fare too well (too straight, I guess). A comedienne perhaps, a comic never. But the resulting fun was worth the effort.

Tony Martin was the momentary "real" Tony. But the *real* Tony in my life—Curtis—and I were increasingly inseparable. Those bells were ringing louder and louder. I met his family: "Momeleh" (in Yiddish, adding "eleh" to a word makes it a term of endearment), another Helen, the bow of the ship, the leader, the force— under the aegis of dependence; "Papeleh," Manny, the stabilizer, mild, warm—desirous of being a hard worker but unsure how without direction; Bobby, the rowboat, beautiful, sweet—and too young to know yet he could never be a part of the mainstream.

I fit in easily. We were all simple people. (But are any of us, *really,* simple people?) I was uninformed in the traditions of Judaism, however, so, innocently, when I heard that the Schwartz family had never experienced the beauty of a Christmas tree and presents, I appointed myself as the bearer of glad tidings. I brought over a tree with all the trimmings and gifts to put underneath. Little Bobby's huge eyes grew even larger. I supposed this was somehow related to finances. I was having such a good time playing Santa Claus, they didn't have the heart to dampen my enthusiasm. Eventually, tactfully, they explained they normally observed Hanukkah, which occurs around the same time. But because they were not strictly Orthodox, they allowed Christmas to enter their home. In the following years, I would study the history of Judaism to better understand Tony and his kinsmen. (And as before, I would find that *any* knowledge of any religion is a gain of more peace and comprehension for one's inner life.)

I managed to squeeze in a visit to Tony's set at Universal. He looked wonderfully dashing in the swashbuckler costume: the

---

derogatory; and I wouldn't dream of hurting anyone, much less Annie. Annie was just being Annie, and I love her, and her beguiling humor makes me laugh. It always has and during the shooting of *Two Tickets* was no exception.

harem pants, turban, and vest with no shirt. Rudolph Mate was the director. He was an honorable and nurturing man, and was supportive to the two novices, Tony and Piper. Everett Sloane and Jeff Corey were seasoned performers. Only one tiny problem during the filming. In his insecurity, Tony would look to Rudy after a take to seek his approval. And each time he would see Rudy slightly shaking his head. Poor Tony thought he was doing badly, even if the take was a print. He couldn't stand the feeling of failure and garnered enough courage to confront Rudy and ask what was wrong, how could he improve and please him. Dear Rudy was baffled. "But I *am* pleased. You are doing so *well,*" and all the while his head was contradicting his words. Then the realization dawned. Rudy suffered a minor tic, twitch (the cause unknown). What a relief! In a couple of years I would work with Rudy on *The Black Shield of Falworth,* and thank heavens I knew, or I would have been thrown into a tizzy then too.

While I was visiting the set, Leonard Goldstein made a casual remark to me. "Don't keep him up too late, he has to learn his lines." A casual remark or a veiled warning of things to come?

I met Tony's friends: Meta and George Rosenberg, his agent, also brother of the Universal producer Aaron Rosenberg; Marty Ragaway, writer; Larry Storch, actor; Danny Arnold, the now very powerful producer/writer; Jeff Chandler and Rock Hudson, fellow Universal contractees; Jerry Gershwin, young MCA agent; and Jerry Lewis and his wife, Patti. They, above anyone, were most influential people in Tony's life at that time. Perhaps the New York hard-knocks syndrome, the ethnic compatibility, the scrimmage for achievement, formed the basis for this alliance. The new girlfriend was suspect; "Is she good for our bubeleh?" Concurrently there were my buddies asking, "Is he right for our little chum?" We both survived the trials. I don't need to tell you what acceptance meant to me—my insatiable need to belong had not abated in the least.

Mom and Dad and I gave a party that December of 1950, combining all factions. Partly because we wanted to, partly because of the holidays, and partly because the RKO affiliation was over, done, (well, almost). In the course of the festivities, I stood on a chair and said, "Ladies and gentlemen, I have an announcement to make." There were murmurs of "Uh–oh, here it comes, they're going to do it. Lay you odds this is it," filtering through the room. I said, "I am pleased to tell you—dinner is served!" Now wasn't I the cute one?

Tony and I made our first public appearance as a twosome at the star-studded opening of MCA's *Ice Follies of 1950*. As we were walking along the red carpet with accompanying photographers, the crowds lining the sidewalks and streets were yelling, "There's Janet Leigh! There's Tony Curtis! And they are *together!*" I guess one might say this was the genesis of the affair of the heart between us and the fans. It just came about. It wasn't planned or calculated on our parts. Actually, we couldn't have been more surprised at the mushrooming effect of our togetherness.

In my four and a half years in Hollywood, the magazines and newspapers, prompted by the MGM and RKO advertising departments, had been extremely generous to me. I appeared on the outsides and insides of the periodicals as often as anyone in the industry. When Tony's popularity erupted, he too was covered extensively. And collectively, it was near impossible to pick up a tabloid without our faces looking at you from somewhere.

I am aware that at the time, Tony and I were severely criticized by the hierarchy of the celluloid kingdom; we were accused of being publicity seekers, upstarts who capitalized on exploitation rather than talent.

I would like to comment on this, not in the form of an excuse, but more as an explanation of a belief, as a tenet I still adhere to today.

God smiled on me and saw fit to place me in an incredible industry. The primary action in my tenure as an actress has been to learn, to expand, to increase my proficiency. That was—and is—always the premier objective. And very early it was also revealed to me there were other responsibilities related to this business, one of them being information. It is not only advisable, but necessary, to use friendly persuasion on the moviegoing public (the horizon also includes the television audience, the music devotees, legitimate theatre lovers—all the categories of entertainment enthusiasts). It is not favorably regarded, or practical, to give an outstanding performance to an empty house; hence the publicity departments—at studios, networks, recording companies, as well as privately operated agencies. So I rendered thanks for the publications that asked for my participation. And *they* asked, *I* didn't. I can unequivocally state that I have never asked to have my picture taken or to be interviewed. I only tried to comply with requests, whenever possible.

And I have a similar attitude toward admirers, the fans. They are the ones who spend their earnings on a ticket, or tune in the TV set, or purchase the tape or cassette. They, through their communication to the controlling powers, are the ones who, figuratively speaking, pay our salary. So how can they be ignored? Normally they are decent and kind people who want to show their appreciation for the pleasure they have received from their favorites. Sometimes even, a gap is filled in their lives—a touch of the unattainable brought a bit closer. I'll never ever forget a sweet young girl, one of hundreds greeting Tony and me at the train station in Boston, who took my arm and confidentially asked me, "Now, when are we going to have our baby?"

True, occasionally, this overidentification can be excessive and violate the privacy and possible safety of the adulated one. In which case, you have to deal with it as you would any out-of-line friend or foe. I have a rule about the sanctity of my home: The welcome mat is not out for intruders. This is our haven, belonging to us and invited guests. And when I have explained this, it has usually been graciously accepted and understood by those venturing into our territory. The criteria are different outside those boundaries. I've been in a restaurant's powder room and had a pen and paper passed under the stall for an autograph. So what—it didn't hurt anyone.

Unavoidably, over so long a time, my trust in the journalistic process has been periodically violated. But I'm not one to allow one disappointment affect my outlook on an entire media. On the whole I believe I've been fairly reported. It's the same principle in life. A disillusionment in work or in a personal relationship shouldn't cause a withdrawal from a profession or the human race. If you shut yourself off, because of an injustice, you are also shutting yourself off from a possible wonderful experience. You should exercise the increased wisdom, but not in a shell of suspicion.

Nineteen fifty-one was a big year for work and for life. *Strictly Dishonorable* (the film with Ezio Pinza and Millard Mitchell) commenced principal photography in January. Upon its completion, I was called to RKO for added scenes on *Jet Pilot.* And on location!

As much as I dreaded it, MGM and I were honor-bound to acquiesce. Back I went, donned my uniform once again, and tried to recapture some semblance of the character.

We were shooting at George Air Force Base in Victorville, and toward dusk, a plane kept circling, spoiling the shot. Duke (Wayne) made a crack, "It's Howard, Janet, checking up on us." Ho ho, ha ha! " 'Tain't funny, Duke!" The Phantom (another label for Howard Hughes) had kept a low profile since I started dating Tony; maybe he intuitively guessed it was serious. So I was unprepared when the plane landed and out stepped Mr. H. This must have been the last-ditch effort. Jules Furthman and Duke insisted we all have dinner, and—what else—the dinner was in Las Vegas. Tony was furious with me when I came home the next day because I hadn't been in when he called, and he was even more livid when I told him why. It took him a while to understand the whole history, and the fact that he was not competing with Howard Hughes.

But something in my deportment that night, other than my usual detachment, must have indicated to Howard that, indeed, it was useless to prolong this pursuit. The Hughes chapter was at last at an end. I never heard from him again.

Once the ordeal of maintaining my independence was over, my thoughts about Howard mellowed. I really felt sorry for him. With all of his wealth, his lackeys, and his notoriety, I sensed he was a very lonely man. He was never sure if he was liked for himself, and was unwilling or afraid to find out. His solace was his empire, his machines—empty replacements for humanity. I am grateful for what *he* considered to be my opportunity of a lifetime.

The Morrison bout with poverty had not equaled the Schwartz encounter. We might have had trouble paying the rent, but we had never been thrown out into the street. Our abode might have been tainted with someone else's debris and crowded, but it wasn't a cold-water flat. And sadly, the Schwartzes' situation had been aggravated by religious prejudice. Jeanette might have felt like "the outsider," but she never had to walk blocks out of her way to avoid a neighborhood where she might be beaten or abused. She maybe couldn't afford certain activities, but she had never been excluded because of her faith. Her ancestors had not been tortured and placed in concentration camps because they were Hungarian Jews. Yes, she had read about it, seen newsreels, but it hadn't happened

TOP: with Alex Romero, in rehearsal for *The Red Danube*. "My knee hasn't been right since." BOTTOM: *The Red Danube*, 1948.

TOP: on the set of *Holiday Affair*. From left to right: Robert Mitchum, Janet, Elizabeth Taylor, and director/producer Donald Hartman. BOTTOM: Cary Grant visiting Robert Mitchum and Janet on the set of *Holiday Affair*, 1949.

With Lex Barker on the set of *Holiday Affair*.

OPPOSITE: on the set of *Holiday Affair*. ABOVE: with Gene Kelly on the set of *It's a Big Country*.

HAPPY BIRTHDAY GOWIE BOY

TOP: a birthday party for Gower Champion on the rehearsal set of *Two Tickets to Broadway*. On my left is Dick, our pianist, and on the other side of Gower are Marge Champion and Robert Sheerer. BOTTOM: visiting Elizabeth Taylor on the set of *A Place in the Sun*. From left to right: Stewart Stern (Arthur Loew's cousin), Elizabeth, Montgomery Clift, Janet with Arthur Loew, Jr.

TOP: with Tony, Ezio Pinza, and Hedda Hopper on the set of *Strictly Dishonorable*, 1951. BOTTOM: My shower, given by Marge Champion. Guests included: Ava Gardner, Alexis Smith Stevens, Shelley Winters, Kathryn Grayson, Arlene Dahl, Selena Royle, Patti Lewis, Ann Strauss, and others.

The Midnight Gala in London, England. Rhonda Fleming, Tony, and I; Jimmy McHugh; Frank Sinatra and Ava Gardner.

to *her,* to her *family.* Yes, she had empathy, for *all* suffering. But that was a long step away from actual exposure.

I realized more than ever how we are products of our past. No, none of us are simple people. We are a web of complexities. And as I fell hopelessly, passionately in love with Tony, I knew we would need to give each other unselfish understanding to bridge the chasm that separated our backgrounds. Could we accomplish this? Were we mature enough to meet this challenge? We could only try, wait and see, and hope.

Angels in the Outfield was my next assignment. Directed by the unmatchable Clarence Brown, it starred Paul Douglas, Keenan Wynn, Lewis Stone, Spring Byington, and adorable little Donna Corcoran. The film was about a grumpy baseball manager, an orphan who sees angels on the diamond, and a meddling newspaper-woman (me). It was a charming story, and I had potent professionals as co-workers. And Mr. Brown drove home another valuable lesson. I was to approach the uncooperative manager as he was eating, and interrogate him about his slumping ball club and error-plagued players. There was a long list of names I was to rattle off, and I stumbled over one in the take, and I stopped.

"Why did you stop, Janet?"

"But, Mr. Brown, I made a mistake."

"Never, *never* cut a scene. I will say cut when it is the appropriate time. This girl would not have these names at the tip of her tongue. Your stammering made it believable, normal. The importance is the intent of the scene—the makeup of the character—not to show the audience how well you memorize."

I felt like such a fool—again. You can rest assured I have continued my participation in a scene, no matter what unrelated nonsense was coming out of my mouth. Or what my klutzy feet were doing.†

In April the company moved to Pittsburgh, where the real Pittsburgh Pirates were to portray the reel baseball team. There was much ado connected to our association with the home team and a lot of press coverage. I was asked to attend the season's opening

† In *Prince Valiant* I jumped off my horse and ran toward the downed Val. And then *I* was down. But I kept trying to get up. In this instance, however, the director stopped rolling film. Val was the one supposedly injured, not Aleta.

game and make an appearance on the field. My high heels sank in the soft turf, and I kept losing my shoes with each step. Ralph Kiner, the home-run king, gallantly carried me off in his arms. This was a P.R. person's dream and the media had a heyday. And of course, rumors sprang up about a romance. We had fun together, but his eyes were for the girl he married, Nancy Chaffee—a tennis whiz—and my heart belonged to Tony, who was on an extensive studio tour promoting *The Prince Who Was a Thief.* And his reception was phenomenal—better than anticipated—huge turnouts in all the cities, screaming girls tearing at his clothes. Now sometimes stunts are planned and sometimes people are planted, but even with all that plotting, the desired results are not assured. But in Tony's case, the actuality of the fans' enthusiasm far exceeded Universal's contrivances or hopes. He was understandably overjoyed and a bit taken aback by all the attention he received. It didn't take him long to adjust, however, and ride the wave.

He was due in Pittsburgh, and we had an all too short day and a half. We were so much in love. This affair of the heart surpassed any previous experience. It encompassed friendship, gaiety, intellectual respect, and a flaming ardor laced with tenderness and abandon. It is so difficult to describe the totalness we felt.

Love: "An insatiate thirst of enjoying a greedily desired object" (Montaigne); "The heart's immortal thirst to be completely known and all forgiven" (Henry Van Dyke); "Nature's second sun" (George Chapman); "Tyrant sparing none" (Corneille); "The blood of life, the power of reunion of the separated" (Tillich); "A spiritual coupling of two souls" (Ben Johnson).

We began considering the ultimate commitment.

I returned to California and finished *Angels* early in May, and Tony came home for a breather. We had a period of two weeks before he was to leave town again and I was scheduled into New York for publicity purposes.

The obvious obstacles to wedded bliss were discussed. Religious. Financial (Tony would always be the support of his family). Careers. Naturally, I wanted to pursue my craft, but my husband would come first. And there are the unavoidable pressures, demands of our profession. Despite all this, we believed we *could* triumph over the known obstacles and over the future hurdles life would put before us. The resolution was determined, the strategy activated. I shopped at Amelia Gray's for my trousseau, but for anyone's information, I was only preparing for the New York trip.

Mom and Dad instinctively knew, and our farewells were especially tender and emotional, heavy with silent thoughts. I was so full of my happiness, I never gave a thought to the effect this move might have on their lives. Even if I had, I don't know if I would have altered the course. I was selfish enough, headstrong enough, and in love enough to have smothered any reservations.

Once in New York I enlisted the aid of John Springer. We squeezed time between appointments, and drove to Greenwich, Connecticut, where we made all the preliminary arrangements for the wedding.

Greenwich was a beautiful choice. The majestic trees and abundant lawn provided a quiet, peaceful background, a sharp contrast to the New York hustle and bustle.

We applied for the marriage license under the names of Jeanette Morrison Reames and Bernard Schwartz. I took the blood test, and was promised Mr. Schwartz could have it done the morning of June 4. The date was made with the court judge, John P. Knox. So far so good, no leaks.

As John and I were leaving the courthouse—which didn't look like a courthouse in those surroundings—just beaming, a couple came up to us, "Oh you look divinely happy. Congratulations to the newlyweds!" We were so flustered and we didn't want to blow our cover, so we sort of sheepishly muttered our thanks and sped off.

On Saturday, May 26, I flew to Tony in Chicago. I rushed into his arms at the airport, not aware of the waiting reporters. It seems Tony had slipped in an interview while there and admitted we were engaged. We fended all the "when?" questions, "Oh—later— maybe in August—not yet—" and hoped we had convinced them.

We cuddled at dinner in the elegant Pump Room in the Ambassador East Hotel. What a fabulous restaurant—ultra chic! Jerry Lewis and Dean Martin were starring in the hotel's Chez Paree nightclub, and we decided to pop in and surprise them. The room was overflowing, so we just stood in the back, enjoying their talent, as always. A waiter was threading his way through the maze of bodies carrying a small table and two chairs, which he deposited on the side of the stage. Props maybe, or else a city official, perhaps the mayor. The maître d' approached and motioned for us to follow him. We thought he must have found seats somewhere. He had— right up on the stage, the setup was for us. Jerry and Dean inter- rupted their performance and introduced the betrothed pair to the audience. We were so embarrassed and had to sit there in full view for the entire show.

Afterward, in the dressing room, we disclosed our plans and asked Jerry and Patti to be best man and matron of honor. The timing was perfect—the boys were leaving for New York in a few days to tape TV's "Colgate Comedy Hour" and play the Copa- cabana, and Patti was meeting Jerry there. Everything was falling into place.

Back in New York, Mickey Loew came with me to pick out Tony's wedding ring. I didn't realize how traumatic this would be for her. If I'd utilized one ounce of brain matter, I'd have known. I was only thinking of her as my friend, not as an almost mother-in- law.

"I'm sorry, honey," she said as she started to cry. "Of course I am happy for you, and I love you, and am proud to be here with you. I just can't help these few tears. I always thought we'd be doing this together, but for you and Arthur." So we both sat our- selves down and had a good cry. (That never hurt anyone!) I don't know what the jeweler thought; I hope he knew his merchandise couldn't have been *that* bad.

That was not the only emotional moment of the week. Tony arrived in New York a little upset. He had confided our intentions to Leonard Goldstein, his producer, and Leonard had not given the expected response. Leonard believed Universal would not be pleased. After all, they had expended time and money in Tony, and being married might dampen his appeal, lessen the box-office re- ceipts. Why not wait a few years?

Now we were both confused. Neither of us had given this aspect any thought at all. Could our love, so precious to us, hamper the progress of his burgeoning career? That possibility *did* remotely exist. I remembered Mr. Green's reluctance to introduce my mari- tal status in the very beginning. But then, it actually hadn't mat- tered one iota.

We visited Jerry at rehearsal. *What was Leonard doing there?* We soon found out. Jerry took us aside, and proceeded to parrot Leonard's views. My eyes got bigger and bigger in disbelief. What was I hearing from our friend? Well, this Jezebel had had enough. I left. And in a highly hysterical state.

I ran back to the Waldorf, barely dodging cars and people, and started to pack. The previous weeks hadn't exactly been tranquilizing and I guess I had used up my quota of composure. Tony was in hot pursuit. Breathlessly he burst into the room and poured out his feelings. "When you went out the door, and I thought I could lose you, the answer was clear. I told Leonard that if being single is my only chance for success, then I'm in the wrong business! I don't care what he thinks, or Universal, or MGM, or RKO. *We* are what is important."

Jerry called. "My God, honey, I'm sorry. Don't misunderstand, I was only trying to help. Leonard knew the two of you would probably listen to me, and I really didn't weigh what he said. I'm up to my neck in work, and I didn't think. When Tony spouted off, I knew he was right."

Leonard called, contrite, with apologies and regrets. ". . . No ulterior motive . . . complete misjudgement on my part . . . of course I have faith in Tony's ability . . . you have my blessing."

My poor head was a cacophonic jumble. I had enough guilt and self-doubt and fear plaguing me, I didn't need any more put on me.

We needed to be alone, to soothe our anxiety and have a quiet moment to think. We went for a drive, to his brother Julie's grave, and prayed. For guidance. For understanding. For forgiveness. A serenity enveloped us, almost like a protective shroud, against the precariousness of existence. Tony said it was almost as if Julie had sent out his voice of approval to us.

June 4, 1951

It was a beautiful spring day. The small wedding party gathered on the green outside the courthouse. John Springer, Dorothy Day (confidante from MGM, New York), Robert Sterling (Anne Jeffreys was working), Paula Stone (producer and friend through the Champions), Tommy Farrell (actor and friend through Jerry), Mack David (songwriter and friend through Jerry), Joe Abeles (portrait photographer and Tony's oldest friend from New York)—but no Jerry and Patti. I wore a simple pale aqua linen straight-skirted dress, with matching shoes and hat. And with the heat, it was wilting a little. Nerves added to that, I'm sure. After an hour of strained waiting, we were about to proceed with Paula and Joe substituting, when a limo came screeching around the corner and delivered a disheveled Jerry and Patti. He had worked late, overslept, and run into traffic. No matter. All was well now.

Dear John! He had seen to everything: arranged for *one* photographer to service the media and us, ordered bouquets for Patti and me, and even set up a wedding brunch with champagne.

The ceremony was short, sweet, sedate, and solemn. We gave each other our plain gold bands, and I was Mrs. Bernie Schwartz. Then all hell broke loose. Jerry couldn't contain himself any longer, and when he kissed the bride he pulled a Rudolph Valentino, bending me backward to the floor, with my knees buckling as I tried to hold onto my chapeau. That set the tone for the rest of the day. And for a lot of years as well. It was glorious, it was happy, it was fun, it was volatile, it was crazy—it was wonderful!

On the way back to the city, we passed through Tony's old neighborhood in the Bronx; a relative was sitting on a stoop. Tony told the driver to stop, and we bolted across the intersection and embraced the bewildered woman while Tony yelled, "We just got married—this is Mrs. Schwartz." The studios had alerted the wire services that morning and telegrams and flowers had started to accumulate when we returned to the MGM suite at the Waldorf Towers. Tony carried me over the threshold of our first "home." The afternoon papers were ablaze with the story and pictures. We were somewhat unprepared for this amount of hoopla. Ironically our marriage produced more attention for *The Prince Who Was a Thief* than Universal could. They were delirious.

We called Mom and Dad, and Momeleh and Papeleh. "Hello, Mrs. Schwartz? This is Mrs. Schwartz." A lot of screaming and crying and long-distance hugging and kissing. A lot of love.

We each then had to attempt to adhere to our individual schedules. Not easy, when all we wanted was to be together, but we were primed to pay the piper.

I came back to the hotel before Tony and fell victim to one of the many gags perpetrated for our benefit. The buzzer rang, and I opened the door to a gorgeous girl. "Is Mr. Curtis here? I have something for him. Oh, then I'll just wait—" and she wiggled inside. We sat, staring at each other, interrupted by the telephone and deliveries. I was hard-pressed to make even perfunctory conversation. Something suspicious here . . . What connection was she to Tony? Maybe she was a thief, so I didn't dare leave her alone. Finally Tony was there. "Mr. Curtis, I am your present—from the boys." She was the female counterpoint of the Valentino approach, doubling him over in her arms with an unsisterly smooch. We were completely nonplussed. "The boys" would have been pleased to see the result of their "hired assassin." And I would have been more than happy to reciprocate, if I could have thought of something wicked enough.

Danny Stradella had reserved the entire side room of Danny's Hideaway for a wedding party. A big crowd greeted our arrival that evening. We didn't realize how many people we knew in New York. All of the wedding party; the Universal, MGM, and RKO contingents; Jerry and Dean and all of their associates; Candy and Mel Tormé; Vic Damone; Gloria DeHaven; Cyd Charisse and Tony Martin; Phil Silvers; Robert Preston; etc., etc., etc. The current hit act at the Copa, the De Marco Sisters, performed. Comradeship and love reigned supreme.

Then, at long last, Tony and I were alone. This time, when the hotel door closed and I looked at my husband, there were no barriers, no hesitations, no psychological compromises—only freedom, a flow of tender feelings, an unconditional surrender to unity.

I I I

Mrs. Tony Curtis

(The Way It Really Happened)

CHAPTER TWELVE

How was this for timing?

Nine o'clock the *very* next morning, I had to report to the studio of Philippe Halsman, the world-famous photographer, to pose for my first *Life* magazine cover. I daresay he had more covers to his credit than any other photographer. I subsequently worked with Philippe many times, producing *Look* covers, inside *Life* pictures, and another *Life* cover. What a dear man. Absolute dedication and concentration to his art.*

The resulting cover of June 5 was exceptional. The June 25, 1951, edition (price, twenty cents!) also included pictures of the wedding (a large reproduction of Jerry's exuberant kiss); the reception at Danny's and the Versailles (hostessed by Gloria DeHaven, but actually given by RKO); and rehearsal shots with Marge and Gower. The text was focused on the theme of a new marriage and a new career. Meaning, of course, the image change from the clean all-American girl next door to the sexy siren. I cringed as I anticipated Miss Burns's reaction.

The day of reckoning came, the day of departure. Tony had to continue the tour and I had to return to California to start another movie. I accompanied Tony to the depot and in the compartment adjoining his was Piper Laurie, languishing on a berth, draped in an exotic negligee. Hardly a comforting sight to a new bride. But I swallowed my jealousy and assumed a "secure" posture. After all,

---

* On a later trip, he and his assisting wife drove me to Jones Beach for a sitting. He was so embroiled in explaining the concept of the layout, he forgot he was piloting an auto and gestured with both hands. We careened from lane to lane and missed a head-on by inches. I asked him to pull over, and took the wheel. I had never driven in the East and didn't know where we were going, but I was sure I could at least get us there in one piece.

Tony was traveling with Jack, and Piper with Gail, both representatives from Universal. What could go wrong? And nothing did. But I carried that tableau in my mind until he returned.

There were ample activities to alleviate the emptiness created by Tony's absence: the excitement of coming home a married lady, to family and friends; the preparations for the new film, *Just This Once,* with Peter Lawford and Richard Anderson, guided by a talented new young comedy director, Don Weis; the search for a new dwelling to set up housekeeping. Aunt Pope worked with Daddy and, in addition, handled my fan mail and scrapbooks and occasionally bailed me out when I was just too swamped.† She was the one to find our first residence, a furnished, modern one-bedroom apartment, in a two-story complex covered with ferns at 10600 Wilshire Boulevard. Coincidently, after Elizabeth Taylor divorced Nicky Hilton, she moved upstairs. This building was hot property, and was infested with photographers and reporters once it was discovered. No possibility of clandestine operations there. One false move and you would be on the front page.

Everything was ready for Tony's homecoming. That happy day I was on pins and needles, worrying if he would like my choice, hoping I had put his things away properly. One certainty—it was clean—scrubbed and sparkling and spotless. No need for concern. He carried me over this threshold, and we were home, in our home, in our own special home. And no one or no thing could change that.

In our own special home, the cupboards were bare. Furnished did not mean kitchen equipment or linens. I had bought one set of sheets and pillow cases, and two sets of towels. And groceries. But nothing to put the groceries on.

Marge Champion remedied that lack. She had planned an enormous bridal shower and she made it clear, no frivolous gifts, no ornate silver. Only practical useful items were welcome. The guests followed instructions perfectly, and I unwrapped every conceivable necessity. The guests were Margie, Mom, Momeleh, Gower's mom, Lillian Burns Sidney (Mrs. George), Miriam Nelson (Mrs. Gene), Patty Edwards (Mrs. Blake), Aunt Pope, Elizabeth Taylor,

† The tradition continued. Aunt Pope now handles my daughter Jamie's fan mail and scrapbooks.

Ava Gardner, Alexis Smith Stevens (Mrs. Craig), Lucille Ryman Carroll (Mrs. John), Kathryn Grayson, Arlene Dahl, Harriet Lee, Selena Royle, Patti Lewis (Mrs. Jerry), Ann Strauss, Emily Torchia, Candy Tormé (Mrs. Mel), Helen Rose, Vera-Ellen, B. J. Paley, Shelley Winters, Mona Freeman, and others.

I looked around and was overwhelmed and grateful that these people had so honored us. This grouping was quite a cross section of humanity, mingling knowns and unknowns, but all friends, all there for a single purpose. This was happening for Jeanette Helen Morrison and Bernard Schwartz. All right!

George Sidney took a photo of the few forlorn males who were there, way down by the pool. Gower, Craig, Gene, A. C. Lyles, Tony, Bobby, and George, who knew how to set the camera and run around to be in the picture. A really special day.

I wouldn't have the audacity to liken this period of our lives to Camelot; the real modern-day Camelot was to arrive in 1960 with the emergence of President and Mrs. Kennedy. But truthfully, that is the analogy that flashed through my mind when I first thought back on these times. We were young, in love, and attractive, working and surviving in a highly glamorous profession, and stimulated by diverse circles of friends. We weren't just looking through rose-colored glasses; that's just the way it was—then. Our darkness would come, but that doesn't preclude the joy of the light, or negate the dawn of another day.

We spent much of our spare time at Jerry and Patti's on Amalfi Drive in Pacific Palisades. The always large group would gather and either go to the local movie house, play word games, or eventually make our own movies. Jerry formed a mock company, Garron Productions (named after their first two sons, Gary and Ronnie). He had every known piece of equipment for home use: 16-millimeter cameras, tripods, lights, reflectors, sound equipment, splicing machine, etc. He was the guiding force, the director, writer, editor—with a little help from his friends. Danny (Arnold) worked on the scripts; Dick Stabile (whose orchestra traveled with Jerry and Dean) and Mack David aided with music; Frankie (Jerry's right hand) handled props and everything else. We all contributed to the costuming and to any other necessary task, and we all performed. Definitely not a union-sanctioned endeavor.

Patti was a gem. She put up with the ever-present people, the mess of the accouterment, even participated, and managed to feed "the crew." She had to be greatly relieved when Jerry was working during the week.

Fairfax Avenue and *Watch on the Lime* were our major blockbusters. Quite apparently, they were parodies on the classics *Sunset Boulevard* and *Watch on the Rhine*. In *Fairfax Avenue* I played the Gloria Swanson role, Tony the William Holden part, and Jerry the Erich von Stroheim character. It was hilarious. And under the awning of triviality, we were exercising and experimenting, even stretching in our fields. I know I for one would have been hesitant to attempt certain scenes on a real set. But, as it turned out, I was pleased with the effect of my imitation of Gloria Swanson imitating Charlie Chaplin. I believe I released a parcel of inhibition, felt freer. And Jerry, I'm sure, subliminally used these times as research toward directing and producing.

Fairfax Avenue was so enjoyable we decided our friends should not be denied the pleasure of seeing it. So we had a premiere in their rumpus room by the pool, complete with kleig light and red carpet and star-studded audience. Over one hundred skeptical guinea pigs were held hostage—wisely, the food wasn't served until *after*. The squirming prisoners included Dean and Jeannie Martin, Hal Wallis, Vic Damone, Herbie Baker, Mona Freeman, Mary Murphy, etc., etc. "The house lights dimmed," and we launched our rocket. Maybe we didn't reach the moon, but we didn't fall in the ocean either. The level of entertainment was higher than the viewers had dared anticipate. On the other hand, MGM had nothing to fear. The climax of the evening's gaiety was the surprise presentation of Garron's "Academy Award"—to me. It was in the form of a gold medallion with three star-shaped diamonds and inscribed,

The Jerry Lewis Award
From Garron Productions to:
Miss Janet Leigh
For Her Stellar Performances in
Fairfax Avenue

Watch on the Lime

And for Being a Great Gal.

For me, this was further welcome evidence of membership. It rests among my cherished possessions to this day.

A novel form of fraternization was initiated by Naomi and Dick Carroll (who then owned a small haberdashery, and who now has the largest fashionable men's store in Beverly Hills), Stanley Rubin (producer), Stanley Roberts (writer), and Tony and me. We met one Sunday at Naomi and Dick's small apartment for brunch. The conversation was so succulent and witty and the afternoon so delightful, that we resolved to assemble once a month, alternating residences, and inviting some one new each time. Because bagels and lox had been served, we called ourselves "The Fox and Lox Club." This flourished for quite a while. Joining us, gradually, were Stanley Donen (who worked with Gene Kelly and now is the successful director—*Funny Face,* to name just one credit); Pat and Blake Edwards; and a list that kept growing, like Pinocchio's nose. Elizabeth Taylor was Stanley Donen's date on one memorable Sunday. They had a disagreement—well, a fight—and she picked up one of the desserts, a whipped-cream-covered pie, and shoved it in his face.

The brunch was getting out of hand. Not many of us had a place big enough to house the increasing numbers. One Sunday, when I adjourned to the bathroom and didn't know any of the girls there, I came to the inevitable conclusion that the end was close. And it was. Soon after we dissolved, but it was sure fun while it lasted.

There was a whole other coalition formed around the Champions: Pat and Blake, Miriam and Gene Nelson, Alexis and Craig Stevens, and more. There would be happy weekends of swimming and dancing, and community cooking. I was the cleanup committee —fancy cuisine was not my forte and still isn't.

As I said, we were living in golden times. I was in my element. Our social life was intermingled with work—lots of it. Around August I began filming *Scaramouche,* one of the prettiest movies I ever did. It was a cheerful swashbuckler set in French Revolutionary times, about a young man who disguises himself as an actor to avenge the death of his friend at the hands of a wicked marquis, and starred Stewart Granger, Mel Ferrer, Eleanor Parker, Henry Wilcoxon, Nina Foch, Lewis Stone, Robert Coote, Richard Anderson, and helmed by George Sidney. The costumes, the photography, the sets, were all just outstanding.

A new skill was required for this role—riding sidesaddle. I had had limited experience with horses, left over from the few excursions Mom and Dad and I had made to the mountains. But only with a Western saddle. Sidesaddle was completely different. So, prior to the picture's start, every morning at nine, I reported to the stables located on one of the back lots for my lessons. First, someone has to hoist you for the mount. The right leg loops over the horn, which is high on the left side of the saddle, and the left leg is straight, allowing the left foot to fit into the stirrup. You feel precarious in the beginning, but oddly enough, you are anchored soundly and actually have more stability. The second day the inside of my right knee was raw from gripping the horn so tightly. The trainer quite matter-of-factly suggested I bring a sanitary napkin to pad the spot where it was rubbing. I know today similar items are advertised on television, but in *those* days, no one even mentioned anything that had to do with menstruation, unless it was a mother explaining the cycle to a daughter. For a man to give voice to the subject . . . I was so uneasy, I pretended I didn't hear him. The next morning I hurt a lot. Finally, I abandoned modesty for the sake of comfort. Covertly, I transferred a napkin from my purse to my jacket to the bruise. It worked.

My progress at riding was fairly rapid. I practiced wearing a long full skirt, a simulated version of the riding habit of that period. Sidesaddle presents a beautiful silhouette—the abundant material gracefully flowing, covering the animal's left flank, cascading almost to the ground. An episode dealt with a runaway stallion, so it was necessary for me to master a fast gallop. I guess I was feeling a little too cocky one morning, and I gave my horse too much head. Well, this high-spirited steed said "Whoopie!" and sped off on a never-to-be-forgotten run. It was impossible to rein him in after the control was gone. Trees were a blur as we whizzed by and my legs ached from the pressure of trying to hold on. The trainer took a good ten minutes to stop us. That may not sound like very long to you, but it seemed an eternity to me. Did I catch hell! "Damn it! Who do you think you are, Annie Oakley? Didn't I tell you over and over, never relax on a horse! Always keep your guide! You could have been hurt bad! And I could have lost my job! Come on —that's enough for today."

Jimmy (Stewart Granger's real name was James Stewart, changed for obvious reasons) and Mel had to conquer new challenges too. Grueling sword fights for one, which are choreographed like dance routines. Naturally the blades are not razor-sharp, but a mistake could be dangerous. Jimmy cut a dashing figure, handsome, suave, but he did have an explosive temper.

The days of the grand ball and climactic duel between the antagonists, Jimmy and Mel, were understandably hectic and vexatious for all concerned. We had a huge set, difficult for the cinematographer; hundreds of extras; countless arc lights, which sent the temperature soaring; heavy, unbreathing costumes and white wigs, stunningly resplendent though they were; heated dialogue, making our juices race and our nerves vulnerable; and for Jimmy and Mel, exacting, exhausting physical combat.

The spectacular is a drawing card for visitors, and that set was no exception, which just added to the confusion. Jean Simmons, Jimmy's wife, and Tony were among the guests this one particular afternoon, sitting in director's chairs placed conveniently in front, by the main camera. It is customary to use multiple cameras on elaborate sequences, giving the added coverage and eliminating the necessity to shoot the same master over and over from various angles. The scene was going well. Mel and Jimmy leaping over balustrades, exchanging furious parries, weaving in and out of the banister and up and down the staircase, and the other participants reacting appropriately. All of a sudden, Jimmy tripped, and the take was spoiled. In his frustration and anger, he unthinkingly hurled his sword. The weapon soared, narrowly missed Jean's head, and imbedded itself in a cabinet behind her. A collective gasp exuded from the crowd, followed by a significant hush. An ashen-faced Jimmy made his way to Jean, knelt, and put his head in her lap. You see, the drama is not only in front of the camera.

Tony was particularly sensitive to the mishap, for he was priming another Arabian Nights feature, *The Son of Ali Baba,* in which he would be called upon to perform daring stunts with a sword. The risk was dramatically demonstrated.

With the box-office results from *The Prince Who Was a Thief* tabulated, the studio wasted no time in casting Tony and Piper Laurie in another correlative film. There's an old adage—"Don't fool with success." And that was fine. At this stage of his career, work was the key, so long as he eventually would be allowed to branch out and expand his range. When *Son of . . .* was released, it too was a moneymaker. It also provided friends with ammunition to tease Tony. At one point in the movie, atop a hill, our hero is proudly showing his lady the realm of the estate, and proclaims, "Yonder lies the castle of me fodder!" Just a wee bit of the Bronx.

Family ties were strong. I had found the Schwartzes an apartment in the Fairfax area and moved them. Their lives had hardly been altered. Tony was still very much in evidence and now a doting daughter-in-law had been added. They and Mom and Dad joined in some of our activities. But the usual mixing was at dinner once or twice a week. Mom and Dad were doing okay; they hadn't yet exceeded the acceptable ratio of discord between them, nor had the void caused by my leaving the house fully registered.

At the small office in Beverly Hills, Daddy and Aunt Pope were kept hopping managing his business, my affairs, and now Tony's fan mail and scrapbooks. George Rosenberg took care of Tony's finances. Our arrangement was based on fact and need. Most of Tony's salary went toward his folks, commissions, and personal requirements. My income was considerably higher at that time, so I took responsibility for my own essentials and obligations, plus our living expenses of rent, supplies, etc., with the understanding that he would reimburse his half when circumstances permitted. Which he did; it was important to him.

In early November, 1951, John Haskell, businessman and husband of columnist Dorothy Manners, approached us about appearing in a show in London, sponsored by International Variety Club and benefiting the National Playing Fields Association of which the Duke of Edinburgh was then president. It was to be a midnight gala on the order of a command performance, on Monday, December 10, at the London Coliseum. All expenses paid, of course. Would we be interested? Was he kidding? *Would we be interested?* Does a bear sleep in the forest? We were beside ourselves. *Yes, we would be interested.*

First, we had to clear the trip with the studios. They were quick to realize the potential value of this for their properties, and not only gave their consent but offered assistance. A whirlwind of preparations ensued. What should we perform? A writer at Universal suggested a musical skit he had already written and seen performed effectively. Very lively—energetic—and amusing. This met with everyone's approval, and rehearsals commenced. His time, musical arrangement, and costumes compliments of Universal. I was also asked to sing a medley of popular composer Jimmy McHugh's tunes. Me? Sing on a London stage in the presence of Princess Elizabeth, of royalty? Oh my God! Professors Smith and Bodley and Rosie and Harriet, don't fail me now. Many afternoons were spent under Jimmy's tutelage. What to wear? Universal helped Tony with his wardrobe—tuxedo and all the trimmings, warm coat, etc. And MGM authorized Helen Rose to design two magnificent gowns just for me. One, for the show, was breathtaking: white, strapless, tight-waisted, blossoming into layer upon layer of tulle and organza, creating the illusion of a floating cloud when I moved, with exquisite silk roses draped from the left shoulder to the middle of the waist and gradually disappearing in the voluminous skirt. The other was equally ravishing: deep burgundy velvet, strapless but with a heavy brocaded V attached to the center of the bustline, rising to caress the shoulders and continuing toward its anchor in the back; a cinched waist; and a soft, full skirt. I felt like a princess, even during the fittings. The studio also furnished a fur coat and Miss Burns loaned me an ermine stole.

Passports were obtained. Our journey had been extended. The government had asked the U.S. contingent (comprised now of Frank Sinatra, Ava Gardner, Rhonda Fleming, Dorothy Kirsten, Jimmy Van Heusen, Jimmy McHugh, John Haskell, and us) to continue, after England, to military camps in Germany and France. *Happily!*

Goodbyes are sad, no matter what the promise of tomorrow is. This would be my first Christmas away from Mom and Dad, and I knew they felt depressed. But they were also thrilled for us. We exchanged presents the night before leaving, with departure set for November 27, 1951. I had seen a smart black suit on sale at Amelia's, but with all the other expenditures caused by the trip, didn't think I should indulge. I always took Mom shopping with me whenever possible (continually trying to fill her hours), so she was aware of the suit. It gave them great joy to be able to surprise me with it that evening.

I'm not sure what prompted me, but I am grateful for whatever source guided me to keep a traveling diary of this and subsequent overseas expeditions. When I perused my account just recently, I was flabbergasted by the number of activities we managed to squeeze into one day. I was tired just reading what we accomplished—and remember, we were still newlyweds.

The page of November 29 typified the week in New York:

Lunch at Sardi's. Saw Joshua Logan and Shelley Winters. Also Paula and Mike (Sloan). Went to lawyers (Joyce Selznick and Universal were having contractual differences about Tony). Then to see Sidney Shulman's store on 9th Avenue (a school chum of Tony's). Joe Abeles took pictures. Off to "21" for cocktails with *Look* magazine. Dinner at Danny's with Mike, and Johnny (Springer). Saw Della and Andy Russell, Romo Vincent. Ended up not having tickets for *Paint Your Wagon*. Drink at Sardi's, saw Jule Styne, Lester Shurr. Went to the Bronx in Danny's car. Back to Danny's, played word game (Guggenheim) with Milton (Berle), Jerry (Colonna), Mike, and Paula. Walked back to Waldorf Towers.

We did publicity. We went to the theatre—*Two on the Aisle, Top Banana* (wonderful Phil Silvers), *Don Juan in Hell* (brilliant reading of Shaw by Charles Laughton, Charles Boyer, Sir Cedric Hardwicke, Agnes Moorehead). We nightclubbed at the Copa, the Village Vanguard. We socialized with the Van Heflins, Harry Belafonte, the Mack Davids, the Jerry Livingstons, the Bob Prestons, MGM, RKO, MCA. We even had a party at the suite. We did it all.

Diary, *December 5:* Arrived London Airport, 8:45 A.M., London time, TWA flight 960. Met with newsreels and cameramen. Hadn't hit us we were actually on foreign soil. Initial shock was *everyone* sounded like Olivier or Greer Garson. We were the ones who spoke with an accent. And the driving! Never adjusted to car being on wrong side of road. Always on verge of panic. Sharman Douglas (daughter of the former American Ambassa-

dor to Great Britain—we became good friends), RKO's David
Jones, UI's Doug Granville and Jack Sullivan, MGM's Leslie Williams took us for another news conference and press luncheon at
hotel. Car and maid at our disposal. On way in glimpsed Buckingham Palace, Albert Memorial, Kensington Palace. Now our
eyes started to pop and realization to dawn. Four-thirty to six-
thirty yet another radio, press picture session, this time with the
Emissary and Equerry of the Prince. Sharman took us to the play
The Love of Four Colonels. Theatre different, starts earlier, tea and
drinks served during and at intermission. Dinner *after* at Ward
Room. Peter Lawford and Don Weis joined us.

Still hard to believe we are going to bed in England.

London was a continuation, if not an acceleration, of the pace set
in New York. The first obligation naturally was to the rehearsals
(even a bowing rehearsal was scheduled) and the show itself. An
army corporal, Ted, had been assigned as our pianist for London
and Germany. Poor, sweet Ted. Ours was an intricate number,
timing was paramount, and his experience was moderate. But he
persevered and mastered the difficult composition. Then there were
the interminable press conferences, photo sessions, radio and television interviews to promote the benefit and the performing stars.

But there was no way we weren't going to snatch some hours for
sight-seeing. I was like a sponge, soaking up the wonders of the
days of yore. As Tennyson wrote, "the eternal landscape of the
past . . ." Admiralty Arch, Big Ben, House of Commons building,
Westminster Hall. We gazed at Sir Winston Churchill and Clement
Attlee in action in Parliament. We squeaked a tabooed smile out of
a guard at Buckingham Palace. Trafalgar Square with the pigeons.
Waterloo Bridge without Vivien Leigh and Robert Taylor. Thames
River, Tower of London, Victoria Memorial, London Bridge,
Whitehall. And we were privileged to enjoy magnificent Orson
Welles in *Othello.*

Prince Philip and the chief barker of the Variety Club, C. J. Latta,
hosted a huge party at the Embassy Club. This evening was intended to be the "informal" salute to all the performers in the
Midnight Matinee: Noel Coward, Orson Welles, etc., etc. If Princess Elizabeth had attended, tradition would have forced a more
ceremonial posture. It was still pretty formal by our standards:

black tie, receiving line, dais, and no one allowed to raise a glass or smoke or anything until the Prince had been announced and had toasted his guests. Each place setting displayed an impressive array of crystal and gold utensils. I really watched procedure closely. Please, no mortifying faux pas, I thought. Despite the ritualistic beginning and appearance, however, people did eventually let their hair down, so to speak. The Prince danced with all the ladies and was enjoying himself so much we could have been there for days since we were not supposed to depart before the Prince. At last permission was granted for those of us who had to work the next morning to slip away.‡

The big day, December 10! Picture call was 10:45 P.M. at the theatre. The crowds were unbelievable; all the streets were blocked off.

When I arrived at the theatre I asked where the makeup room was located. Blank stares. "But who is the makeup man? Who puts on the makeup?" I asked with increasing anxiety.

"In *theatah,* my dear, one applies one's own makeup."

I was crestfallen. I didn't know *how.* I didn't even have any supplies. My experience had only been in films. Tony came to my rescue. He had been taught that skill at the Dramatic Workshop, so he borrowed some gear and fixed me up. After five and a half years and seventeen pictures, I was still a novice.

At two minutes to midnight They walked in. We were very nervous. We had to remember to bow to the royal box before starting our act. They set the tone. The audience looked to Them and took Their reactions. Thank God, They liked it! The laughs came in all the right places, and we received a big response. The orchestra was unfortunately terrible. Frank had to stop the band at one point. On the whole, the show went well, maybe a trifle too long. The finale was in front of the Royal Marine Band and Grenadier Guards Band. The lineup in the front row included Jimmy McHugh, T.C., J.L., Max Wall, Orson Welles, Noel Coward, Dorothy Kirsten, Frank Sinatra, Rhonda Fleming, Tommy Trinder. We were presented to Princess Elizabeth on stage. I was terrified I would col-

‡ Fifteen years later, the Prince was in California, and the dais was asked to a private reception. I was confounded when he, without hesitation, addressed me by name and reminisced about that dinner. What recall!

lapse when I curtsied. Scotland Yard was everywhere. The night ended with breakfast at the hotel where Orson entertained us with magic tricks. Welcome sleep was not ours until 6 A.M.

Just as I was getting very British, we were on our way to Wiesbaden, Germany, in a C-47 Goony Bird. Ava and Frank did not go with the group. They had been married on November 7, and were having a honeymoon spat.

The Schwartzer-Bok Hotel (Black Goat) was sixteenth century, with paneling from a castle (but of course), high ceilings, foot-long keys, unintelligible personnel who walked in unannounced, and two johns. I was extremely curious why there would be two in the same bathroom. I leaned over and fiddled with the knobs, trying to make the odd one work. It did. A gush of water hit me in the face, drenching me and the entire room. My premiere experience of the bidet.

Diary, *December 12:* Camp Lindsay Hospital. First good eggs and coffee of whole trip. Can you imagine—guys thank *us* for coming —when we owe them everything—kids are so brave—never complain. Khur House (The Eagle Club)—chandeliers Napoleon gave Josephine—modern German architecture. Band all professionals—only Air Force dance band in Europe. Rehearsed —first show at 4:00. Dinner at Stardust Club. Saw bombed-out places. Wiesbaden bombed only as reprisal. My God—18,000 Germans killed in 20 minutes. Another show at 8:30.

We were finding out what "one night stand" really meant. From Wiesbaden, to Neuburg Air Base, to Munich, to Fursten Feldbrick, to Erding, back to Munich, to Frankfurt, to Rhein Main Base, back to Frankfurt. Sometimes we got a little giddy. I went so far as to commit the unpardonable sin of breaking up into laughter while performing. I was introducing my next song, "I Didn't Sleep a Wink Last Night," and ad-libbed, "I really didn't." I was referring to our travel schedule, but because mention had been made of our recent marriage, the GIs in the audience interpreted another connotation of why I hadn't slept, and started hooting and hollering. The more I explained, "Oh no, I didn't mean *that*, I meant—" the worse it became. They were having such a good time with my discomfort. I finally said to hell with it and chuckled with them. Then I glanced toward the wings, and saw that Tony was horrified at my unprofessional behavior. I tried to settle down and get on with the song, but every time I said, " 'I didn't sleep a wink last,' " we started all over again. It's that awful sensation of knowing you shouldn't laugh, like in church, but when something strikes your funnybone, you just can't stop. I never did finish the number. The boys had a ball that night, and I was in the doghouse.

One absolute we learned: the Air Force was akin to the Postal Service. Through rain, sleet, or snow, or fog, delivery no matter what! On the way to Frankfurt I really could not see a thing outside the window pane. Except, suddenly, a burst of flame. One of the engines had caught fire. We were paralyzed with terror. And helpless. The pilots were outstanding. Calmly and competently they managed to pacify their passengers, cut off the malfunctioning engine, and bring the craft in on an instrument landing. Ambulances and fire trucks awaited us but miraculously were not needed. At least not for us. Tony had a bad reaction, shock actually, and I put him to bed at the hotel. I felt I had to keep moving, not dwell on the incident, so Sharman (Douglas) and I ventured out into the city. I did some shopping: a piece of Dresden china, a suitcase, quaint electric trains. It was cold and cabs were hard to find. When we finally returned we were scolded. We were not to be without an escort—ever. Conditions were difficult in the country and we could be easy targets for robbery or whatever.

MGM had arranged a couple of press receptions for me. Germany was just reestablishing the motion-picture exchanges. A number of my films had been made available and raised extensive interest in the German market. Tony had not yet penetrated their consciousness. Just as well, because inexorable pangs of resentment and anger were fermenting in him. The noticeable nonpresence of Jews progressively fueled his suspicion of every native: Did you know? Were you a part of this atrocity? Were you guilty by your silence? Why didn't you do something to stop the slaughter? The fawning, the hand kissing of the Germans only heightened his mistrust. He was not in a diplomatic mood.

I wasn't immune to parallel thoughts; the degree of intensity was just less. I saw war and its instigators as the enemy, more than a people. I also didn't have the personal element involved. I experienced a general abhorrence of all inhumanity.

Because of the unhinging plane incident, we decided to train it to

Paris. This also allowed us to nibble on more of the atmospheric delicacies Germany offered. But before leaving, we motored to Bad-Homburg Haus and picked up a bit of trivia. The English homburg hat originated in this locale and was brought to London by Edward VII.

There was nothing trivial about the evening's host and hostess, however. Sharman had arranged a dinner with High Commissioner and Mrs. John J. McCloy. He was a wealthy executive who was also active in serving our government. She was a lovely, cultured, erudite lady, a valuable asset in his affairs. They had first been sent to Germany in 1935 for two years, on "business." Their interests put them in Hitler's company very often. Mrs. McCloy professed ignorance of the language but in reality spoke fluent German. Obviously, information overheard was beneficial. Nothing of this was discussed between them because they were aware that they were constantly watched and their facilities bugged. While exchanging benign dialogue in their home, they would pass notes, then destroy them. At the 1936 Olympic Games in Berlin, they were next to Hitler's box. Every time the United States or Great Britain had a victory, especially when Jesse Owens won his Gold Medal, Hitler would lean over to his cohorts and say something like, "Those b——s, just wait, they'll get theirs." Mr. McCloy evidently had the dubious honor of being on the Nazis' top ten "wanted" list.

Diary, *December 17: Gay Paree!* Arrived 8:30 A.M. Woke us in middle of night for passports. Trains very punctual—no water— separate little cars. Redcaps very excitable. George V Hotel *beautiful*—buttons for every service—closets galore—big big bedroom—little little living room—Does that mean they do most of their living in the bedroom? Way in saw Place de la Concorde, drove down Champs Élysées—widest avenue I ever saw. Welcoming flowers all over suite. Sharman had to leave. Grand TWA party—MCA—MGM—UI—RKO—photographers and newsmen. Outrageous group. After met Jules Stein (Chairman of MCA, brother Dave head of Paris branch). Big Jaguar. Went to Left Bank to Chez Allard. Tiny streets—date back to Revolution. Drove down one way street wrong way—saw lots of people in little store—stopped. An exhibition of an old painter—seventy-eight years old—painting three years—Lagru was his name—

style of Rousseau. Went to Arabic place for coffee—strange African-type brass tables—sat on low stools—dancing girl—tipped by putting money in skirt—Ted got so nervous he couldn't find the place in the skirt.

A bit of misinformation, probably a lack of communication, or perhaps just our not understanding correctly, but the Paris stay was not for visiting camps; it was more in the form of a bonus for touring the bases in Germany, coupled with publicity for the three studios, and partially sponsored by TWA. Johnny Haskell was the coordinator. Who cared what the reason, as long as it was legal. *We were in Paris.*

Paris is called the City of Light and a town like "a woman with flowers in her hair." It is one of the world's greatest centers of art, learning, culture, beauty, and pleasure. Romance thrives, and we were no exception. Our thrill and love for each other flourished in this sensual milieu. And we took advantage of the other offerings as well. Gorged ourselves on The Louvre, Les Invalides, Arc de Triomphe, Notre Dame, the Seine and Left Bank, Montmartre, Musée des Arts Modernes, the flea market.

And Versailles! It was difficult to absorb or comprehend this level of opulence. Quite obviously far removed from any sense of reality. Yet, here it was. We were looking at the evidence of what actually had existed—spellbinding to be a modern voyeur. It was enthralling to allow one's imagination to run rampant through this historical retrospective and painfully simple to evaluate what this lack of balance caused a country, a continent. A Jeanette or Bernard would have had no chance then. But what a sight to see now.

We savored the delicious cuisine in the elegant atmosphere of the best restaurants: Maxim's, Monseigneur, Tour d'Argent, Allard, Chez Anna's, and the Lido, where we were spotted by our friends in the show, the Charlevilles.

We crowded in a French movie *Messaline,* the Folies-Bergère, and saw the great Katherine Dunham. Her dress fell off during the performance, but no one was shocked.

On Christmas Eve the group celebrated with champagne in our suite—Vic Damone, Jimmy McHugh, Jimmy Van Heusen, John Haskell, Jackie and Charlie Charlevilles—and exchanged presents. I had sneaked out to find the shop on the Left Bank where Tony had admired a pair of cuff links. A wonderful singing taxi driver stayed with me, enjoying this Cupid caper, and we were successful. We placed calls to Los Angeles and were teary-eyed and homesick. Just before midnight Tony and I went to a small church and walked home in the rain, sharing coins with whomever we met on the street. Our first Christmas together.

Au revoir, Paree! In our peripatetic lives, Tony and I would be fortunate enough to journey abroad many times. No trip, however, could have the impact of this one, our first. The mere fact of its being the first, made it unique. And never again would we be the same age, in the same circumstances. Each succeeding pilgrimage would bring its own marvels, and we would relate to these as the people we would be at that time. Equally rewarding, just different. Not the first.

CHAPTER THIRTEEN

Nineteen fifty-two was a year full of movies and tours for the two of us. Tony was rushed into a boxing picture, *Flesh and Fury,* and a comedy, *No Room for the Groom.* He also studied with Sophie Rosenstein, the drama coach at Universal. She had a program similar to that of Miss Burns's, only at Universal the contract players presented their scenes one Friday a month in the permanent theatre set so that the producers and directors might attend and see their performers in diverse roles. Tony was excellent in an excerpt from John Berry's *All You Need Is One Good Break,* and I'm certain that aided his semiescape from harem pants. Each released film, each tour, resulted in the same public response: fans screaming, girls fainting, clothes torn off and mobs everywhere we went. Tony's popularity was impressive, maybe not to the elite of our fair city, but certainly to the masses across the country.

I was forced to do a forgettable picture called *Fearless Fagan.* None of us wanted to be a part of this, not Stanley Donen who directed, not Carlton Carpenter, not me. It was the first time I had felt any rebellion about an assignment, but I didn't have the courage to make a stand and go on suspension.

MGM had begun its metamorphosis. The seemingly all-powerful L. B. Mayer had been replaced by Dore Schary. Mr. Schary was not the strong disciplinarian Mr. Mayer had been, nor did he appear to have the magic pulse of a Thalberg. He also faced a changing industry: the introduction of 3-D, widescreen Cinemascope, stereophonic sound, independent producers, and television, which had refused to heed the prophecy of doom and just kept burgeoning. My gold-plated lion was slightly tarnished, his crown somewhat askew.

One picture I *did* want a part of was *The Naked Spur.* I tested with a giant—the man *and* his talent—James Stewart. Anthony Mann, the director (fittingly named, for he was a real man's man), and producer William Wright had to determine if we sparked the proper chemistry. I guess we did, because I won the coveted role. Oh glory, was I happy. In addition to Jimmy, there were Robert Ryan, Millard Mitchell, Ralph Meeker, and me as the total cast (give or take a few horses and mules). It was a Western about a bounty hunter, a fugitive and his charge, an old miner, and a drifter. Greed motivated most of the characters. My hair was chopped short as if I had done it myself. I wore old pants and a shirt, hardly any makeup, and I played a tough, spirited, uneducated daughter of a dead outlaw. Lissy Anne was a mountain lass, but this firecracker was altogether different—challenging, evocative, almost an anti-heroine.

The company locationed near Durango, Colorado, and Tony conveniently was free to be with me most of the time. It was beautiful country, in the rugged Rocky Mountains where wild rivers raged, with terrifying boulders jutting high above the whipped waters. The cresting sequence took place on the plateau of one of these cliffs. The climb up, also filmed, was petrifying. But the ultimate panic was being on top and peering down down down at the angry water and rocks below. With no guard rails, with no nothin'! As in any self-respecting climax, there was a fight-to-the-finish encounter. Up there. Dramatic, to be sure. The fear we registered was genuine.

We were housed about twenty-five miles from the town of Durango, in a complex of cabins on the perimeter of the main building, where we ate, and played when we had the energy. Jimmy brought his wife, Gloria. They occupied the same quarters Clark Gable and Lady Ashley lived in when Gable shot *Lone Star* in this area a year or so before. Evidently Lady Ashley had done some remodeling, so theirs boasted the most modern decor. But although they were primitive, the cabins were comfortable and clean. It was a congenial, pleasant, cheerful group, and I believe everyone thoroughly enjoyed themselves. Tony and I celebrated our first anniversary, and Gloria and the majordomo put together a bash. Tony haunted the fishing streams and made good use of a new easel.

Certainly, he was surrounded by a gorgeous palette of natural colors. He also had an inborn flair with a paintbrush.

I experienced yet another manifestation of professionalism. Jimmy, Bob, and I were doing an emotional scene, and Mother Nature was not fully cooperating. The wind was strong, and the sun capriciously played peekaboo with the clouds. Jimmy was propped against a tree trunk; and Bob and I faced him. We were able to shoot the master and Jimmy's closeup without too much interference. But the reverse angle on Bob and on me presented a dilemma. Our background showed the sky and landscape, and the light changes caused the camera crew endless frustration. Howard Koch, the A.D., dismissed Jimmy for the day, since his work was done. Jimmy, as only he can, said, "Well, I can't do that, you see, because, well, that just wouldn't be right, now would it? I think I'll just—hang around—and be off camera—for my friends there." And he stayed the entire tedious afternoon, only to play the scene in back of the camera, while it was focused on us. Now, *that* is a pro! It makes my blood boil when I hear instances of recent "stars" insisting their close-ups and shots be done first so they can leave, thus forcing their fellow actors to emote with a detached script supervisor. You'll never have it reported that a *real* star was guilty of such egregious behavior.

Late that summer, in my new Judy Holliday-style hairdo, I was reunited with Van Johnson in a fetching little comedy, *Confidentially Connie.* * In the six years since *The Romance of Rosy Ridge* he hadn't changed one adorable freckle, or one endearing quality. He was a father now, of a daughter, Schuyler. His eighteen films in the interim had included diverse roles: comedic, such as *The Bride Goes Wild;* musical, with Judy Garland, *In the Good Old Summertime;* dramatic, in *Battleground,* and teamed with Spencer Tracy, in *Plymouth Adventure.* The public seemed to have forgotten and forgiven its initial displeasure over his marriage.

It was toward the end of this that George Pal, of Paramount, borrowed Tony from Universal to play Harry Houdini. He then tried to woo MGM into loaning me out to be Bess Houdini. I

---

* I loved working with Van and had another opportunity in 1962 on *Wives and Lovers.*

begged. I pleaded. There was some asinine question of billing, and I said, "There is no question. My husband should be billed first." And Harry Friedman, of MCA, finally called to tell me the arrangements had been made. He told me later how he always loved to relay good news, anticipating my "Holy cow! Honest to goodness?" I didn't disappoint him.

We were very excited. This wasn't a big-budget film, but it had a fine script, and we would work together. In the beginning it was scheduled for black and white. Edith Head coordinated the wardrobe, and when she saw how beautifully it projected, she asked George Pal to come and take a look. He did and marched right to the front office. Not only did he gain Technicolor, but his operating expenditures were also augmented.

The movie spanned about thirty years, so the designer, hair stylist, and makeup artist had a field day. The various periods involved, the colorful stage costumes, the aging of the principals proved stimulating for all concerned departments.

And then there were the magic and the illusions. Who doesn't like magic? We all revert to childhood when we are dazzled by its feats. Tony bore the brunt of most of the training, but since Bess worked with her husband for many years, I also had my share. A clever magician, George Boston, was one technical advisor, and labored with Tony daily. Tony had amazing dexterity and was a very quick study. His rapid progress astounded everyone. Joe Dunninger, himself a close associate of Harry Houdini's, was another technical adviser. We were both initiated into the Magicians Society, and we were honor-bound never to divulge the secrets passed on to us. And to my knowledge that oath has not been violated. After all, these are the tricks of the trade, and if the mystery is taken away, how can we illusionists make a living!

The opening-day jitters could have been a problem, but director George Marshall would have none of it. He was so funny and sanguine, yet so aware and knowing, he immediately set the tone of the set. Having been the beneficiaries of this approach, we adopted it for our future work habits. The responsibility for the attitude on a set does lie with the leaders and stars, and we always tried to establish a happy but productive atmosphere.

Praise the Lord and pass the ammunition, of laughter. Every family, rich or poor, has been touched by disappointments, sadness, sickness, tragedy, and, hopefully, laughter to help them deal with all of the above. A sense of humor, the ability to plow through adversity and somehow have a smile handy, is one of our greatest gifts. I remember with absolute clarity wonderful moments of abandonment—crazy, silly times—spontaneous or planned. Water fights for some reason seem to have a pattern in my life. At home, it could start with Mom flicking water at Dad while doing dishes. Then Dad would get Mom with a glassful. A while later, Mom and I would trap him with a bucket outside. And inevitably we would all end up in the grand finale at the wrong end of the hose. I could dwell on less happy images of Mom and Dad together, but I prefer this one.

On *Houdini* George went further. He began throwing paper cups of water at Tony and me whenever possible. Naturally, we retaliated with ice down his back. And on and on, until he pulled the *pièce de résistance*. We were shooting in an empty auditorium, and Bess was pleading with Harry not to include the dangerous Water Torture Cell Escape in his act. George kept positioning me farther away from Tony, and I was complaining that the distance seemed wrong for the intent of the scene. "Well, try it, see if it works." So, after the lights were set and everything was ready, he rolled camera. The cameraman had warned me it was crucial to hit my mark because lighting was difficult in such a vast area. So I did. And was absolutely drenched, head to toe, by huge buckets of water strategically placed in the rafters. Obviously the whole crew was involved in this cleverly conceived plot. Ho, ho, ho, it took two hours to get me back in shape. But, no one cared. We were on schedule, and the laughter and friendliness were important. Everyone worked hard, long hours, arduous setups, unfamiliar and complex apparatus to handle and operate, but when the chemistry is right, it all pays off. George Pal understood as well: A contented company bodes well for all.

In the midst of the first-day congratulatory wires and bouquets I received a basket with a big bow. Inside was a satin pillow, and a ball of black fur. Tony had surprised me with a baby poodle. It was a female, so I named her Houdina. She was the cutest, most loving puppy. I adored her and lavished all my motherly instincts upon this innocent. And my desire to have a child intensified daily.

Tony and I worked well together. We were perhaps a trifle tentative in the beginning, even oversolicitous, but gradually we established a smooth interaction. Because we were in love, because we were married, we could be uninhibited with each other, which, I think, added another dimension to our performances. The reviews on *Houdini* were, for the most part, quite good. Interestingly enough, almost all mentioned the interplay between us as a fruitful commodity. *Daily Variety* explained it this way: "Paired, they are a harmonious, ingratiating team. First-rate in every division. This is going to be one of the big numbers of the year. Will give top audience satisfaction." The paying public proved them correct; it was a box-office bonanza. We must have done something right because *Houdini* was the first of six features we made together. Tony always said, "I like working with Janet. She's the only leading lady who also cleans my dressing room every morning."

Jerry and Dean were at Paramount the same time, so it was a lively lot. Our set attracted heavy traffic. George Boston and Joe Dunninger were in their glory and held court for all the intrigued visitors.

It was not Utopia, however. My sensitive stomach was subject to colitis, which struck me in fits. I had pushed myself a little too far with working and keeping house and family obligations and socializing. And poor Tony suffered severe burns over most of his body from being submerged too long in ice. But we all had to pay the piper to some degree. Still do.

The All-American and *Forbidden* quickly followed for Tony. And just after the new year, 1953, I went to Universal to start rehearsals for *Walking My Baby Back Home,* with Donald O'Connor. What a versatile talent in that human dynamo! He could dance up a storm, sing, deliver a serious scene, or have you rolling on the floor in spasms. One day, during rehearsal, he took off an outer T-shirt. Or he tried to take it off, and one of his arms was being stubborn. He improvised a fifteen-minute comedy routine with that shirt, getting one hand caught, then a leg, then an arm and a leg, until the shirt was stretched beyond recognition. It was a priceless performance, and a crime it wasn't recorded on film.

Louis Da Pron choreographed some memorable numbers, including a sand dance and a marathon amusement park acrobatic exercise in endurance. I also sang with the Modernaires, in harmony if you please. I asked for Betty Scott to return as my dance-in.

Not only was she an excellent dancer and a pleasant companion, she was also an adroit teacher who could make my feet do wonderful things.

This was Buddy Hackett's first picture. You know, the Chinese waiter bit: "Two from column A, one from column B—wait a minute—who ordered one from column A and two from column B?", etc. A very funny man who went on to make a big name for himself.

Universal was sometimes referred to as the "country club" studio. There were many grassy areas, and bungalows replaced the usual large, stern administrative buildings. Bill Goetz, who was married to L. B. Mayer's daughter, Edie, was in charge, and preferred a relaxed environment. In those days we toiled six days a week, with Sunday off. Bill was one of the few executives I had ever seen on a Saturday. He always made the rounds, dressed in casual clothes, to say hello and give his tired employees a word of encouragement.

Strange—well, not really—but every time a mishap occurred in which I was injured, especially on musicals, it always happened on a Saturday. The body and mind just become careless when fatigued.

Tony came by often, with Jeff Chandler or Rock Hudson or Howard Duff, another buddy. He brought Harry Belafonte on the stage one day, and the set photographer took a picture with me in the middle, an arm around each of them. It appeared on the cover of *Ebony*. I'll never quite get over my shock and surprise, and yes, *resentment,* when I received a small quantity of hate mail because I had my arm around Harry!

We moved to a larger apartment, a penthouse, at 10814 Wilshire, and I had a sweet lady to help me, Ida Mae. She would come in the afternoon to clean and fix dinner. What a luxury! This apartment had more privacy, spacious rooms, and boasted a good-sized terrace. Houdina liked that aspect of our new home—a lot.

Harry Friedman called for his customary "Holy cow!" when he told me Twentieth Century-Fox just signed me as Aleta of the Golden Isles in *Prince Valiant.* Tony wanted to play Val, but Twentieth producer Robert Jacks and director Henry Hathaway chose newcomer Robert Wagner. So Tony was put into *Beachhead,* a South Pacific war story, to be shot in Hawaii, on Kauai. Damn! I couldn't be with him the whole time. But I did wangle permission to accompany him on the Princess Line for the voyage over and the few days he was to spend in Honolulu.

Before leaving I had the preliminary wardrobe and head measurement fittings. Aleta was to have long golden tresses in elaborate styles, so numerous wigs were required. And the sketches for the costumes were spectacular. The work could begin while I was gone.

I was harboring a secret, a faint hope I was afraid to mention in case talking about it might scare it away, make it not true. I thought I was pregnant. I had to wait a while longer to be positive before I said anything, even to Tony. Ironically, we had just done a Sunday piece with Louella Parsons and stork rumors were emphatically denied. It's peculiar the way the media functioned. Every few months speculations came out that this star or that star was expecting. Then came the refutations. And years later, when the personality announced she *was* pregnant, the columnists always said, "Remember, you read it here first." If my expectation was confirmed, I knew I would call Louella and give her the exclusive, so as not to make her look foolish, or us liars.

Sailing day was exciting with all the streamers, confetti, and gay throngs of travelers and well-wishers. Tony was really turned off to flying after Europe, and only wanted to travel by ship or train. That was fine with me, as long as the vessel stayed on *top* of the water. My fear of the unknown ocean depths had lurked in a recess of my brain since Elizabeth's beach party years before. As we pulled away from the pier—whistles tooting, horns blowing, people cheering— we glanced along the rail of waving passengers and saw Van and Evie Johnson. Such a welcome coincidence, such a wonderful, unexpected bonus. He was on his way to Hawaii to make *The Caine Mutiny.* We spent every waking hour with them and enjoyed all the pleasures of the cruise together. Sunning, dining at the captain's table, dancing, even taking hula lessons (with no visible success). Oh, am I grateful it was a smooth crossing, because I was a little shaky, not bad, just somewhat queasy.

By this time I was certain. *I was going to have a baby.* The joy, the wonder, the realization of what our love was going to produce. Tony was thrilled. He wanted to shout it from the highest mast, to all the noisy sea gulls, to the strangers on board, to the entire world. But we restrained our impulses and decided to wait until we were ashore. There is nothing quite like the inner glow I felt when I looked across a table, or over the heads of guests somewhere, and my eyes locked with my husband's, and without words, we participated in an almost spiritual communication of a preciously shared confidence. We had never been so intimate.

Arrival in Hawaii was a pageant. Everyone was up early to catch the first glimpse of the outer islands in the dawn light. As we drew closer to Honolulu, smaller boats and yachts converged upon us. Layers of leis were piled around our necks, the fragrance almost suffocating. Beach boys were diving for coins. And the dock was swarming with humanity. When we disembarked we were crushed by the crowds. Security for the four of us was nearly impossible. The heat was intense and the pressing bodies allowed no air. I was afraid I was going to do a stupid thing and faint. The police and the studio reps finally managed to get us to the cars, safe and sound and intact. I've always been amazed when visiting a new locale to find people know me. It's as if we have friends in each state, in different countries all over the world, even though *we* don't know *them*. A warming thought.

The island was everything it was supposed to be. There was tropical humid weather, with flashes of wrathful rain to ensure against complacency; lush, profuse growth, palm trees, coconut trees, many varieties of exotic foliage, acres of pineapple plants, fields of swaying sugar cane; and the beaches and turquoise jeweled water and sprawling grand hotels. A paradise.

Our suite at the Royal Hawaiian on Waikiki, with Diamond Head in the distance, was classic "island": wicker furniture, airy rooms, panoramic windows, wide verandas, and fruit bowls overflowing with pineapples, bananas, papayas.

It was customary to dress formally in the evening at the Royal Hawaiian. The men looked handsome in their white coats and the women beautiful in light, wispy gowns. A romantic and festive aura prevailed. Even a cocktail was exotic. And a hand-holding stroll along the moonlit ocean assumed magical importance.

We indulged in all the typical tourist activities. Shopped—I bought several muumuus, thinking those loose garments would be useful in a few months—and we had two straw hats made on the beach, the kind that have a house and garden on top. We toured the island, and attended a luau under the stars, a Hawaiian feast prepared in an underground oven called an *imu*, with platters of roast pig and yams wrapped in taro leaves amid a rainbow of flowers. We paddled on a board in the tepid water, but only where I could see bottom, and we rode in an outrigger canoe and a twin-hulled catamaran.

And then it was aloha, Hawaii. And worse, aloha, my darling. We arranged to call only twice a week or the long-distance bill would be astronomical. But we would write constantly. I boarded the plane with my leis and cried all the way home.

I did Louella's radio show to pacify her. There was no problem with the studio because the picture would be finished before my shape started to change drastically. The families, of course, overreacted in their enthusiasm.

The wardrobe fittings were tough. There were so many outfits and it was hot, and the hours of concentrated standing got to me. Dorothy Jenkins, the brilliant designer, tried to space the sessions, even though she was battling a deadline.

About two weeks after I returned, I started to spot, then bleed. I was concerned and called my doctor, Dr. Sarah Pearl. At this point all she could do was say, "Rest, stay off your feet." I kept an appointment with Miss Burns, and I know now she had tried to talk to me that day and comfort me, and prepare me, for the inevitable.

My Uncle George had come back from working in the oil fields of Kuwait and had agreed to stay at the apartment so I wouldn't be alone. That evening I began to cramp and hemorrhage. He bundled me in the car and took off for St. John's Hospital. "It was the only time in my life I prayed for a cop to stop me. I did everything wrong—drove too fast, ran every light—and I'll be damned if I saw one policeman," poor George lamented later. Dr. Pearl, Mom, and Dad met us there, and I went into the operating room. Where my dream was lost.

This was not Tony's night to make contact. But when George went back to the apartment, the phone was ringing off the hook. An intuitive Tony was given the news. A heartbroken Tony called me immediately. I was still groggy, but aware enough to know what had happened. I was in such despair. I felt that somehow I had failed. Was I being punished for my earlier transgression? The one I had almost put out of my mind? Or was there another outstanding debt? Tony did everything he could to reassure me, of his love, of future attempts—we were both young and had ample time to raise a family. All of this while trying to disguise his own disappointment and the frustration of his absence. A hysterical Momeleh standing in my room didn't help at this particular moment.

It took some time before I could sort things out. I came to the conclusion that ours was not a vengeful God. For whatever reason, this, the baby, was just not meant to be—now. Nothing was permanently damaged; I would function normally again, and I had to have faith I would be given another chance.

Prince Valiant proceeded on schedule. Robert (R.J.) Wagner was probably one of the nicest human beings in this, or any, city. Well-mannered, straightforward, humorous, eager, he good-naturedly submitted to the indignity of being with the ladies in the hair department every morning to don his Prince Valiant pageboy wig. Actually, the whole cast was first-rate: James Mason, Sterling Hayden, Victor McLaglen, Donald Crisp, Brian Aherne, Debra Paget, and Primo Carnera (biggest man I'd ever seen).

Henry Hathaway was an excellent director, a charming host, and a good friend. But he did have a few quirks on a set. Occasionally he enjoyed being mischievous, goading someone, baiting, to get a reaction. His pet peeves were the makeup artists and hair stylists. He claimed every time he was ready to shoot, "they" would come in and fiddle around his actors. I learned very early to use the time between setups to repair or touch up my makeup and hair so I would be prepared for the next shot. But if there is another long rehearsal under the lights, an added touch-up is necessary before rolling camera. As a matter of fact, the cinematographer normally would call "N.G." (no good) if anyone was too shiny. Henry really yelled this one day, and I was compelled to defend the offending parties. But he tried another approach. I was studying my script, and he pulled his chair up and said, "You know, Janet, this makeup is really a racket. You are a beautiful young lady, what do you need with all that junk!"

Oh, you little devil! I said to myself. To him, "Why, thank you. What a lovely compliment. Tell you what. Tomorrow, instead of reporting to makeup and hair at 6:30 A.M., I'll come directly to the set at 8:30 *au naturel*, looking just like I do when I get up in the morning. It will be great for me, two extra hours of sleep. Only one slight complication, I don't think I'll look very much like Aleta." No more was mentioned about the evils of makeup or hairdressing.

R.J. and I were rehearsing an active fiery sequence and in the throes of the heated argument, I grabbed his arm and swung him around so violently I startled him, and he laughed. Oh boy, Henry lashed into him for that slip. "Why aren't you as involved as Janet?" Oh *dear.* "Take a lesson from her professionalism!" Oh *my.* "We're supposed to be rehearsing so we can get an acceptable scene!" Oh *hell.* "I'm sorry," I whispered. R.J. flashed me a quick grin, so I knew we were all right. My deduction was that Henry ragged R.J. a bit much. But on reflection, I decided he was really helping him, protecting him, tugging on every string, pulling out all stops, making him better than he thought he was. Because R.J. was young, relatively inexperienced, and his was the demanding, pivotal role.

Tony's homecoming was poignant. I was in the midst of jammed King Arthur's Court. Long before he was due, my eyes were darting here and there, hoping to see his face. And finally—finally—I saw him on the outskirts of the crowd. I ran and we just clung to each other, no words needed.

The A.D. mercifully yelled, "Lunch! Crew half hour! Cast one hour!" And we were alone in my dressing room to cry, to kiss, to hold, to touch. We couldn't stop touching.

In May of 1952, Grandma and Grandpa Westergaard celebrated their fiftieth wedding anniversary. I had a luncheon at the studio, their only visit, and the clan gathered at Bit of Sweden for a gala dinner. I'm grateful they were so honored, because Grandma died of cancer on August 16, 1953. August would prove to be a dark month in my life.

Mom was hit hard by her death. So was Aunt Pope. And Grandpa was lost. Mom drove herself mercilessly, caring for Grandpa, handling all preparations and decisions, maybe to the point of neglecting Daddy. (I wondered later . . . Mom was so strong and authoritative during that trying period, why couldn't she have drawn on that strength at home? Did she only feel needed then, and not with Dad and me?)

Tony was pushed into *Johnny Dark,* and then a musical, *So This Is Paris.* I went back to Paramount to make *Living It Up* with Jerry and Dean. I wondered what my studio was doing. Was I never going to work at MGM? Not that I was unhappy with my present projects, it just seemed odd. But I rationalized it at the time that MGM had given me my chance and nurtured me all these years. Now I was paying them back, bringing them revenue in return for their investment. I could accept that, maybe not forever but certainly for a while.

Edith Head was delighted to dress me in modern fashions and designed a stunning wardrobe. And Norman Taurog was a perfect choice as director. The part of the sob-story reporter indicated a style not compatible with me. The dialogue was laced with caustic one-liners; Eve Arden manages this so effectively, but it isn't my way—glibness doesn't sit well on my shoulders. Comedy for me has to come out of a situation, not just delivering witty lines. Norman agreed completely, recognizing what was natural for me. Not much rewriting was required; it was in the playing, and the director had to be in accord or I would have never heard the words "Cut! Print!"

Norman understood comedy, and he knew his people. He allowed Jerry and Dean to have their heads, when that served the purpose. But he also reined in when *that* was necessary. He didn't lose sight of the balance, the overall continuity, which is so important when dealing with strong personalities who can pull away off tangent. Dean was a natural—relaxed, easygoing, open, and sexy—and it resulted in a seemingly effortless, honest, warm portrayal. Jerry came across as an inventive buffoon, and more. He's a much better actor than he has been given credit for. The die had been cast, however, and the creators and public wouldn't permit him to deviate from his familiar image. That had to wait until he directed, where he could explore through other actors.

The film debuted the following July to excellent notices. Without any dissenters, it was proclaimed the best Martin-Lewis production. Paramount hosted a three-day-weekend shindig in Atlantic City, bringing the press in from all over the country. The 500 Club, where Dean and Jerry had begun eight years before, was reopened for the occasion. The boys were in rare form. I guarantee no one present ever forgot those three nocturnal "days."

The Black Shield of Falworth was the second teaming of Tony and me. This was Universal's answer to MGM's *Knights of the Round Table,* Twentieth's *Prince Valiant,* and the current crop of knight pictures. Yes, another loan-out for me. The picture was well-mounted and exhibited a convincing sense of medieval custom. I was back in my (side) saddle again. And we had another opportunity to research our give-and-take relationship. It was a tonic to see what special nuances we could bring to a scene, because we were us. Slowly, yet progressively, we stripped away camouflage, continually experimenting, always searching to improve.

During the heavy shooting days and nights—you don't know what cold is until you've worked on Universal's back lot at night—we decided to live in our bungalow dressing room at the studio. Traveling time was nil, and it was big and comfortable and in picturesque surroundings. With trees and expansive lawns, rabbits scurrying about in the early morning, Houdina had a ball. Anyone who has been on the Universal Tour recently, or is familiar with the lot today, will cry, "It ain't so!" But, I promise you, that's the way it was.

Our idea was a success. Mainly because it allowed more sleeping hours. And Tony had a heavy athletic load in this picture. There was a close call in one of the fencing bouts. His opponent missed his timing and grazed Tony's cheek with the sword. It drew blood, but luckily caused only a superficial abrasion. A quarter of an inch to the left, and we would have had serious problems. Dave Sharpe, Tony's stunt double from the beginning, was berating himself. But this was a close-up, nothing he could have prevented. Dave was such a sweet character. He always had a cigar in his mouth, even in rehearsals, only removing it for an actual take. I asked about that, because he didn't smoke.

He explained, "I was really a babe in the woods when I started in this business. I knew my job, but I didn't know the ways of the world. I was hired for this one particular leap off a cliff. I got it all prepared and everything, and the director wanted to see how it looked through the camera, just a run-through. So I did the jump. Then he wanted to see it again. So I did it again. And then he said he changed his mind and didn't want to do it after all. Well, that's his right. But when I saw the picture, the stunt was in it. That

S.O.B. had filmed my rehearsal, and I didn't get paid. We get our money when the camera rolls. So now, I keep this cigar in my mouth, do all the practice they want, and I don't take it out until *I* know the camera is turning and it is official." Pretty good reasoning.

Nineteen fifty-four was a year of change. The pundits of MCA and I had a conference. They knew of my questions concerning MGM's intentions, and they were fully informed of the conditions at that studio—indeed, every studio. In my habitual state of insecurity, I was too intimidated to consider being an independent contractor, not trusting my employability. Tentative discussions had already been held, however, and I was assured I had nothing to fear. But the umbilical cord had to be severed before further progress could be made.

A meeting was set up with Benny Thau, who couldn't have been more understanding. I think he already suspected the contents of my prepared statement. I was quite emotional. I felt I was asking to leave my family, my roots. Deep down inside he and I both knew, though, that our family had changed, it just wasn't the same. He made it very easy for me. In essence, "Janet dear, you have paid your dues. I can't hold you any longer, you have a right to spread your wings. There is one more picture I would like you to do, and then you have your release." I was overjoyed. I was grateful. I was sad. I was afraid. Was it an end, or was it a beginning, or was it both?

My swan song was not too memorable, except that *Rogue Cop* paired me with Robert Taylor. He was a beautiful man, always modest and self-effacing. To quote him: "I was a punk kid from Nebraska who's had an awful lot of the world's good things dumped in his lap." I could relate to that. Appropriately, Roy Rowland was the director. The first, and the last, at the alma mater.

As I walked out that big iron gate for the last time, the flood of memories brought a flood of tears. A broke, bashful, untrained tenderfoot named Jeanette had entered through those gates, and now Janet Leigh was leaving—leaving behind eight irreclaimable, unbelievable years. Years of an era that was no more. No more base camp. No more haven under the protective arms of the giant. No more being eighteen. No more being a little girl.

And what was I taking with me? I hoped a smidgen of knowledge, of skill, of sophistication, of security. And I was certain of one glorious gift: A constellation of events had placed me in Hollywood, at Metro-Goldwyn-Mayer, in the twilight of the Golden Years. I had been there. And no one could ever take that away from me. It was a place in my heart forever.

MCA had been correct in their prediction. I signed two nonexclusive pacts. One with Columbia for five pictures spread over a period of time. One with Universal for four pictures, also spanning a few years. The accumulated projected compensation was more than satisfying, it was titanic.

Tony had been agonizing over a contemplated change of his own. Our chum from MCA, Jerry Gershwin, had been talking to him about the benefits of being represented by a major agency—namely extensive studio coverage, effective influence, and packaging possibilities. I could only support his logic from my own experience. Other input warned of the danger of being lost or forgotten among a long list of clients. Both views had validity. The bottom line has to be the *degree* of actual interest and belief the agency has in the artist. For if this is a major factor, then you have the best of all worlds by being under the auspices of the more powerful organization. Bit by bit Tony became convinced of their determination to act enthusiastically in his behalf. His decision was made. Now he had to drum up the courage to tell his friend George. He was in a state for days, before and after the discussion. Some contractual arrangement was made between the two agencies. And it was done. And a new career was in the works for Tony.

Later, in the sixties, when MCA was deemed a monopoly and forced to divest to "free the slaves," we had no desire to be liberated. We were in an ideal situation, securely lodged, and we didn't want to budge. I had never been with another agency. Many of us were now balloons, floating in the air without anchor. I've never quite understood why success is penalized. Of course, the ruling was not ours to make.

We had a shift of residences as well, to a rented house at 2018 Coldwater Canyon, two doors away from the home of Charles Feldman, whom I had finally met. It was a scale higher in available space, and had a studio for artwork, and a brick patio with a pool.

Change also included signing with an independent public relations company. Teme Brenner, married to MCA's Herb Brenner, had been a Paramount publicist. Our first encounter was on *Houdini*, but it was during the press work for *Living It Up* that she confided to us she planned to move to Rogers and Cowan, and planted a seed for us to join her. There was no need at that time, but now I was no longer under the watchful eye of MGM. Teme cited the pragmatic reason. A studio has the responsibility of selling its picture, but the actor is only part of that. A retained P.R. firm's allegiance on the other hand, is primarily to the hiring actor, and on a sustained basis, not just during the shooting of a single film. We respected Teme's judgment. When we became acquainted with Henry Rogers and Warren Cowan, her judgment was further substantiated. They were a quality operation.

Our social life was changing too. Rosemary Clooney and Jose Ferrer were good friends. I had met Rosie at Paramount while she was filming *White Christmas* (Bing Crosby, Danny Kaye, Vera-Ellen), and I was in *Living It Up*. We were on the same wavelength immediately. Rosie was open, earthy, funny, thrilled about her career break.† And Joe and Tony were simpatico from the word go. Tony admired, we both did, Joe's aristocratic polish along with his dramatic finesse. He exemplified the patrician manner for which Tony yearned.

Sammy Davis, Jr., had also come into our lives in a big way. And we, the world, almost lost him in a big way as well. Jeff Chandler called frantically. Sammy had chosen to drive back to Los Angeles after his last show in Las Vegas. It's not clear if he fell asleep at the wheel, or became confused and took the wrong entrance ramp to the freeway. Anyway he had a horrendous collision and was in surgery with a fifty-fifty chance of surviving. We hovered over the telephone, waiting for word. When it came, there was good news and bad news. The good, the best news was he was going to pull through. The bad, he had suffered severe injuries and lost his left

---

† As close as we were for so long a time, there was never an indication of the shadow that darkened Rosie's future. But what a gutsy lady! To come out of the bleakness and glow even brighter.

eye. When you're young, you never believe accidents can happen to you, or your contemporaries. Only to some unknown, unseen, someone "out there." So it's a jolt, a rude awakening to discover you are not invincible. But the young can also adjust more quickly to a setback, recoup faster, and bounce right back. And that's exactly what Sammy did. The embryonic Will Mastin Trio, comprised of Sammy, his father, and his uncle, saw Sammy exhibit a variegated display of virtuosity—dancing, playing every musical instrument, singing, impersonations. He literally attacked the audience with his energy and versatility. So much so that I wondered sometimes if he knew who Sammy was. And then, when he achieved maturity and trust in himself, hastened by the brush with death, the real consummate person emerged. He didn't have to be anyone else. His stamp, his mark was indelible, and then *he* was being imitated. Yes, he certainly did bounce back, higher than ever.

Why, I never knew, maybe because we were "the" new couple in town, but we had been invited to a dinner at Joan Crawford's. We were in awe. Her children were in brief impeccable attendance. And I remember everything being perfect. Joan was beautiful and charming, and somehow a little more interested in Tony than me. But was I jealous? Of course!

We were guests at a Rocky and Gary Cooper dinner party, a star-studded evening. I felt we were in the company of royalty. Actually we were—Hollywood royalty. In that context we met a king— Humphrey Bogart. Rumor had it that Bogart took delight in verbally attacking a vulnerable victim with the zest of a witch doctor sticking pins in the proverbial doll. I had no desire to be the recipient, so I kept my distance. After supper, around the piano, guess who wandered in and stood next to me? I was quiet as a mouse, but fascinated at the same time. Here was the legend, so close. He wore a little gold earring, and I tried to look without staring because I hadn't seen a man wear an earring. But he caught me. "Oh, admiring my earring? Don't get any ideas—I'm all man, sweetheart. Who are you?" I stuttered. "What's the matter with you? You afraid of me? I won't bite you." And he didn't, perceptively realizing that I was no opponent.

A producer friend, Milton Bren, took us for a Sunday ride on Bogart's ship, the *Santana,* toward the end of Bogart's illness. There was a pall, a sense of doom, as if the ship knew its master wasn't coming back. It sounds weird, I know, but I couldn't shake the feeling that the ship was mourning, crying, with each creak and shudder of the bow against the waves. I hardly knew Bogart, yet I ached for him. He would never come and play with his friend the ship again.

Edie and Lew Wasserman began including us in their Sunday get-togethers. Of course we had seen them previously, but these Sundays were reserved for their inner core of friends. Everyone gathered for cocktails, swimming, and barbecue. This was a completely different Lew Wasserman: fun-lover, prankster, joker, throw-in-the-pooler. The brilliant executive disappeared. The shrewd, hard-bargaining wielder of power was absent; instead you knew an affable, regular guy. Edie was an invaluable partner for him. She established a rule—and God help those who broke it and faced her wrath—*no* business discussions; *no* pulling Lew aside and talking deals or getting advice. His haven was not to be disrupted. This probably preserved his sanity and health, for leading the MCA army was a stressful, tasking, pressured position.

Our social credentials and acceptability were slowly being established.

Boston was next on our agenda, where Tony filmed *Six Bridges to Cross,* a gangster story roughly based on a Brinks robbery caper. It was a fairly good part for Tony, but an interesting, and a little frightening, development occurred. The script described Tony's character as coming from Italian heritage. The timing of the movie was unfortunate, because the Italian community was up in arms about the rash of movies made in recent years depicting hoodlums of Italian descent. The newspapers were ablaze with the controversy. The location sites were picketed, sometimes slightly sabotaged. Threatening letters were received, resulting in round-the-clock surveillance. No real damage was done, however, and the problem was eventually smoothed out, but it was hairy for a while.

I returned home in the middle of shooting to start rehearsals for the first project on my Columbia contract, *My Sister Eileen.* The original picture starred Rosalind Russell and Janet Blair and later became the stage musical *Wonderful Town.* In the beginning, ours was to be a version of the Broadway show. Somewhere along the way negotiations between Columbia and the New York production were stymied, and Columbia decided to go forward with a musical remake of the movie *My Sister Eileen,* to which they owned the rights. The problem presented was to not even remotely resemble any material exclusively created for *Wonderful Town,* and thus infringe on *their* property. Fred Kohlmar was producer, Blake Edwards and Richard Quine the writers, Richard Quine director, Jule Styne and Leo Robin the songwriters, and Bob Fosse choreographer. All of them had a team of lawyers looking over their shoulders constantly. Everything had to be cleared and approved legally. Headache time!

Harry Cohn, head of Columbia, was one of the last movie mogul breed—gruff, tough, domineering, contrary, capable of vindictiveness, head lined in roguery—and smart. A tenacious maker of movies and builder of stars, he loved to put his subjects on the defensive. And had to know every move of every person within his domain. He checked minute details, down to inspecting to be sure that lights were turned off at night in offices and dressing rooms. I liked that old bear. Oh, we clashed several times. But once you understood his *modus operandi,* you could deal with him.

Bob Fosse had inquired if I was amenable to working out with him prior to the actual scheduled start date. I sent back the answer with a question, "Is this afternoon too soon?" I had seen his *Pajama Game* in New York and understood why he had won the Tony Award and why he was hailed as the newest talent on the horizon. He was accustomed to professional dancers, and I guessed he wanted to assess my range of capability. I was worried. I couldn't measure up to his standards. So the sooner we started rehearsing, the better. Harry liked this part, getting something for nothing.

I was apprehensive when I reported to the temporary practice hall. I had no clue as to what to expect, no identifiable face or form to put with Mr. Fosse. Would this insecurity ever end? No!‡

What I found was an attractive, slight, light-haired young man limbering up in front of the mirrors. He had a sensitive, almost angelic face and a mind that I would discover never rested. I filled him in on my limited background, and we started to work. He introduced some combinations, testing how far I could be

‡ It was comforting to read recently that Laurence Olivier still experiences that actor's nemesis, stage fright. At least I am in the best company.

stretched. At the day's end, he said, "We both are aware you are not Pavlova. But I am elated by what you are. I was prepared for the worst—a two-left-feet lazy movie star. But you move well, learn quickly, and very important, you work hard—we can do some exciting things."

I was walking on air. We labored every day for nearly a month. Then, one by one, the remainder of the cast joined us, signifying the official kickoff of Operation Eileen. Betty Garrett, Jack Lemmon, Kurt Kasznar, Dick York, Tommy Rall. Betty Scott again as my dance-in, and the wonderful "gypsies" for the massive conga number. About three weeks into formal rehearsal, Bobby came to me, with something serious to discuss. My heart stuck in my throat. I wasn't good enough. I wasn't shaping up. "I, ah, wondered if you would, ah, object to Betty being my assistant? She would still be available to help you, but we would hire some one else to be the dance-in." I was so relieved, and so happy for Betty's promotion, I threw my arms around him and gave him a grateful kiss. At least it was meant to be a grateful kiss. But it turned out to be a little more than either of us bargained for. I suddenly was embarrassed; this was certainly not the reaction I'd intended. *Be careful, Janet, you don't want any complications in your life,* said a wee inside voice.

Fortunately, my spontaneous burst of appreciativeness was not misinterpreted. He didn't think I was being flirtatious or suggestive. I could tell. It had been an innocent gesture and was considered accordingly. Still, there was no denying that our friendship courted more than a business affiliation. Proximity, mutual respect, genuine affection can do *that.*

Nothing daunted the synergy of the company. Not any edicts from Harry Cohn, not any puny squabbles over camera angles, not the lengthy days or schedule. We were a young, spirited, talented, ambitious conglomeration of energies. It was a six-month labor of love. No one wanted it to end, and it was a sobbing group who gathered for the farewell party.

Our efforts were rewarded. The reviews were excellent for all the individuals concerned, and the picture was very successful.

Only one time was I excused from the set early. Late in November, Tony and I were slated to do Edward R. Murrow's prestigious "Person to Person" television show. Even Harry Cohn recognized the value of this. Coldwater Canyon and the driveway up the hill to

TOP: a "calm" Janet being presented to Princess Elizabeth on stage of the Midnight Gala. BOTTOM: breakfast with Orson Welles after the Midnight Gala.

TOP: on location for *The Naked Spur,* 1952. Gloria Stewart, Jimmy Stewart, Millard Mitchell, Janet, and Ralph Meeker. BOTTOM: learning a few tricks from Joe Dunninger on the set of *Houdini,* 1952. Jerry Lewis was a frequent visitor.

With Dean Martin and Jerry Lewis on location for *Living It Up*.

With Betty Garrett on the set of *My Sister Eileen.*

TOP: at the Waldorf-Astoria in New York, accepting an award for Grace Kelly. In the middle is Oscar Hammerstein, who innocently asked, "Do you sing?" Also attending were Jackie Gleason, Mary Martin, young Patty McCormack, and Mitch Miller. BOTTOM: left, a photo of me taken by Tony in Paris, 1955. Right, on location in Kenya, Africa, during the filming of *Safari,* 1955.

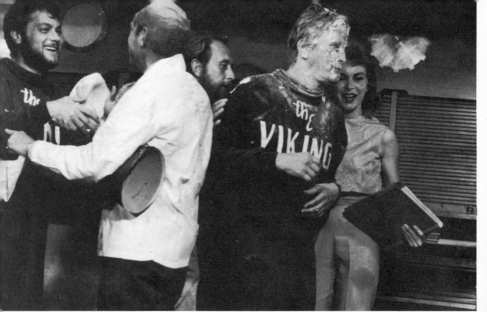

TOP: on board *Brand VI;* Director Richard Fleischer (with megaphone), Tony, Kirk Douglas, and Janet are attempting to boost morale during the filming of *The Vikings.* BOTTOM: with Blake Edwards and Tony on the set of *The Perfect Furlough,* 1958.

Jamie's debut. Photo taken of the Curtis clan for the cover of *Look* magazine.

With Anthony Perkins for the premiere of *Psycho*, 1959.

our house were a blanket of trucks and generators and whatever. It never rains in California (as you know if you read any Chamber of Commerce literature), but *something* from the sky was coming down in buckets, accompanied by flashes of lightning and the roll of thunder. So the plan to conduct a portion of the show outside and portray the California casual life-style had to be scrapped. We reorganized for an indoor show. Countdown and—air time. Mr. Murrow did the introduction, asked one question, and that was all we were able to hear from him. The storm had caused a malfunction in the audio, and we had no voice contact with him, none. Tony and I gave each other one of those "What the hell!" looks, took a deep breath, and plunged onward, leading the camera from room to room, trying to remain poised, and racking our brains to recall the topics that were to be discussed, without the bridge of his regular commentary. By the end, we were both drenched, and not from the rain. Mr. Murrow called at the conclusion, and was full of apologies and gratitude and wonderment that we had pulled it off. So were we. Live television was a whole different ball game from movies, and our admiration for the brave souls who did this week after week grew by leaps and bounds. "Playhouse 90," "Texaco Star Theatre," "Your Show of Shows," etc.—my God, how did they do it?

New York, in early 1955, was a site of serendipity for me. On the personal front, this is when I met my cherished friend Fon Tayne. At Edie and Lew's a few months back I had admired the dress Polly Bergen was wearing (she was then married to Freddie Fields of MCA, later producer and studio executive). She gave me the name and number of a rising young model and designer in New York. Tony and I visited her on our next trip. Fon modeled her collection; each ensemble was exotically named. I would have ordered every outfit if finances had permitted. But we settled for three. Tony said, "Let's see that Shapiro."

Fon was confused. "That—what?"

"You know, that velvet with the criss-cross back and funny sleeves."

"Oh, you mean Sapphire. Yes, that would be lovely on Janet." And she disappeared behind the curtain barely able to hide her laughter.

A relationship was launched. Fon designed a first-birthday dress for my older daughter, Kelly, and a high school graduation gown for my second daughter, Jamie, and everything in between.

She had an unbeatable sense of humor and the two of us always seemed to have amusing adventures. One quick illustration. At a cocktail party, a gentleman had given me a gold Harry Winston pen. It was a perfect size for a handbag, and I used it constantly, until it was dry. No refill in Los Angeles could be found, so I waited until a succeeding journey to New York. Fon and I were strolling along Fifth Avenue on one of those rare "ladies' days," dressed to the hilt, and we passed Harry Winston. I remembered my pen and thought they might suggest who would carry the refills. Winston is probably the best-known house in the world for world-wide expensive, exquisite jewels. I had never been inside. Two armed guards opened the outer doors, and we were ushered into opulence. A distinguished-looking man glided toward us. "Ah, Miss Leigh, what a privilege to see you. How may I serve you and your beautiful friend?" Before I could open my mouth, he continued, "But, of course, not in *here*," and he escorted us to another door, defended by two additional pistol-packing patrolmen. The quiet private room was lined with recessed cases each displaying a magnificent multicarat stone. "Now," he purred, "what is your pleasure?" Our pleasure would have been to get out of there, but we were trapped.

"Well, ah, you see, ah, several months ago I was given this pen," and I fished around and found the culprit at the bottom of my purse. "And, oh dear, I wanted to know where I could get a refill." There, I had managed to spit it out.

A lethal silence. Then, masking his disappointment with a false heartiness, "I believe I can be of some assistance. Let me see." He quickly led us out of the inner vault, went to the drawer of a side-board, grabbed a handful of slim plastic packages, and presented them to me. I reached for my wallet. "Oh no. *Please!* We give these little pens as tokens to our valued customers. There can be no charge. Do come again." Fon and I mumbled our thank-yous, stumbled outside, and almost collapsed on the pavement. Do I have to say I've never been back?

A ready-to-wear dress company approached Daddy about my endorsing their product. I didn't care too much for their samples when I conferred with them in New York, but I had an idea. Until recently I had always dressed on a really cramped budget. Even now I was careful, although I enjoyed a more generous allowance. It was nearly impossible to find a plain, simple inexpensive garment. Everything was loaded with bows, or fake flowers, or glitter. I assume the purpose of so much trimming was to hide the actual lack of quality. Would they be interested in manufacturing a line of my design? I couldn't draw very well, definitely couldn't make a pattern, but if I roughly sketched my thoughts, perhaps one of their trained personnel could finish it properly. We signed a contract and I waded into new waters. I would be independent from their operation and have complete autonomy. I also wanted to incorporate helpful hints I had been given earlier: basic colors, double usage, a black sheath, separate skirt to put over dress, bolero to give a different look, all at minimum prices. The concept caught the buyers' imagination. I put in a lot of hours, modeled the clothes, and talked to the delegates from department stores throughout the country. I attended the mart in Dallas. *Life* magazine did a four-page spread.

Everything was rosy and sales were going nicely. Eventually, however, the bloom came off the rose, and the waters became murky. Dad and I were not able to be watchdogs continually. There are means, common to any particular business, by which an associate can be manipulated to a disadvantage. Not out-and-out cheating, just obliquity. In this instance, we uncovered information that in the sales salon, gradually only their fashions were in evidence. And, my line was being "knocked off," the vernacular expression for copying a dress, altering one tiny detail, and including it in their collection. Talk about a cutthroat profession!

We didn't have the stomach for these shenanigans. Or the time. Or the inclination. The partnership was over.

The venture had necessitated several brief shuttles between California and New York. On one of these I had been asked to accept an award for Grace Kelly. A luncheon was held in the Waldorf-Astoria, and honored Grace for *The Country Girl,* Mary Martin, Jackie Gleason, young Patty McCormack for the play *The Bad Seed,* a writer, a maestro, and Oscar Hammerstein. I was seated beside

Mr. Hammerstein, and we had a wonderful tête-à-tête. Out of the blue he asked, "Do you sing?"

"A little. Why?"

"Would you sing for me?"

"I don't sing that way. I mean I don't have an act or a routine."

"Doesn't matter. Dick [Richard Rodgers] and I are writing a new show for this fall. You would be perfect for the ingenue."

I clutched at any escape. "I'm leaving tomorrow and won't be back in New York for two weeks."

"Fine. Any couple of songs will do. I'll have a pianist meet with you when you arrive, and our staff will prepare a scene or two, just so we can see you on stage. Then it's settled?" I nodded meekly, not quite clear how this had all evolved. Mr. Rodgers telephoned early the next morning, delighted by the prospect, and gave me a number to contact immediately upon my return.

What had I let myself in for? Tony was passive, somewhat reluctantly indulgent about my news. He hadn't been enthusiastic about the clothes business either. I called Harriet Lee and prepared two vocals. The time flew by, and I was flying East. Joe and Rosie (Jose Ferrer and Rosemary Clooney) loaned me their New York apartment for these short commutes. The script and scenes were delivered. I rehearsed with their musician and director. The audition was set for the next morning at ten. Bobby (Fosse) was doing the groundwork for his new show, *Damn Yankees,* but he came over after his conferences to lend moral support. It was intoxicating, and I felt so—New Yorkish. Here I was in a rather bohemian apartment, on the eve of a tryout for a Broadway musical, a Rodgers and Hammerstein Broadway musical. My high lasted through the taxi ride to the stage door and until I saw the dark, empty stage. Then I was nearly anesthetized with trepidation. The piano player and director greeted me confidently (easy for them, I thought), and motioned me onto the stage. The piano was in place, and there was that single glaring dangling work light one hears so much about. I scanned the deserted auditorium and could barely focus on four figures sitting in the middle of the ominous ocean of seats. The soothing voice of Mr. Rodgers floated up to me. "Don't worry, Janet, we understand how strange this is for you. We're not expecting perfection. Start whenever you are ready." I had decided to get the singing part out of the way first. I nodded to the accompanist, sent up a silent prayer, and dived in. Afterward, I likened the experience to a cold shower. Difficult to take the initial plunge, but invigorating once you've gotten over the shock. I felt more comfortable doing the scenes and really cut loose. The reality of the whole adventure wasn't as disconcerting as the anticipation.

Tony had followed *Six Bridges* with *The Purple Mask* and *The Square Jungle.* I was readying *Pete Kelly's Blues,* a fun romp about musicians and gangsters in the Roaring Twenties, with Jack Webb, Edmund O'Brien, Peggy Lee, Andy Devine, Ella Fitzgerald, Lee Marvin, Martin Milner, and me as a wealthy flapper. About two weeks after tossing my hat in the New York ring, I received a wire from Rodgers and Hammerstein. "We are pleased to offer you the role in 'Pipe Dream'. Very excited. Welcome to Broadway. Love, Dick and Oscar." I read it over and over again, until the paper was limp. MCA had negotiated the impossible, obtained permission from both studios, *and* convinced Rodgers and Hammerstein to settle for a six-month commitment in New York in place of their usual minimum of two years.

I could have played *Peter Pan* without the wires I was so happy, and could hardly wait until Tony came home. I sat him down, made him close his eyes, and put the telegram in his hand. "Now open. Well? Say something!"

The furrows on his brow deepened. "You can't do this! I should have spoken before, but I honestly never thought (a) that you would get it, (b) that the studios would agree, and (c) that Rodgers and Hammerstein would allow a six-month clause. What happens to us—to me? My work is here, and I don't want you away all that time. Ten to eleven months, counting rehearsals and out of town, of separation, and *we'll* be separated."

There was no question he was right. I knew it as soon as he started talking. Janet, when will you learn? When will you start to grow up and think? Priorities, girl, what are your priorities? You were so caught up in the act of auditioning, of being asked to audition, you didn't consider the consequences of the next step, didn't even consider the next step. Of course your husband comes first. And if you are ever blessed to have children, *they* will come before your career. You have always believed that, and the first time the situation presents itself, you fumble the ball. Never fear, I swore, it won't happen again. And it didn't. Ever!

My letter of regret was painful, but not melancholy. I was content. I had the satisfaction of knowing I had tried and won. *Pipe Dream* was not one of Rodgers and Hammerstein's most successful productions, but that really is beside the point here. My decision had to do with our partnership.

CHAPTER FOURTEEN

Easily the most significant series of events now occurred in Tony's life, and thus in mine. Harold Hecht, James Hill, and Burt Lancaster had previously asked Universal to borrow his services for their United Artists picture, *Trapeze*. Universal had flatly refused, saying they couldn't spare him from their projects for six months. Tony was despondent, because this could have been a giant step up the importance ladder. H, H & L were dogged about using Tony and persevered with MCA, who also wanted this for him. Now here is where a big agency officiates best. I was not privy to the negotiations between the two parties, but *some* use of power, *some* interchange, or swap was employed. Because, lo and behold, Universal did an about-face and okayed the loan-out. What a coup! To co-star with Burt Lancaster and Gina Lollobrigida, be directed by the internationally respected Sir Carol Reed, and have the film shot entirely in Paris! I accepted the next Columbia bid, *Safari*, to be done in London and Africa, to ensure our presence in the same vicinity, except for my few weeks in Africa. At the conclusion of *Safari*, I would remain in Paris with Tony. Everything was wonderful.

The family front was not so wonderful though. Papeleh had had a mild heart attack, and Bobby was not progressing well, which increased the pressure on us from Momeleh. My Mom and Dad were at low ebb in their war of attrition.

I had a brainstorm. Mom should come with me for the duration of my shooting. She would have the trip of a lifetime, I would have company and a helper, and maybe the time apart would enable my parents to evaluate their situation, and give them some breathing space. The mere idea, the preparations seemed to clear the air a little. Mom was vital, busy, stimulated. I was encouraged.

Mom and I departed first, to New York and then London. Tony followed shortly, train to New York, ship to France. We would meet in two weeks in Paris. Mom was wide-eyed during the entire tour. All of this was so foreign to her: the photographers, the press, the reception committees, the limos, the Columbia suite at the Sherry Netherland. The two days in New York were filled with work, but I managed to bring her to Danny's with some buddies—Judy and Jay Kantor, June and Johnny Springer, Marvin Levan, Mickey Loew, Fon Tayne, and others.

I didn't call Bob Fosse. Somehow, when I confronted "the play or not the play" crisis, I addressed another issue as well. An occupational hazard, providing fruit for juicy gossip, was the "set romance." There were numerous reasons for these dalliances—proximity; mutual goals; mercurial, thin-skinned personalities, chemistry; even fantasy—all tempting conditions to lure the unguarded creative soul. I knew I was sitting on a time bomb, whose explosion could send lives hurtling every which way, and so I decided it was best to just get off.

London presented the same scenario as New York. We had a beautiful suite at the Savoy overlooking the Thames, with a view of Big Ben and the House of Lords. The little pages were adorable. They would bring one message, or one bouquet, or one package at a time, rotating so that each one had a peek. And a tip.

I was whisked to wardrobe by Andy Worker, the producer; Terrence Young, the director; and Cubby Broccoli, the financial figure. Elstree Studios is a lovely ride from town, nestled in a pictorial residential area. Filming is different in London—not in equipment so much, or in achieving a performance, but more in attitude and custom. It's more formal. Maybe it's the accent. There is a matron for your dressing room. Tea is served religiously every day on the set. There are very civilized hours, including a five-day work week, which Hollywood fortunately adopted soon after. But in spite of the formality, there is an easy feeling, relaxed, and much is accomplished. It was a productive atmosphere.

I met Victor Mature, Roland Culver, John Justin at the jammed press conference. Vic and I were the quota allowance; only two American imports on any English film. He seemed nice enough, and said he was nervous with all the crowds. Some children had rounded up a ladder and climbed to the second-story windows of the hotel to see us. They were so exuberant when we went to say hello we were afraid they would fall off. English fans were quite demonstrative and persistent. Not the reserve you would expect.

Strikes were common occurrences at the studio. The electricians walked off at one point because of too much dust. Unlike the States, the administrators displayed extreme calm, almost resignation. "We'll jolly well have to do something about that, won't we?" Another time there was a general "token" strike by all the guilds. These interludes were used to work on script changes and have visits. Gene Kelly dropped in, Paul Douglas, Compton Bennett. We watched Clifton Webb on the set of *The Man Who Never Was.*

As great luck would have it, Uncle George finished his second hitch in Kuwait and landed in London. Perfect! Mom and Unc made all the sightseeing rounds and he would fill her time on my weekends with Tony. I squeezed in some fun too, between shooting and the endless publicity. My Rosie and Joe had been in England for a few months, so we spent many hours together catching up. She was playing the Palladium, a very imposing, colossal theatre, and I was thrilled for her success. The audience wouldn't let her off the stage. We attended Guy Mitchell's opening there as well, in the Queen's box.

A highlight in the entertainment department was Marlene Dietrich's closing night at the Café de Paris. She was the quintessence of glamour. Noel Coward delivered her introduction. (As if she needed one.) The dramatic impact of her change into a full dress suit from the famed body dress lingers with me still. As does another image. At the Academy Awards a few years later, the beautiful ladies of Hollywood had arrived at the podium lavishly bedecked with glitter and gold. When they announced Marlene Dietrich, she walked from the wings in a simple form-fitting black gown, with a slit to her thigh, on the *viewer's* side, and the place went crazy. Showmanship A+!

Tony had cabled and called every day from the ship, and at last he was in France. Our plan was that I would fly to Paris each weekend until I finished at Elstree, and then leave for Africa from there. After two weeks' separation, it was quite a reunion for the French press. United Artists had rented an apartment for Tony, 2 Rue Spontini, just off Avenue Foch. It looked like an old castle, but then everything did. Lift to the fifth floor, and our French maid, Jeanne, opened the door to an elegant, spacious, antique-filled home away from home. Tony showed me each room, one at a time, like opening presents at Christmas.

Much of *Trapeze* was filmed at the Cirque d'Hiver, the permanent winter circus. My first impression was of the smell, but after a while, I didn't notice. The second was the cacophony of many languages. Dialogue directors were needed in English, French, and Italian; assistant directors qualified in German and others as well. The circus families represented most of the countries of Europe, and the crew was also a mixture. The animals seemed fiercer than in American circuses. A new lion tamer was in training—the last one had recently been chewed to death! Yikes!

On the Sunday of the first weekend, a huge parade had been planned, featuring the entire cast and circus ensemble and animals. Milton Greene, one of the most artistic photographers in the field, and a good friend, was on assignment from *Look* magazine to cover the movie, the parade, and us. Amy (his wife) and Milton and I kept driving ahead, with the police, then stopped and took pictures. There were over two hundred thousand fans lining the streets, and finally Burt and Tony pulled us up on their float, for protection. What fun!

The next stop, for the cover shot, was a picnic spot miles from the city. The time machine had put us back in 1869, in a Renoir painting named *La Grenouillère*, a popular boating and bathing spot on the Seine. Cool, crystal-clear light filtered through the willow trees, harmonizing with the tender green and blue-gray of the water. Each bend of the river was a tableau. Milton was wallowing in his art, and we were drunk with the ethereal grace.

How sad to have to return to reality and the airport.

The next weekend Terrence Young arrived in Paris with me. I liked him a great deal. He was a cosmopolitan gentleman, and a very resourceful director. I couldn't imagine him in the wilds of Africa. But the closer the time came, I couldn't imagine myself there either.

That week I saw Tony work out on the trapeze with Burt. He only had been at it seven days, and he already looked good. Ed Ward, Burt's double, and Fay Alexander, Tony's, filmed one of the intricate maneuvers. Watching was so nerve-racking I forgot to take snapshots.

Tony was miserable in the apartment, because it was too isolated, and so we moved to a large suite at the George V, where most of the company was staying.

Monday was a holiday in France, so Tony swallowed his fear and flew back to London with me on Sunday night, which surprised everyone and caused a stir at the studio. Who cared? We had an extra day together.

The following weekend was the last before my (hopefully only) six weeks in Africa. The inoculations were all over; they are really powerful. Especially the one for yellow fever; the night of receiving that one I fainted dead away.

Mom and Unc and I landed in Paris with twenty pieces of luggage, most of which we would leave there. Tony had asked Uncle George to go with us to Kenya, and he almost did, but the company didn't have the facilities. He would fly to the States after Mom and I left.

We did have a smashing good time. Mom and Unc took in all the wonders of Paris. *Cinamonde* magazine arranged for us to receive two little scooters, and we went all over the Bois de Boulogne, to Parc de Saint Cloud, to Château Bogatelle, with pictures naturally. Sir Carol had a dinner party for Burt and Norma, Gina and her husband Milko, René Clair, Maria Schell, etc., at Laurents in the Bois. More of the *Look* layout, at the Rodin Museum, to an island underneath the Pont Neuf, which was a gathering place for lovers, fishermen, and great characters.

Hateful day, August 30. Tony Howard, the P.R., and Euan Lloyd, the associate producer, had boarded the plane in London, and were waiting for us. I prolonged the departure as long as I could, but like death and taxes, the moment came. My diary records, "I've never *not* wanted to go somewhere so much in my whole life! It was really all I could do to keep myself from getting off the plane and telling everyone to go to hell."

We refueled in Rome, and had dinner in Cairo, where I had an unexpected reception. I felt like the blond goddess. We were presented with flowers, gifts, jewelry—and lots of stares. The food was divine, served by waiters in red turbans and white robes and belts. Balmy, beautiful weather, and we now understood what was meant by "seeing the Egyptian moon." It pains me to know of the turmoil in the whole Middle East region now, and it grieves me to think of the costly conflicts that took place, and are taking place, at our next destination, Africa.

A secret society named Mau Mau, the members of which were under oath to practice torture, murder, and terrorism against those who opposed them, erupted in Kenya in 1952. Late in 1952 Jomo Kenyatta, the alleged leader of the rebellion, was imprisoned. The uprising continued, however, subsiding by 1956, and was declared officially over in 1960.

When we arrived in Nairobi, Kenya, on August 31, 1955, the main thrust was over, but a state of emergency still existed. The attacks by the Mau Mau then were more in the nature of forays for food, weapons, and ammunition, rather than military offensives. Not that that information made us feel a lot safer. Dead is dead, whatever the reason behind an assault.

Life seemed fairly normal in Nairobi, except for a few telltale signs. It is a little strange to walk into a pharmacy and below the white laboratory jacket see a holster and a gun protruding. And the ladies' evening bags couldn't disguise the bulge caused by their small pistols. The heavy barbed wire enclosing the native quarters was a menacing reminder too. We almost jumped out of our skin when an arm reached in our window at the one story Norfolk Hotel and dropped something. It turned out that was how telephone messages were delivered.

The safari clothes were "fitted," a loose term since Mom looked like a head sticking out of a tent, and I a pregnant barrel. Our caravan of cars started the six-hour trek north and inland to our location site. We stopped at one village that had been a repeated target of the Mau Mau. It was a fortress now with barbed wire, a moat with spikes at the bottom and tall spearlike sticks around the perimeter. There were throngs of ragged children whose thin little bodies were covered by sores caked with dirt. Women with shaved heads and wire bangles worked in fields carrying babies or carrying baskets, contents up to two hundred pounds, and babies as well. The men were the prima donnas, painting themselves, dying their hair, wearing bright colors and feathers.

About three hours and seventy-odd miles later, we came to our last bastion, Nanyuki, at the base of Mount Kenya. The Mawingo Hotel was lovely and modern. I believe this was the real estate

William Holden eventually purchased for his Kenya Club. It's easy to understand why.

Victor Mature had elected to stay at this hotel and drive the two and a half to three hours each direction to our tent city or to the day's location. There was no way I could do this since I had to cope with hair and makeup. That arrangement lasted until Vic's room was bombed, at which time he decided that maybe the camp would be more convenient after all.

Animals were abundant: zebra, giraffe, impala, water buffalo, camels, ostrich, Grant gazelle, Thompson gazelle, oryx, the rare eland, and monkeys. The bigger game we gradually saw later. The geographic features changed from dense mountainous foliage and craggy crevices to a plateau covered by tangled scrub.

We crossed a barrier, the base for local Kenya forces and the Kikuyu "Home Guard" (the predominant tribe of the area), and were on the last lap. This was a checkpoint station; no one was allowed out after dark (who in their right mind would want to be out at night!), and lorries of soldiers were sent scouting for anyone missing. Finally, the camp loomed before us. A sizable center pavilion served as the mess hall, kitchen, and recreation facility. Then there were various tents for equipment, garage, repair shop, wardrobe, makeup, wireless, etc. On the outskirts were the individual dwellings. Separate, in the distance, were the native huts. Ours had a canvas floor, a rickety dresser, two single cots with mosquito netting, two unstable nightstands with kerosene lamps, *and* the only enamel white tub to be found in the vicinity. Only one hitch—there was no water system. But plenty of ingenuity had been used. A big tank had been installed on a wooden tower, the workers would heat tubs of water and pour them into the vat, and gravity carried them through a hose to the tub. A hole had been dug underneath for the drain. You notice I didn't mention a john. That was about fifty yards straight into the wilderness.

Sleep was out of the question the first night. So many "dont's" to meditate. *Don't* drink any water that hasn't been boiled. *Don't* go anywhere alone. *Don't* put your shoes on without knocking them against something, in case any creatures had crawled inside. *Don't* stick your hand in a drawer or any place blindly, look first. Scorpions and tarantulas were prevalent, and a spitting cobra was killed nearby. *Don't ever* swim in the river. (Rumor had it that a second-unit man had been lost to a crocodile.) And the sounds! A lion's roar. Hyenas laughing.

Filming was definitely, distinctively African. The intense heat, the windstorms, the red dirt rendered makeup almost impossible. We gave up after a while and only used mascara and blush and lipstick. All we could do with hair was keep it washed and let it blow and wear a hat as often as possible. Moving around to different locations was really hard work for the crew. The animal and action sequences posed tremendous problems. The company had to be flexible because so much depended on animal movements and availability. For example, in the middle of a morning a Land-Rover careened toward us, Andy (Worker, producer) yelling, "A white hunter just bagged a rhino about thirty miles from here. Let's go!" This was needed for the picture, so everyone dropped what they were doing, grabbed the camera and a few reflectors, and off we went through desolate country that lacked even dirt roads. Some places we had to throw wood over gullies in order to pass. As we drew closer to the mountains we were nervous as hell, because that was where the Mau Mau hid. The rhinoceros looked like a prehistoric monster, poor beast. Permission had been granted for the kill. Then some warriors just appeared, done up with war paint and carrying spears; we froze. But they were from the Samburu tribe and were "good guys." I dearly hoped we would never see how the "bad guys" looked.

Another day, while we were shooting near the Vasonyeri River, one of the white hunters scurried to Terrence, motioned for silence, and whispered there were several elephants with calves heading for the river. There was a sequence in the movie in which I take out a tiny rubber dinghy, against orders, and go for a float. To have the elephants so naturally in the background would be a coup. Quickly we prepared. A group of natives was sent far down the river, forming a human chain to stop me in my raft. The camera crew, Terrence, several white hunters, and I hiked quietly upstream. Everyone else slid away. The hunters with their rifles stationed themselves along the bank, out of sight, in case of any trouble. The current wasn't too swift, but I could capsize. Terry and the cameramen ducked behind a big bush, and I waited like Moses in the rushes. When the signal came that the elephants had reached the other side, I released my hold and glided along, taking in the sights. The elephants weren't aware of me for some time because we were on the right side of the wind, and we got the shot. When they did see me, they started running along the edge of the water, also in the camera's eye. It was thrilling.

When the time came for the first stunt, my stand-in and double— a local English girl from Nairobi—disclosed she was three months pregnant. Damn! The memory of my loss was still tender territory. I couldn't let her risk her condition, and I knew she needed the money or she wouldn't have accepted the job. I struck a deal with Andy and the production supervisor, Max. As long as the feats weren't ridiculously dangerous, or didn't call for extraordinary expertise, I would perform them myself. But the girl had to be paid. They assured me nothing planned was too bad because, after all, she wasn't a professional stuntwoman either.

The battle siege, where a jeep blew up and burning trees fell and blank bullets popped all over, was dirty and smoky and hot but bearable. My Waterloo came in the rapids and falls. The excursion in the dinghy naturally led to near disaster, with the peaceful river becoming rapids and leading to a mammoth fall. A real dummy (not this one) went over the long drop. The close-up was done under controlled conditions at a chosen "baby" cascade. Hunters and natives organized a circle to catch me at the bottom. The camera was low, aimed upward to give the illusion of great height. "Action!" and I started paddling, frantically trying to maneuver in the swirling mass, and bingo, over and down I went. I struggled in the water, tossed around like a cork, and then was stopped by my masculine net. Everything really went well. Except—a fatal slip— when I overturned I inadvertently gagged and swallowed some water. The results of that escapade are still with me. There wasn't an immediate reaction. The entire group had been afflicted with various degrees of stomach troubles, me included, but when this bug began operating, there seemed to be no remedy. Ultimately I couldn't keep anything down, and the camp nurse couldn't help much. A quick flight to a doctor in Nairobi relieved the condition somewhat. Later, in London, Sir Neil Hamilton Fairley, a specialist in tropical diseases, diagnosed bacterial dysentery. The bugger was gone but had caused considerable damage, and I would likely always have a sensitive abdomen. He was correct!

The finale of the dinghy adventure was filmed at Chandler Falls.

Farther north, almost impassable rut trails, into tsetse fly area, terrain modulated from an oasis to black lava rock to rising bluffs to flat barren plains. Some of it looked like the land that God forgot. We had to walk about two miles and then wind our way down a precipitous cliff. The equipment had to be lowered by pulleys. But what a panorama awaited us! Breathtaking Chandler Falls in the background, rugged mountains, the tranquil runoff from the distant falls. Here was where I supposedly landed, dazed and flopping in the water, and as the crocs moved in, Vic rescues me. Our trusty white hunters had been there hours before us, firing into the shallow river to scare away the crocodiles. (They didn't tell us then that they had actually shot one.) I noticed that the Africans holding the reflectors in the water kept jumping. "Nothing to worry about, Janet, just little fish that nip." And seeing my look, "No, not piranha!"

Ready to roll! "Okay, Janet, go out in midstream, submerge, stumble around, almost unconscious, you know what you've experienced." Did I ever! In I went. "And Vic, I'll give the cue when you bang away at the crocs, second unit will show that angle, rush in, pick up Janet, and carry her to shore. Everybody ready?"

Vic shook his head. "I'm not going in there."

"Why not? It's safe. Several rounds of ammunition have been pumped in there."

Vic said, "So what? What if one of those S.O.B.s is hard of hearing?" Everyone doubled up. And then I thought, could that be? And then I got out of there! The white hunters and Africans thrashed and churned the waters to placate us. Finally, we were convinced and did the scene.

Jacob, our personal shepherd, awoke us every morning with breakfast, and because he had mastered a smattering of English, served as our local newspaper. One early dawn he had much to report. The strongbox of money had been stolen from Max's tent. Footprints, bare feet, were found on the outside. It was none of our people. We supposed that a renegade had slithered into camp. The Kenya police were conducting a search. Mr. Max was fortunate he didn't hear the intruder—or—and Jacob indicated the fate with a finger across his throat.

Two nights later, I had one of the harsher bouts with my bug. I dozed on and off; the cramps were awful, but I was scared to venture into the inky darkness and howling wind. When I thought I heard Mom stirring, I asked if she were awake. "Keep quiet," she hissed.

"Why?" I whispered.

"Someone crept around the flap, into the tent, flashed a light on the dresser. You moaned and groaned and he ran."

"*What?*" I screamed, lashing out and knocking over the lamp, which started to burn. Now we were both shouting hysterically and the whole place was aroused. Poor Mom was petrified, positive we were going to be murdered in our beds. I was not exactly intrepid. Everyone came on the double, extinguished the blaze, attempted to calm us, and discovered more footprints, similiar to those made by Max's visitor.

Vic brought his mattress, threw it between our cots, and slept there for the remainder of the night. Two white hunters positioned themselves by the flap exterior. From then on, a hunter stayed every evening, and Kikuyu guards roamed the circumference, brandishing Arabian scimitars. Anyone who had to go to the latrine carried a lamp for identification, otherwise those men were trained to strike first and *then* ask questions. Mom and I had to be flattered. Evidently the hunters argued for the privilege of protecting us, and finally settled by alternating. They were a rare and wonderful breed. We adored them all.

A last *Perils of Pauline* tale. Andy and Max commuted to Nairobi in a small bush plane a few times a week. That is how we sent and received mail. Correspondence meant so much out there. Overseas telephone calls had to be radio-booked from camp and took place the next day at the Mawingo Hotel in Nanyuki. I managed to call Tony about four times on my off days. We were so lonely and missed each other unendurably. Our conversations were fraught with anxiety and filled with yearning. I hurt with desire to leave. Soon, soon.

Mom and I always shopped for the crew on these trips. The little niceties of life: toothpaste, shaving cream, clothespins, shorts, all those exotic items. By the time we made our purchases in every small store, the entire population would be following us. Arabs and Africans both, wanting autographs. It seemed so strange, that even in Africa . . .

On this one long ride back, about dusk, we were relishing the array of colors of the sunset, when *pow,* a tire blew. Where it chose to blow was smack at Ambush Alley, so named because it was at the bottom of a steep incline where a U-turn led the road to an upward climb, forcing vehicles to drive slowly; with the thick forest providing concealment, it was the ideal setting to waylay an enemy. It had been utilized by the Mau Mau numerous times since 1952. Ivor, our white hunter, was not happy, to say the least, but we couldn't just sit there. He handed his rifle to Mom, explained how to use the thing, and set her at the rear of the car. I was given his pistol, with instructions, and stood at the front. He cautioned, "Any movement at all, any wiggling in the leaves, shoot—*do not hesitate.*" And he proceeded to fix the tire. Surprisingly, we were relatively composed. Our eyes darted in every direction, guns were cocked, our fingers on the triggers, ready. I don't know what device served Mom, but I pretended this was a scene, and my imaginary character could handle this emergency with aplomb. Darkness was almost upon us when Ivor called, "I'm done. Get in!" And we took off as if we were in the Indianapolis 500. He was proud of his trainees and made us Honorary White Huntresses.

Just before we reached the barrier, truckloads of armed police met us. We were past curfew and the alarm had gone out. The company was in an uproar, the white hunters and other unit members were close behind the police in jeeps and Land-Rovers to aid in the search; it all looked like an army poised for battle. But there was relief in their faces, and Mom and I were passed around for hugs and squeezes of jubilance.

I don't mean to leave the impression that this location had only trials and tribulations. There were scores of pleasant memories. The absolute basicness of a country such as Africa left vivid imprints on our minds and hearts. The sharing of these experiences created relationships. We had gatherings each twilight at assorted tents with lively conversations in which we often explored subjects suggested by our unique surroundings. We were invited into the native quarters and marveled at the frenetic gyrations of their dancers and the provocative rhythms of their drums. We had a collection of souvenirs—local paintings, carved wood replicas of the existing tribes, three of those sexy drums—all cemented these unforgettable moments.

As eager as I was to depart (and I was eager), the goodbyes were sad. We gave Jacob and Hassan, our driver, the safari equipment. (They had to have documents proving these were gifts, not stolen property.) The white hunters were especially hard to bid farewell. They really had opened their arms to us in friendship.

From Nairobi, to Entebbe, Uganda, to Khartoum, Sudan, to Cairo, Egypt, to Nice, France, to Paris, France—and twenty-seven-and-a-half hours to the waiting arms of Tony. This was a Wednesday, and I didn't have to work until Monday. We couldn't stop talking or holding. There was so much to tell. The doorman at the George V presented us each with a rose. Then the elevator operator. Then the maid. And the apartment was filled with treasures: flowers, perfume, candy, etc.—but the real treasure was close, close, close to me.

The next day, as I was trying to function and sort things out, Tony called from the lobby (I still couldn't accept that he was so near) and told me to come right down. There, in the midst of a crowd, was a bright red Messerschmitt, one of those three-wheel two-seater cars that had the appearance of a resting insect. It was cute, made me giggle. Another coming-home present. But I had a sneaking suspicion someone else I knew would really be playing with the new toy.

Tony had some John Levee paintings on approval. John was a Los Angeles boy, brother of the successful agent Michael Levee, who had moved to Paris to study art. He was gaining a fine reputation, and he and his French wife, Jeanette, had become good friends of ours.

They injected us with an additional transfusion of art appreciation, and opened a door to aspiring artists: Oscar Chelimsky, another American, as yet obscure, and Karel Appel, a Dutch painter who had won a Guggenheim Award. We purchased one of his pieces when we visited his studio.*

Jeanette and John showed us where to buy the best gouaches and lithographs, how to look for the painter's authentic, not reproduced, signature, and how to evaluate the numbers of editions. We

---

* In 1960 he came to the United States and Tony commissioned him to do a canvas for one of our walls, about twenty feet by fifteen feet, depicting his impression of his drive from New York to California. It made an unencumbered bold statement of the divergence of our land.

owned now a Picasso, a Chagall, a Roualt, a Matisse, a Marini, a Braque. An original of any of these masters was astronomically priced, then completely unattainable. (In a few years, we were the proud possessors of some of the real creations.) But this way we could enjoy genius for a sum within our means. Investment was not our purpose; however, their value did increase about one hundred times eventually.

Irving Allen, Cubby's associate, called from London to alert me of a situation, certain the press would be calling for a reaction. They did. Vic had landed in London in his cutoff safari shorts, carrying his native drum, and had escaped on a New York-bound plane, off on a spree.

These were heady days. *Trapeze* was filming at Billancourt Studios, ten minutes from the hotel, and Tony would come back in between shots, or I would be there. The luxury of reaching out and knowing we could touch each other!

Edie and Lew, Joy and Edd Henry (of MCA) were in town. Terrence came for the weekend. Lunch at Berkeleys was similar to Romanoff's in Beverly Hills, with Darryl Zanuck, Gregory Ratoff, the Ali Khans, Bob Cohn, Alain Bernheim, and Donald O'Connor in attendance.

Of course it had to end, and once again, we were apart. But now we could see the light at the end of the tunnel. Vic had come back, reported on the set Monday, as scheduled. And in two weeks *Safari* was finished. Mom went home by ship, another adventure for her. Fortunately I was able to get her a booking on the same sailing as Vic, so she had a familiar face around. She told me afterward he had been absolutely marvelous to her, treated her like a sister. I knew she had had a good trip and hoped the home front with my father would reap the benefits.

October 21, 1955. I was now "Sadie, Sadie, married lady" in our new apartment at the Elysie Park Hotel, 2 Rue Jean Mermoz, a block off the Champs Élysées, between Fouquet and the Arc de Triomphe. Cozier, still roomy, quieter, and less expensive.

Life was a whirl of activity. Shopping, sight-seeing (always more to examine in Paris), always publicity to do too, socializing. On November 16 I went to see a Dr. Lipsitch at the American Hospital. On November 18 I had thrilling news for Tony. I was pregnant.

We hoped to keep it a secret until we were home, but in just a few days Sir Carol congratulated Tony on the set. At Tony's startled look, he said, "You really didn't think you could keep this confidential, did you, dear boy?" I must have had the most gossipy rabbit in France. We called the families immediately, and cables began arriving. Rosie (Clooney Ferrer) to me, "Copycat." She was with child too. Joe to Tony, "You can borrow my maternity wardrobe." Jackie and Jerry Gershwin, "We have the name picked already!" And they did, too.

Now that I had been given this second chance, I made a covenant with myself. No filming, no overdoing, lots of rest, and restoring of health. I was considerably run-down and debilitated, from the bug that wanted free transportation from Africa, and from all the work and travel. From this moment on . . .

Tony nonchalantly slipped in some additional tidings. He had ordered a gull-wing Mercedes, 300 SL model, metallic gray with red leather. We would drive to Italy and leave by ship for home. At the rate we were buying we would need a boat just for us and our belongings. I wasn't as joyful about his news. I was concerned about finances, if we could afford all this. Why did I have to be so damn realistic? Why couldn't I relax and just "let the chips fall"? I spoiled his fun a little, I think, but I tried to rally and pass it off. "Blame it on my 'condition'," I countered.

Thanksgiving, November 24, 1955. Tony had to shoot, no holiday in France. I went to the army base near Versailles to entertain the boys. The Commander had been very kind to us, making the PX accessible for supplies, and this served as a small thank you. Earle and Norman Krasna (writer and producer) threw a Thanksgiving bash at Fabien's Restaurant for stranded Americans, and what a wingding it was. We spent the majority of time with the Krasnas, Julie and John Forsythe, dear Mike Mindlin (who then was in charge of P.R. for *Trapeze,* and who now is a producer), Pokey and Tommy Noonan, Norma and Burt Lancaster; but there were many others to toast and give thanks too: Olivia De Havilland, Adolphe Menjou, Edward Arnold, Marion and Francis Lederer, among others.

The last shot was done, the last line dubbed, the last still taken. The skyscraper of cartons and trunks and the Messerschmitt had been dispatched to Genoa. And on November 30, with two suit-cases, maps, and dictionaries, Tony and I migrated toward Italy in our spacemobile. The deeper our penetration into the feudal coun-tryside, the wilder the reaction to the car. Children pointed and screamed and jumped up and down. We must have looked as if we came from Mars as we sped along the quaint, narrow streets.

Around Orange we started seeing Roman ruins—hilltop forts—part of a dado. Avignon, called City of the Popes, had the old wall around the nucleus of the city. And the massive austere Palace of the Pope, with prayers and organ music coming from the interior via loudspeakers, seemed like a hidden voice of some big monster booming out at you. Aix-en-Provence boasted statuesque fountains. Even in the off-season, Cannes and Nice, the entire French Riviera, were beautiful: the highway carved out of the mountains, following the frolicsome blue and green Mediterranean; cities tucked in lay-ers from the cliffs to the sea.

We crossed the border into Italy just before San Remo. The first words were, "Ah, Jawnet Lee–egg–a and Too–ne Coor–tis!" Our new names.

Italy appeared less affluent, but warmer and happier. It took over an hour to drive through the large, industrial Genoa. At Sestri, the road left the coast for the mountains. The fog in the valleys looked like cotton candy stuck on the trees. La Spezia returned us to the coastline and then to Pisa. And there almost stood the Leaning Tower, in the middle of the Piazza dei Miracoli (Square of Mira-cles).

There was a freeway to the old city of Florence, and then on to Rome. Remnants of the war were still in evidence. Many of the inevitable ancient stone houses were half demolished. Machine-gun holes defiantly glared at us, daring us to ignore or forget. Ostensi-bly, the people must have come back after the fighting and settled in any place, or part of a place, left standing and with alacrity pur-sued their main priority, cultivating and farming the land, for the fields were fruitful and luscious.

The Hassler Hotel, atop the famous Spanish Steps (I recognized them immediately from *Roman Holiday),* welcomed two weary trav-elers. Two angry, weary travelers. Tony was feeling lousy, sympa-thy symptoms maybe, because I was punk too. Add fatigue, and you come up with one hell of an argument. What a battle! I was gradu-

ally developing an intense dislike for that automobile. Flashy and
streamlined, yes! Fast, yes! One of the problems was that it made
me nervous; it reminded me of an out-of-control stallion. Comfortable, no! Too difficult to navigate entering and exiting. I wasn't big
and cumbersome yet, but if it bothered me now, it could only get
worse with time. Probably the expense factor lurked in my subcon-
scious too. But Tony was not to be swayed—that was *his* baby. We
had had quarrels before—tons—but this was a lulu.

Sleep, a healthier attitude, and Rome evaporated the tension by
the next day. We absorbed as much Roman history and culture as
we could in our four days, until we were dizzy with our minds'
conjectures at what the city had been like so long ago.

One whole day was devoted to driving along the Appian Way to
the villa owned by Gina (Lollobrigida) and Milko. The mansion
was grandly, yet tastefully, appointed, but the grounds were spectacular. We explored the entire premises. If a property adjoined the
Appian Way, you are not permitted to build closer than eight hundred feet, so the view remained constant. They had tombs and urn
altars in residence. Often when they dug to plant a tree or whatever, they would find bones, or earrings, or playthings, or utensils.
The unexpected discoveries were kept very hush-hush, for if the
government verified these plums, the spot would immediately become a national museum. With my thirst for history I was a kid in a
candy store. All this in your own backyard!

Naturally there was more shopping (add another new suitcase),
and the *paparazzi* trailed us everywhere. Abbe Lane and Xavier
Cugat, via United Artists, hosted a shoulder-to-shoulder cocktail
reception for us that turned out to be one of the most enjoyable of
that kind of event I have ever experienced.

"D" Day was fast approaching. We backtracked to Genoa, having driven over fifteen hundred miles on the trip. It took a day to
wade through the endless clerical chores pertaining to our quantity
of cargo, particularly the two cars and painting crates. But at long
last, on December 11, we boarded the relatively new ocean liner
Cristoforo Colombo and we were on our way home. There was a brief
stop in Cannes, and the next day we docked at Naples for six hours,
with ample time to tour the city and drive to Pompeii.

In A.D. 79, Mount Vesuvius erupted and lava buried the city of
Pompeii. Not much attention was given to the sporadic finds until

1748. Gradually then, the archaeologists had uncovered and re-stored a large percentage of the original town, enabling visitors such as we, to see how it was two thousand years ago, to walk in and out of houses and up and down narrow lanes, just as the Pompeians did, see the ancient public square, temples, pillars, stat-ues, markets, and baths, see the jars, plates, ovens, and hearths. In a wealthy estate, there was a room called the "love room," where a wall mural illustrated different positions assumed during copula-tion. One picture graphically showed a man's organ being weighed, to prove he was "worth his weight in gold." Very enlightening!

Back on board ship, watching the preparations for departure, we witnessed a moving scene. About seven hundred tourist-class pas-sengers had boarded. We learned that this number filled the quota for the States for a period of time, and the farewells we saw were heartbreaking. Families evidently were being separated, and the air was heavy with sobbing and hysterics. One poor girl looked as if she would throw herself off the pier. The contradiction of attitude was so vivid—their misery about embarking, and our joy.

On Wednesday we docked outside the Rock of Gibraltar to load a few travelers, went through the Straits of Gibraltar, and left the Mediterranean for the Atlantic Ocean. Big mistake! The calm, the appetizing cuisine, the insouciant days came to an abrupt end, and the pitching and rolling and gales began. A storm battered us with wretched constancy until Monday afternoon. No gala evenings, only Rice Krispies and crackers and crossword puzzles in our cabin. A notice circulated we might be a day late arriving in New York because of the weather. Several times we had thought the ship would splinter, so we felt grateful hearing we would arrive at *all.* But the turbulence waned somewhat, a little of the lost time was made up, and we did dock in New York on Tuesday, December 20. Two patriotic, flag-waving, glad-to-be-home Americans greeted and embraced and kissed the bevy of waiting friends. In the excitement, I took the news that our house had been robbed as if someone had told me I dropped my hankie. Who cared? We were home!

The last entry in my diary, Friday, December 23, 1955, written on the train the night before Los Angeles:

Such a mixture of emotions I am experiencing now. When I look back and think of the many different kinds of days I wrote about

—and the various places I was in when I wrote—and the state of
mind I was in when I wrote—I realize what a full five months it
had been! No wonder I feel like crying and laughing and screaming all at once. Tomorrow will be a day I shall never forget—and
a Christmas that has given me the best presents I could ever
receive—home, our families, our friends, five months of being
exposed to continuous education and culture and growth as an
individual, *and* the miracle of expectant motherhood. How does
one say how full one's heart is? I can only hope when I read this
over in the years to come I will be allowed to experience again
this delicious excitement that is all over me now.

I've been forced to learn many things on this trip—some historical, some material, some geographical—but the most important lesson has been our added knowledge of each other and life
—and I hope we never lose the little progress we've made—I
hope it's been a stepping-stone to more and more understanding
of what makes us—us—and someone else—someone else—! After a quiet day we went to bed very early—hoping that would
make tomorrow come sooner—that wonderful glorious happy—
tomorrow!

Strange, isn't it, how little has changed in my outlook and values.
People, circumstances, surroundings have been altered. But the difference really is that a lot of tomorrows have come, and gone.

CHAPTER FIFTEEN

Early in 1956, we followed a pattern set by innumerable prospective parents before us: We bought a house: 1152 San Ysidro Drive, Beverly Hills. It was a charming French country house, completely enclosed by a low stone wall, with a nice-sized yard, a pool, guest cottage, conventional living room, dining room, paneled den, new kitchen, maid's room, large master bedroom, a study for Tony, and a nursery with an added workroom completed the upstairs. And how very *empty* it all was. Furnishings came slowly, just bare basics in the beginning. Actually, we never did decorate the living room or dining room, but that didn't matter. It was wonderful. It would be ready six weeks before my due date, July 1, and it was our home. Well, I guess it really belonged to the bank. Back in the old debt trap again; it didn't seem to bother anyone but me.

At least Tony was working. He started *The Rawhide Years* with Arthur Kennedy. We each signed for a television show, mine to be filmed after the baby. These were packaged by MCA and provided us with the redone kitchen. Around March I appeared on Rosie's (Clooney) TV show, and that furnished the nursery. A simple duet and some dialogue, nothing strenuous. The director had the toughest task, shooting in a way to camouflage both our jutting tummies. Despite the easiness of the performance, the mild backache that had plagued me worsened and progressed to the lower front right. By the end of the day I could hardly stand. Dr. Pearl prescribed some pills for relief and subdued my surging fear by her belief this was not a preliminary sign of aborting. Please, please, please not again!

The pain did not subside; on the contrary, it became excruciating. Dr. Pearl thought it might be a kidney infection and called in a

specialist. Dr. Schlumberger took one look at my agony and ordered an ambulance for St. John's Hospital. The growing fetus had
pushed the kidney against the pelvis, causing the pressure. I don't
know all the steps that were taken to alleviate the condition. I was
in the haze of torment. I do know it was four days of hell. But even
hell can go down in defeat, in flames, so to speak. For I didn't lose
our baby, and the misery did fade. When the fog finally lifted, I saw
poor Tony. He was a basket case.

For the duration I had to lie down with my legs elevated several
times a day to keep things in place. This curtailed moving operations, but my volunteer elves took commands well.

Charitable organizations had previously entered my sphere in my
early Hollywood life. The Civitan Club of Monrovia had adopted
Le Roy Boys' Home as a pet project. In 1947 I attended the Christmas party given for the seventy or so "lost" children and became
Aunt Janet to the boys for many years; Arthur Loew and I organized a benefit at one point and raised a few thousand dollars. Lydia
Lane, who wrote a beauty column, visited the Long Beach Hospital
every week, and I became a regular companion. First Arthur, and
then Tony and I enlisted the aid of our friends and presented several shows at the George Air Force Base in Victorville. Along the
way I've been associated with Cedars-Sinai Women's Guild, the
Crippled Children's Society, the Kidney Foundation, City of Hope,
Care, Seeing Eyes for the Blind, Deaf Ski Team, and the Multiple
Sclerosis Foundation. There are so many who need assistance, so
many worthwhile causes that need funding. If my good fortune of
my being a celebrity could and can help focus those needs, just ask
and you've got it.

It was that April, 1956, that SHARE surfaced for me. Seven
ladies—Mrs. Dean Martin (Jeanne), Mrs. Jeff Chandler (Marge),
Mrs. Sammy Cahn (Gloria), Mrs. Gene Nelson (Miriam), Mrs.
Gordon MacRae (Sheila), Mrs. Bill Orr (Joy), and Mrs. Robert
Blythe—decided in 1953 they wanted to become active in community affairs, to do more with their lives. In the words of Leo Rosten,
"The purpose of life is not to be happy. The purpose of life is to
matter, to be productive, to have it make some difference that you
live at all." They went to the city's social service office for information, seeking an area of acute need, where their efforts could best
serve. ECF (Exceptional Children's Foundation), servicing the men-

tally retarded, was recommended, and the alliance was formed. The first goal was a guidance center. The official name became SHARE, Inc. (Share Happily And Reap Endlessly). The motto: all volunteers, no paid employees—and beg, borrow, or steal to keep expenses at a minimum. Tony and I had been at the first "Boomtown" party at Ciro's. It had a western theme, chicken in a basket, and a performance by Jerry and Dean. Twelve girls (the membership immediately swelled to twenty-five) swayed in back of a picket fence singing special lyrics by Sammy Cahn. The profit was $5,036.27, and the group was hatched. (On the recent thirtieth anniversary of SHARE, our ranks stood at eighty-six, and the evening's net was over $500,000. But it is still—beg, borrow, or steal—!)

Jeanne Martin invited me to a recruiting meeting. My closest friend, Jackie Gershwin, brought me. I needed moral support. Because I had worked most of my adult life, and consequently not had the time for many daytime social affairs, I was uncomfortable with "ladies' luncheons." I was not sure if I would fit in, or even if I was inclined to. My consternation was unnecessary. There was the usual chitchat, of course, but these women had business on their minds and determination in their voices. A short film on mental retardation was shown. Every mother-to-be sends up a constant prayer— Oh please, dear God, let my baby be—all right—! I could feel the life stirring in my womb, and I was looking at some families who had been chosen for whatever unknown reason to carry a burden. I wanted to reach out with long arms and gather them to my bosom and comfort them. Is prevention possible? Are they receiving enough clinical and emotional council? Questions, questions. Mental retardation was a grossly overlooked field, widely misunderstood. Obviously qualified trained personnel were needed to do research and administer the treatment. My job, our job—because there was no doubt whatsoever that I was now committed to this crusade—was to provide the required capital.*

---

* Since then I have danced and sung in the chorus line, learned to play the banjo, swung on a trapeze, twirled a rope, anything and everything for SHARE! The presentations have become progressively more sophisticated and our contributions to ECF have coincidently increased. Most of the major stars of Hollywood have been lured, or badgered, into appearing for us. High-powered individuals and companies have been approached and wheedled into underwriting costs. Spouses have had no

I couldn't participate in the show that May. All of the sixteen gained pounds resided in my blimpy front. I could only manage to blow up the decorating balloons and man the cigarette table. I was ecstatic when a guest gave fifty dollars for a package just because I was selling.

Edie and Lew gave Rosie and me a novel baby shower. Novel because it was actually a dinner, a party with men included, not a "girly-girly" function. Our future heir or heiress was supplied with every conceivable essential and nonessential item. What fun it was to fold each wee garment and place it carefully in the big drawers, to read the instructions for each mysterious piece of equipment, to wonder how such a little person had need for all of this—stuff. I found out sooner than expected.

Early in the morning of June 17, 1956—Father's Day—pains roused me. I said to myself, "But it's not time—whoops—maybe it is time. No regular intervals yet. Might be a false alarm; better pack —whoops—my things just in case. What if the nurse isn't free— whoops—this early. Thank gosh we hired the couple. I think my whoops are not going to stop."

I gently awakened Tony and called Dr. Pearl, and we were soon en route to St. John's. It's true what has been said about "labor."— that the mother doesn't remember any of the pain afterward. The kidney pain could be vividly recalled, but I have no memory of the twelve hours and sixteen minutes of labor, only that at 2:14 P.M. it produced a healthy beautiful girl, six pounds six and a half ounces, eighteen and three-quarter inches long. Named Kelly Lee Curtis by her godparents, Jackie and Jerry Gershwin.

Could anyone be as tiny as the bundle handed to me? I was afraid I would break her. How could she breathe through that nose? How could those hands clasp my finger so strongly? How perfect was every detail, the fair skin, reddish blond hair, huge blue eyes—she even had finger nails and toe nails and cuticle and eyebrows and lashes—There aren't words yet invented to define the emotion a mother feels as she cuddles her newborn child. It defies description.

choice but to donate their particular talent. "Death or divorce" is the sole escape for a husband of a SHARE girl!

Because it is spiritual, ethereal, beyond humanity. Nothing earthly could compare.

The father, on the other hand, clearly recollects the labor spell. The obligatory waiting. The nurse, impersonal as a customs officer, doling out the progress report. The worry, the anticipation, the frustration of exclusion, but Tony had company during his ordeal: both sets of our parents, Rosie and Joe, Jackie and Jerry, Edie and Lew, and Ronnie and Warren (Cowan). When Dr. Pearl announced the news, great cheers went up. We would have been thrilled with either sex, but we had both hoped for a girl.

The days at the hospital were a blur of the baby, Tony, the baby, visitors, the baby—deliveries. Over one hundred wires and floral arrangements arrived and over one hundred and fifty gifts.

Home! And Kelly made three. And Kelly's nurse made four. And couple made six. And callers made—? The parade was halted for a while. I developed a headache as a result of the caudal block. Some fluid escaped because I hadn't kept prone for a long enough period. So for a week I really had to behave. In our state of euphoria we could not be daunted—so a week, so a headache, so what?

The first nurse's day off! Alone, by myself, I was accountable for that delicacy lying in the yellow dotted-swiss frilly bassinet, for feeding, bathing, diaper changing, comforting. This was my challenge of a lifetime. She sensed the hesitation and reacted with her own brand of uncertainty. By day's end we were both irritated, and I was ready to negotiate a truce. "I promise not to treat you like an eggshell if you promise not to treat me like the enemy. Okay?" The loose head bobbled and I took that as agreement. Sealed the deal with a kiss, and then our collaboration functioned smoothly.

There were constant important revelations during the following months. "Look! She raised her legs! Isn't that remarkable!"—"She's positively brilliant! Just said 'Ah goo'!"—"Really quite gifted—see how she keeps time with the music!" She was photographed from every angle. Tony singlehandedly, supplied all business for the camera shop. No baby could have had so many pictures taken, unless of course, it was our next baby.

Somewhere and somehow in here, MCA negotiated a nonexclusive contract for Tony with Universal, and we formed CurtLeigh Productions. Henceforth our business affairs would be merged, under the guidance of managers Guy and Dick Gadbois. I was in the awkward position of explaining the situation to my Dad. I worried that Daddy might think I was deserting the family ship. But I recognized the prudence of establishing our own unit, and logically knew Daddy was not equipped to officiate in this specialized environment. Why does everything have to be so difficult? Even when one is being reasonable? Daddy's business did not solely depend on me, but I still felt culpable, and I fretted that maybe this could be unsettling for an already precarious situation between Mom and Dad. I wanted so much to be all things to all my loves, and I was confronted with the probability that I wasn't capable.

In five years I would live forevermore with an unanswered question. Was this afternoon the beginning of an end? Or was the destined seed germinated long before?

Early 1957 found us in New York, with Kelly and nurse, in Edie and Lew's SherryNetherland apartment. United Artists, Norma, Curtleigh, and James Hill co-ventured a wonderful picture, *The Sweet Smell of Success,* starring Burt Lancaster, Tony, Martin Milner, Sam Levine, Susan Harrison, Barbara Nichols, and Emile Meyer. As the crooked press agent to Burt's megalomaniac columnist, Tony took a giant step forward in credibility in the eyes of the industry. He had just completed Blake Edwards's, *Mr. Cory,* a comedy drama, which further displayed his versatility. MCA was laying the foundation for a solid house, brick by brick, carefully teaming Tony with major talents, so that the burden was not entirely on him. Yet he was always in a role where his contribution was definitive. This was a synchronized, well-planned, well-executed architectural design, but it could only be effective if the subject had the basic ability, plus that elusive quality, appeal. Tony had both.

My maiden work detail was the already committed Revue TV Show "Carriage from Britain." I was eager to flex my muscles again after sixteen months, and on the other hand, I didn't want to miss one new development of my eight-month-old wonder. She was crawling all over and making funny sounds and was just delectable. But I also didn't want to place a liability on her unsuspecting shoulders. I knew it was important for our future together that I maintain my status as an individual, or how could I respect her individuality? That I pursue my interests, or how could I be interesting to her?

Free with her? Moderation was the key. And interpreted priority. I reiterated my stand of equitable balance. Formerly: 1. Career. Then: 1. Husband 2. Career. Now: 1. Children 2. Husband 3. Career.

Tony and I returned from dinner one evening in March. There was a telegram waiting for me. "Delighted you are in our picture. Looking forward to seeing you. Regards, Orson Welles."

Orson Welles? What picture? I couldn't wait until morning, so I called Edd Henry, my agent, at home. "He wasn't supposed to contact you. We don't have the finished script. This might be the first film on your Universal contract."

"I don't care about a completed script. I would like to work with Orson."

Edd sighed, "That's just what Charlton Heston said." The shell of a text arrived the next day. The novel titled *Badge of Evil* was now to be a movie, *Touch of Evil*. Orson was in the process of writing and hoped to rehearse with us soon. I only had two more days on "Carriage," so soon was good for me.

The day before the end of the film, I did a skirmish scene with Jesse White, who played a would-be robber. Doubles did the actual tussle, but in one of the close-ups, I was draped around his neck like a fur stole, pummeling his body with my fists, and while waltzing around, he stumbled. I landed across a short step and his full weight landed on top of me. Jesse was crestfallen, sweet man. No need, it wasn't his fault. The initial concern was directed toward my head, for I was stunned. Then that cleared and the attention shifted to my limbs. I couldn't move my left arm without pain. Remember a long time ago I mentioned I was a klutz? X rays showed I had broken the ulna bone.

Now what to do? Dr. Leventhal said he could wait a day before setting, providing I didn't jiggle it. So I sat upright all night and finished the few remaining restaged shots the next day. One problem solved. Now what about *Touch of Evil?* I asked the doctor to set it at a 135-degree angle, much less conspicuous than the usual 90-degree set. I carried a jacket over my arm, had a shoulder-strap bag hanging, and went to Orson's office. "I thought you hurt your arm!"

"I did," I said, unravelling my disguise.

"No problem! We can mask that easily. When I first heard of

your accident, my inclination was to have your character actually wear a sling. But then I thought, a girl on her honeymoon? The connotation was even too bizarre for me!" So I did the entire movie with a broken arm, and no one knew. During the motel sequence and less clothed scenes, Dr. Leventhal sawed the cast in half lengthwise. We would take it off, do the shot, and strap it back on.

We do take our bodies for granted. Who ever gives an arm much thought, unless you don't have the use of it. Routine procedures became complex—dressing, fixing hair. The most bothersome aspect of it for me was that it limited my ability to care for Kelly. Grandma helped a lot, and Aunt Pope, and we coped.

Orson, Chuck Heston, Akim Tamiroff, Joseph Calleia, and I were involved in the prerehearsals. Chuck and I were the new disciples and were absolutely fascinated. I was the court stenographer, without the skills of shorthand and typing. We would discuss the scene, explore where we wanted it to take us, improvise (each playing two characters if necessary). Then, feverishly, I would scribble down what we had done and give it to the real secretary. A lot of what we accomplished was used in the filming. Just as much was discarded. If a particular background intrigued Orson, he would alter his plan to take advantage of the virgin locale. He was always ready to extemporize.

He was a clever one! Universal's production heads were leery of his wild reputation. Adherence to the schedule was uppermost in their thoughts, and they buzzed around him like worried bees. The opening day's shooting took place in the accused's small apartment. It was a complicated piece, with streams of milling police and reporters, Orson and Chuck parrying, significant dialogue, and intricate points to be made. The production department had allowed four days. Orson brilliantly engineered the whole sequence in *one* day. He wove his camera through the crowded rooms, zeroed in for a telling close-up, sauntered through the atmosphere, paused for an over-the-shoulder. Dazzling! And he had the apoplectic drones eating out of his hand. "He has changed, he can conform. We've got him on the right track now."

We were to do five nights on location in Venice—California, not Italy—and the old, run-down Venice—not the renovated version. We spent the greater part of the movie in that vicinity, at night.

Orson was in control; he had lulled the brass into a false sense of security.

The actual opening shot of the picture took a full night, but covered five pages of script. The pink dawn was nearly upon us when the printed take was completed. It was done in one continuous shot and was a classic. The camera faded in on a time bomb, a shadowy figure installing the mechanism in a car, picked up a man and a blonde exiting a honky-tonk cafe and driving off in the doomed car, followed the auto toward the border of Mexico and Texas, included Chuck and me approaching the checkpoint, waited through our exchanges with the official and the passing through of the drunken, gabardine-garbed man and his sexpot bimbo, lingered while we kissed, and zoomed to the convertible and the explosion in the distance. The technical prowess needed for this was beyond my comprehension: the constantly changing and dual focus, the elaborate tracking system, the whisking of lights in and out, the sound, the timing, and the special effects. Obviously if any component went awry before the end, we cut, because there could be only one blast. This concept, this teamwork, deserved to be commemorated. I can't unequivocally say that two cameras were not employed. Maybe for insurance, but I do not think so. Another angle would have allowed someone else to slice the shot at a later date. Orson was too smart to offer that opportunity.

Orson called upon his friends to do capsule appearances *not* in the script. I think, for him, rules were made to be broken. Perhaps he didn't verbalize this view. Perhaps the creative urges, the juices, just wouldn't let him accept the ordinary, the usual. Like young painters straining to break the mold, perhaps he automatically mutinied against a limit. However he arrived at his choices, we, the audience, were the richer.

Marlene Dietrich appeared as a madame, a confidant of Orson's detective. He fell in love with a dilapidated house in a part of Venice and invented a reason to have it in his picture. It became Marlene's brothel.

A decaying hotel caught his eye and that was where I screamed for help from the balcony. The A.D. had to stay with me because the room, if it could be called that, was occupied by the saddest broken specimen of a man I'd ever seen. There were so many irreclaimables within those walls.

Dennis Weaver was luminous as the caretaker of the isolated motel where I was abducted. And Mercedes McCambridge, in a cameo role as the leader of the gang who attacked me, chilled my bones when she uttered that one line, "I want to watch."

Joseph Cotten and Keenan Wynn were part of his stock company. We never knew for sure who might turn up at night or where we might be shooting. Chuck and I were mesmerized.

Not so the studio, however. I guess they felt they had been "had." At the conclusion of the picture, after Orson finished his contractual "first cut," they came to us for retakes. They did not understand all of the detours and believed the flow was disjointed. To some extent their argument had validity, but to tamper with the content meant to devitalize what was Orson. As much as we contested, we were compelled to acquiesce because of the Screen Actors Guild code. So we did some "linking, explanatory, dull" shots. I don't even remember what they were. The release of *Touch of Evil* was disappointing. But it warms the cockles of my heart to at least know that it now is considered a cult classic and honors Orson Welles.

Tony tired of the 300 SL Gullwing and traded it for a more conventional white Mercedes. About the same time we acquired a white handful of fur, a toy poodle, so we named her Mercedes, which became Mercy. Houdina now belonged to Momeleh and Papeleh. They dog-sat during our five-month hiatus and we couldn't take her away. Kelly and Mercy had great times together. Mercy was the only living creature in her world smaller than Kelly, who enjoyed her superiority.

It was such a special privilege to observe the blossoming of our child, to praise and see her pride in each new achievement, and to ease her through the disgruntlement of learning the "no no's." The process of growing up is hard, for everyone. Some of us never do grow up.

Tony's brother, Bobby, was showing increasing signs of disturbance, and Tony had placed him in therapy. Momeleh and Papeleh couldn't cope with his erratic personality. We didn't know if his problem was physical or psychological or both. Tony too had begun analysis. The strife of the early days had left scars and fears and questions, and he sought the solace of psychic probing. I wasn't completely convinced of the need, but I supported any effort to strengthen his sense of well-being.

CHAPTER SIXTEEN

May 14, 1957. Gulliver had nothing on us; the Curtis clan was off again. This time with an entourage of Kelly and nurse Ethel. Taking the baby, and then babies, was an essential of my 1, 2, 3 formula. I wouldn't go unless we all went. I'm talking of major trips, not a week here and there. And this was a major trip.

United Artists and Kirk Douglas Productions had signed the two of us for *The Vikings,* starring Kirk Douglas, Tony, Ernest Borgnine, me, Frank Thring, James Donald, Maxine Audley, and Eileen Way; produced by Jerry Bresler; directed by Richard Fleischer; and photographed by Jack Cardiff. Coincidentally, the narration was done by Orson Welles. The itinerary sounded as if someone were "country dropping": England, Denmark, Sweden, Norway, France, and Germany. This was an ambitious undertaking. As a Dane, I had the distinction of being the only true Viking in the cast, and inappropriately, I portrayed an English princess.

Forty pieces of luggage were dispersed to various destinations, some with Tony on the train, some with Kelly, Ethel, and me on the plane, and some directly to the *Île de France.* There was always an "absolute" when we traveled: lots of people and press. P & P when we left, P & P when we arrived, and P & P in between. I don't offer this as a complaint, just a fact. On the contrary, it would have been impossible to address the myriad of details without their aid. But it is fortunate I was, and am, a "people person." A loner would have never survived the constant crush.

Kelly captivated every one of these P & P's, and proved to be a good globe-trotter. The time changes disrupted her schedule somewhat, but we adjusted as we went along. At the SherryNetherland in New York, during a press party, she opened her arms to the editor of *Parents Magazine,* and the woman melted. Was she a charmer!

New York never disappointed. The hum was diligent, as was the pace. The calls, the work, the New York based chums. Fon Tayne had made some new outfits for me and one for Kelly, so *we* had several fittings. Teme Brenner, Henry Rogers, Mort Viner, Harold Mirisch were all in town, plus Sammy Davis, and Amy and Milton Greene. I couldn't bypass the theatre. I saw Judy Holliday and Sydney Chaplin in *Bells Are Ringing,* and Gwen Verdon in *New Girl in Town.* Even managed a little dancing at El Morocco and the Stork Club.

Tony's train chugged in the night before we sailed. What a bon voyage gathering we had. The three-bedroom three-bath suite was filled with bodies, ice buckets for champagne, trays of caviar, and trunks. The big whistle, the kisses and waves goodbye, and we glided away past "the Lady."

This crossing was the gem of the ocean, so to speak. A slight rolling was all we felt. Kelly even made it from Daddy to Mommy on her own two feet. The *Île de France* had a complete children's facility: dining room, playroom, and Punch and Judy shows. A four-year-old cutie adopted Kelly and hovered over her like a little mother hen. It was interesting to watch Kelly relate to the other youngsters, to the puppets, to the parties.

We were able to participate in the festivities on this cruise and we made up for our previously missed fun. The captain's dinner, numerous cocktail parties, the gambling games, the grand ball. Mr. and Mrs. Boris Karloff were on board and were quite pleasant, but no matter how I tried, I couldn't shake the monster image—I was scared every time I saw him. Tony continually apologized to one and all for his own appearance. He was growing a beard and long hair for the picture and felt shaggy and unkempt. I thought he looked handsomer than ever. But it did scratch and tickle!

We disembarked in Plymouth and took a train to London and the Dorchester Hotel, where we had a penthouse apartment called the Audley Suite. Very sleek. And then the tempo accelerated. We had wig measurements, wardrobe conferences, the inevitable publicity obligations, and meetings with old and new friends.

Kirk and Jerry were sticklers for authenticity, and Berman's, the costumer, was bursting with artistic delights. 1066 was a flattering period, the women flowy and feminine, the men rough and very macho.

We spent time with Helen and Howard Keel (he had a smashing show at the Palladium), Gloria and Sammy Cahn, Arthur Jacobs, Terrence Young, and our old traveling companion Jimmy Van Heusen. And Joe and Rosie were vital and stimulating as always. Nedra and Cubby Broccoli and we showed off our babies to each other.

We were introduced to some new restaurants—The Guinea, the Mirabelle, L'Escargot in Soho, the Ivy—and visited some familiar haunts.

June 3 was Tony's thirty-second birthday and June 4 our sixth anniversary, so there was a series of celebrations. Elizabeth Taylor and Mike Todd were our neighbors at the hotel, occupying an even larger penthouse suite. To start the events, they had a cocktail party. Michael Wilding, Debbie Reynolds and Eddie Fisher (they had just arrived, he opened at the Palladium the next week), Quique and Louis Jourdan, Harold Clurman, Anne and Kirk were some of the guests. Noel Coward greeted Tony, "Hello, you bearded beauty!"

Elizabeth seemed more content than I ever remembered. Mike was the strong force she had needed. Who knew then what fate had planned!

We popped in to another affair of the "racing set" and met Lord and Lady of This and Lord and Lady of That. At one point, a weary Tony said, "Nice to know you Lord." More. To Les Ambassadeurs with Rosie and Joe and Anne and Kirk, where we danced until the wee hours. My Hungarian was in rare form.

We had an opportunity to see some plays: *Sailor Beware, La Plume de ma Tante,* and the wizardry of Paul Scofield in the mediocre *A Dead Secret.* Our biggest disappointment was Tallulah Bankhead at the Café de Paris. Maybe we were expecting too much, but she just didn't have the magic.

I don't know why these things have always had to happen to me. I was in the bathroom at the hotel when I heard a noise. I looked up at the window opening to our small terrace, and there was a Peeping Tom. I screamed, he ran, Tony dashed in and called the house detective. Within seconds he was there, and within an hour he had dragged every member of the staff in front of me for identification. I was so embarrassed I couldn't have pointed anyone out even if I had recognized the culprit. If I had been in a luxurious glamorous bubble bath or something, but on the potty!

Directly across from the Dorchester was Hyde Park, a haven for Kelly. She adored the ducks and pigeons and thrived on the clear air and sunshine. What a character she was! Now she was toddling around like a drunken sailor, trying to feed herself, when actually she was feeding the room. Holding court with all the traffic, laughing and clapping her hands at everything, and passing out kisses whenever we said, "Give a love," and playing in the john—this was a new trick. She did have one bout with a cold, which I promptly caught. But for the most part we found having her with us was not unmanageable. And it certainly was *well* worth any small extra effort.

June 14. Kirk, Ernie Borgnine, Tony and I left on a five-day good will tour of Scandinavia, after which the guys would begin filming on the coast of Norway. I would return to finish wardrobe for a week in London and join them for the last three weeks on that location. The baby would stay in London for this period.

Tony had decided to fly. Nervously to be sure, but he did it. What a welcome in Copenhagen, Denmark. The countries were so hyped because a major motion picture was being made about the Vikings that we were regarded as national heroes. And a Dane was returning to her Fatherland. An entire village, Frederikssund, had donned their full Viking regalia, with two ancient instruments similar to oversized horns, and put on a show at the airport.

Copenhagen was everything we thought it would be: charming, clean, quaint, clean, beautiful, clean, gay, clean, full of bicycles and bridges and silver shops and porcelain shops and fish markets and monuments and myths. Our lavish suite at the Palace Hotel had a balcony overlooking the oldest town hall in the world and a large square in which stood the statue of the Virgin Viking with those special horns. Legend had it that the horns would blow every time a girl lost her virginity. The horns remained silent, which told us a little something about legends.

Before I left the States, Grandpa Westergaard had asked me to make inquiries about his brother. He had lost track of him after the war. At one of our news conferences I requested aid from the media to track him down. This made dramatic copy and was headlined in every edition. I did receive a call, and the interpreter excitedly told me it was my great-uncle and set a meeting time at the hotel. A sweet, shy couple timidly accepted my eager welcome. Through the translator I learned that this apparently reserved pair had been quite active in the underground movement. They had deliberately become untraceable for security reasons during the occupation and then had just become accustomed to anonymity. No telephone, no papers. A friend had alerted them about my search and that was how they knew to contact me.

I looked at these unlikely brave activists and marveled again at people's quiet courage. I always have wondered, what would I have done under similar conditions? Would I have fought, or been passive? Would I have faced death or torture, or been submissive?

They wouldn't accept any offer of help. They did take Grandpa's address before they left. I was very proud, and I knew Grandpa would be extremely relieved and happy.

From the air, Sweden looked as though it were made of a million islands. And when we landed in Stockholm, on the way to the Grand Hotel, it still looked like that. Water and bridges and boats everywhere. A pretty city. Luncheons and banquets were the order of each day, with each Lord Mayor in each country, each providing elaborate tasty smörgåsbord, and each having lengthy and numerous toasts. These were warm and friendly gestures, true, but not very conducive to sobriety. Akvavit (Aquavit) is a clear Scandinavian liquor flavored with caraway seeds. It was served in a small tumbler with a knob base which forced you to "bottoms up" before you could put it upside down on the matching glass dish. It also packed a terrific wallop. The four of us exited some of these mandatory functions with some loss of equilibrium.

Oslo, Norway, continued the pattern. The guys were particularly observant of one feature, the big percentage of buxom beauties. Defensively, and clinically of course, I did note the male population wasn't bad either.

Red "captain's hats" were the trademark for university students until graduation, when a black one was substituted. A dense canopy of over two thousand crimson caps stood as we were made honorary members, and then—bedlam—not destructive, just great enthusiasm. The townspeople appeared to understand, showed diplomatic patience and tolerance, and there was no "incident." We were impressed.

A visit to the Viking Museum was both interesting and invaluable for research. The sets and props were already prepared, but this was for our personal awareness, familiarity, an opportunity to simulate habits, customs, appointments. Every item there had been unearthed in various areas of Norway. Some had been repaired, and some were exactly as found. It didn't seem possible that these crude crafts could have withstood the vicious oceans, or that men could have existed for the long intervals in these cramped quarters. The carvings and detail and scrolls were also amazing. The Vikings may have been called pagans, but they were in no way unintelligent. The use of brass and copper and iron in their designs was highly skilled.

The final stop before we went our different ways was the Olympic Ski Jump, Homenkollen. We took a lift to the top of the hill that overlooked the entire city. And I almost got sick when I peered down the incline toward the catapult for the jump. It was only used once a year when around one hundred of the best skiers in the world were invited to participate. No practicing, just two tries. This was supposed to separate the men from the boys. And I daresay it did.

I spent the week in London at the costumers and during her every waking moment, with Kelly. I worked with our English secretary, Joan, on business and correspondence, and set up lists and telephone numbers for any conceivable anticipated question or problem. Joan would be available, MCA's Laurie Evans, United Artists representatives, plus countless friends and other offices, a trusted doctor. I believed I had covered all angles until the nurse, Ethel, and Kelly were to meet us in Dinard, France.

The baby waved bye-bye, the *nurse* cried, which didn't help, and I departed for Bergen, Norway. The plane was loaded with press and a surprise passenger, our close friend, Stan Margulies (then a publicist, now a producer), so it was a jubilant group that landed at the rudimentary airport. We inched our way out of the pressing crowd. Some persistent fans followed us on motorcycles, a few all the way to the location hotel three hours away, over bumpy, twisting, narrow roads. Oh, did I feel sick—through rugged, primitive, breathtaking scenery. The fjords wove in and out of the thrusting cliffs; waterfalls gushed at every turn.

We straggled in to the Tunold Hotel in Strandebarm, Hardangerfjord, Norway. Considering where we were, it really wasn't too jarring. Spartan, austere, but spotless and livable. Ours was like the Queen's Chambers, because we had a private bath and lavatory. I was frozen, my bags had been misplaced in the confusion at the airport, but I borrowed Tony's sweat suit and snuggling with my honey thawed my frosted body.

Tony left for work early. The luggage finally appeared. I scrounged around for breakfast—if the two English-speaking staff members were unavailable, you were out of luck—and bundled up for the trip to the shooting site. The government had been very cooperative, in all phases of the filming. Two navy speed launches were provided for transportation. The thirty-minute ride offered a contrasting comprehensive view, from down to up. The sheer bluffs loomed even more threatening, the tombstone clouds buried their peaks. It was mysterious, eerie, and gave an insight about the original Vikings. I could understand why they were superstitious and believed in signs and symbols and worshiped strange gods.

I was in this frame of mind as we rounded a bend, and, I caught my breath when I saw a Viking village, Viking inhabitants, Viking goats and chickens and breed of horses, Viking ships. The spell was so powerful I found it hard to realize this was now, not then. A closer examination of the village further strengthened the enchantment. Each hut had a different dragon head and an emblem of the Viking god Odin. The roofs were covered with animal skins to provide warmth. This was the actual station of an old settlement, the workmen had discovered ruins and a king's burial ground. We were at the Maurangerfjord, a smaller version of the Hardangerfjord.

The crew had put a sign on the side of a hill, WELCOME JANET. They had built a hut for a dressing room with a lean-to for a john. I had the feeling they were glad to see me. Behind the picture village they had a regular studio of huts—wardrobe, makeup, props, etc.—and that "street" was called the Champs Élysées. The coffee hut was Romanoff's. Most of the crew and staff lived on the *Brand VI*, the largest ship of the company's "navy." Our Vikings and rowers had been engaged months ago, and had been in training since, even though many were already schooled in and brawny for the sport. Magnificent specimens they were.

Weather was our foe! Atrocious! There was continual cold rain, which resulted in spattering mud. But Jack Cardiff was a downright dream man and a genius. He could shoot in any adverse circumstance, unless the winds interfered with the equipment or the swells pushed the boats out of position. Like an actor, he "used" the uncordial elements to create a mood of the time. His camera became an integral part of the script. Dick Fleischer and Jerry Bresler and, since his company was involved, Kirk, deserved kudos too. Because of the climate-caused delays and the scope of the shots, it would have been tempting to gloss over the intimate scenes, sacrifice performances, in the name of expediency. But they didn't allow that to happen. We enjoyed in-depth rehearsal to flush out every nuance, every shading of our characters and the scenes. And that took courage!

By the time I arrived, wardrobe had only size eight rubber boots left, so I waddled around in my elegant costume with these conspicuous huge tanks on my feet, changing into my delicate slippers before each take. I had my usual mishap on the first day. Kirk was transferring the booty, including me, from the smaller marauding boat to the larger vessel. I had my foot on the rail to make the step up and the rough water flung the two crafts together, pinning my foot in between. I treated Norway to a few choice American words. When we had finished a stunt man carried me through the mud beach to my tent. Where the doctor said, no break, just badly bruised. Why me?

One day stands alone as the worst. We had an early call, and the transportation was mucked up, so we had to trudge three miles in the rain to the launch. This navy branch was rather relaxed in regimen. No strict dress code. No ban on civilians, because the sailors kept a girl on board. They had overslept, we had to wake them, and everyone came scrambling out of the cabins, bleary eyes, tousled hair, and sheepish grins. At least it was funny.

The real nightmare began in makeup. Jerry came running and said there was a call on the *Brand VI* phone for me, which was only used for emergencies or production needs. I stumbled through the mire to the concrete dock that had been constructed for the ferry service to the ship and sped toward the telephone. It was Ethel. "The baby is sick, vomiting, no temperature. The doctor hasn't come yet. You should come back or bring us up there." Was she

crazy? Obviously! We placed calls to Laurie Evans, to the manager
of the Dorchester, to Joan, to the doctor. How could I tell Ethel
what to do when I didn't know what was wrong? Why hadn't she
brought Kelly immediately to the doctor's office? Why had she
called me before she knew anything? How? Why? Why? Why?
Tony and I each alternated on the phone when the other one wasn't
working.

In terms of Kelly I had thought of everything except the human
angle; I misjudged Ethel. She lacked certain necessary qualities,
which I had overlooked, because I believed she would be dependable. Now the first time there was a problem she had panicked,
coudn't handle a single thing on her own. Over the phone the
doctor assured us it was a minor throat infection and with a penicillin shot she would be fine. Laurie said the same thing. The manager
said the nanny had gone to pieces. We hired Joan full time to stay
with Kelly and that person, and accompany them to Dinard. By the
end of the day, back at the Tunold, where the connections were
somewhat better, we sorted it all out. It became so clear. One, T.P.
(that person) was incompetent and lazy. Two, T.P. was lonely and
didn't want to be stuck in London, she wanted to see Norway.
Three, T.P. purposely dramatized the whole affair to get her way.
Four, T.P. was fired the minute we arrived in Dinard. Five, Tony
asked for the privilege. Fine with me, because I wouldn't trust my
reactions if I faced her. I couldn't even talk to her.

Everyone had been working seven days a week, and the boss
men decided a Sunday off was warranted, weather be damned. I
admired their attitude, because *that* was the only sunny day of the
whole stay. No ranting or raving, just a shrug and a "What can we
do?" look. We organized the show we planned to do for the cast
and crew. Since the rain was depressing and miserable, we thought
the show would boost morale.

Tony and I stayed on the *Brand VI* for the next few nights. I was
grateful we hadn't chosen those lodgings from the beginning—no
privacy, no space, and no one slept. I didn't shoot Saturday, luckily,
because I was in charge of all arrangements for our "production."
This was going to be the most mixed-up mess ever seen. No one
knew what they were doing, and if they had, we weren't sure it
would be understood. In any case, we'd have laughs. And it was my

thirtieth birthday. Lots of hugs and kisses and gag presents and a cake and messages from home and good news on all fronts. Kelly was better and Joan was a godsend; the rushes on the picture looked spectacular; *The Sweet Smell of Success* had received excellent reviews; our Jerry Gershwin had been made a vice president of MCA; and our families were status quo.

After dinner, chaos. Tables moved, curtain hung, props placed backstage (stage, ha!), frantic last-minute rehearsals. Showtime! Highlights included:

Jerry Bresler saying good evening in all the languages represented; Danish, Swedish, Norwegian, Italian, French, German, English.

Tony, Kirk, and Ernie sang a ditty, risqué lyrics naturally.

Tony introduced Jimmy Donald as a great escape artist. Bound him up; put him behind a sheet; counted to fifteen; opened the sheet and he is still struggling; repeat, still struggling.

Ernie sang "Shine On, Harvest Moon." Tony and Kirk marched out and just wrapped him in a big roll of gauze, Ernie still singing, and carried him off.

Dick Fleischer and Jack Cardiff did a quick bit about the bad laundry service on board.

A quick flash of Jimmy still struggling.

Kirk and I did the strongman bit. I was the girl assistant. He lifts the thousand-pound weight with much grunting and groaning and fanfare. After our exit, I run back and carry it off with one hand.

Edric Connor, an actor, was the only legitimate act. He had a lovely voice and sang three songs.

Tony, Kirk, and I did the Professor Lombardi skit. The men are downstage doing juggling, handstands, a little magic, and the girl does a striptease upstage. They think the applause and "More!" shouts are for them and keep on performing, while of course the urging is for the girl to take off the next layer. Wanda (wardrobe) had sewn beads on my bra, coffee-dyed white muslin, and made a bikini bottom with VIKING in beads. This was quite a hit.

The last look at Jimmy in the chains and ropes. Only this time, when Tony counted fifteen and pulled back the sheet, I was inside with Jimmy.

The finale was the age-old stand-in gag. Tony was the star, Kirk the stand-in, Dick the director, Jerry the make-up man, Jack the cameraman, I was the script girl. The idea is whenever anything physical is to happen, the director yells cut, the stand-in comes running, he receives the pie in the face, the water, the stool over the head, and afterward all congratulate the star and the poor schnook stand-in is forgotten in the locked trunk. The only difference this time around was the stage was so tiny we *all* got everything—the pie, the water, the powder, the stool—we were splattered. We were a smash. Dirty and exhausted, but a smash. And we had a group of very happy people, including us.

For a while! Then greed reared its ugly head and some of the Vikings and rowers threatened to strike if they weren't given a bonus, thinking the company had no alternative but to acquiesce.

Yet another angry storm made filming impossible. But that and the pending strike did prod the company to a tactical change. An all-night reappraisal was held, and a revised schedule resulted. There was enough footage. The shots left unfinished in Norway could be done in Munich with no forfeiture of quality. It would just add to the time in Munich. The producers thumbed their noses at the weather and the strikers.

So July 9 was liberation day. The *Brand VI* sailed to Dinard, France, with some of the cast and crew and equipment. We drove to Bergen, flew to London, the island of Jersey, Dinard—and Kelly. Pictures *are* worth a thousand words. The photo taken when I held her told all—the joy, the anguish, the love.

She looked fine and healthy. But the emotional havoc was unmistakable; she was nervous, insecure, spoiled—in just fifteen days! Damn that woman's hide! She had done exactly the opposite of every procedure I had so painstakingly established: held her constantly, fed her day and night, did not take her out for walks and air and communion with others. She had made the baby utterly dependent. When Tony removed Ethel and her things to another hotel until a plane left, Kelly wouldn't let me out of her sight, wouldn't accept Joan or even Daddy alone. We were a paragon of patience the next few days, which was difficult because our stomachs were churning so. I played games, popping out of the room and then bouncing back in, hoping to assure her that it was all right when I was out of her view because I wouldn't be far. I diverted her sporadic fits of temper by interesting her with toys, changing the attention. We took her to the beach where she could play with Peter

Douglas and Anne and his nurse and Joan and other children. And get sandy and dirty like every child should. At night we didn't pick her up or give her a bottle just because she was awake. We soothed her and lulled her back to sleep, or sometimes let her cry it out. Gradually, the tantrums lessened and she responded to the cheerfulness, the regularity, Daddy or Joan's solo presence.

The company was shooting the siege of the castle where I was held prisoner, so I had some time off. Fortunate planning for me. The saga of Ethel persisted. I kept receiving calls from her every time she had a layover. She bothered the airlines and hotels with arrogant demands, and they would call me for confirmation. She had her ticket and generous compensation, and I had no intention of paying extra for an extended tour of Europe. So I made it clear to all we were not responsible for any side excursions, she was on her own, and as far as I was concerned she could take a trip to hell, as long as she paid the fare. That seemed to end the matter.

The next blow. A stray arrow from the battle scene hit Tony in the eye, and he looked awful. It was a blessing he had shut his eye before it struck. There wouldn't be permanent injury, but the impact was severe. His beautiful eye looked like the red, white, and blue flag, all discolored and bruised and bloodshot. Tony said Kirk was so unnerved by the accident that he had to give him the tranquilizer the doctor had given him. Shock did set in later, so I had two to tuck in and watch over. I don't know how the news spread so quickly, but that night calls came from all over to verify the incident. Rumors ranged from Tony's losing his sight to his being in a coma at the hospital. I spent hours putting the record straight.

Bastille Day weekend in a French resort town means *packed.* Add a movie company and their visiting families and you are packed like sardines. But we really liked Dinard; it was very informal, very European, very whimsical, very unpretentious.

I was just beginning to relax a mite and enjoy the surroundings. We still had a way to go with the baby, but I could see the progress and felt a touch more at ease. I guess that little letdown was all it took, because I went to pieces. I was sick to my stomach, cold, hot, dizzy, weak, and cried my heart out for no reason. I was scared and so was everyone. The doctor gave a unique diagnosis, "Your head is tired, your system overworked," and he prescribed some medicine to "strengthen your head."

Well, my head improved, Tony's eye healed, and Kelly was approaching normality. She had her first ride on a merry-go-round, a priceless reaction. One day she tried to catch a sunbeam on the floor; how I wish I could have captured that moment. Fragments of new words spewed daily. Joan agreed to stay with us through Munich; she had fallen in love with the baby. She was not experienced in baby care, but then neither had I been. But Joan was intelligent and self-assured and not possessive. We were a good team.

Fort La Lotte was a legitimate castle with a moat, a drawbridge, formidable walls, and a high tower, making its stand on an isolated point overlooking the Gulf of St. Malo. The wind whipped with reckless velocity. Two strong arms had to hold me going across the drawbridge or I would have been Mary Poppins without the umbrella. A narrow old spiral stone staircase threaded a snaky path to the top of the tower, where there was an unobstructed bird's-eye view of the rocky surf, the courtyard, the countryside. We utilized this vista well. Spectacular, but not easy shooting. There were slots around the perimeter (no handrails or bannisters) to pour boiling oil on invaders. It was a wonder people weren't pouring down— one slip or trip and goodbye. The grips did cover the slots with boards, except where they showed in the camera. Kirk and I had a dramatic scene encompassing the entire 360-degree circle. And Tony and Kirk fought their duel to the death up there. The two of them were remarkable athletes, but the stunts they undertook made me sick with worry.

Kelly and Peter Douglas made their movie debuts, and even received credit. Anne and I found ourselves in the unfamiliar role of stage mothers. We judged the best time for our children to work would be after lunch and nap. All arrangements were poised for the babies' arrival. They had little chairs with their names, just like the big folk. Script covers, wardrobe. They were to be English peasant children, snatched up by their mothers to flee the advancing Viking hordes. Everything went perfectly. Appropriately they yelled when yanked up and carried off by these two strangers. Anne and I were nervous wrecks.

Travel schedules from Dinard to Munich did not offer much variety. We decided Joan and Kelly and I would brave the eight-hour drive to Paris for the direct 5 P.M. flight to Munich. Tony had to work the morning of the last day, so he caught a late-night train from Paris.

The packing made me crazy—stuff to be sent, stuff Tony would take, stuff we needed with us. The thought of unpacking in Munich made my head tired again. We had shipped trunks from London, bags from Norway, and now from Dinard. All would be accumulated and waiting for attention when we arrived. And I was on the sick list again. I had started feeling punk a few days before departure, and peaked the day we left. The ride was tedious. The baby behaved admirably and succeeded in amusing us with her "cutes." (Some hunters that fall were going to be surprised by what they found in the bushes—disposable diapers.) At Orly Airport I started having violent pains in my stomach and wasn't sure I could continue, but concluded it would be better to press on to Munich.

To top off this day, we had a very unfortunate incident in Munich. A group of people rudely pushed through the door out of customs, and bumped into a lady, who knocked Kelly over. The domino effect. Then those same parties allowed the heavy exit door to just swing loose, and I caught it an inch from the baby's face. That did it! I saw red and followed them, ready to kill. Those jerks didn't say, "Oh, we're sorry, we didn't see," which would have stopped me, but acrimoniously hollered at me, "You aren't the only ones who landed in Munich!" What the hell that was for, I never knew. They were told in impolite language my opinion of their behavior. I would have gone on, but Ernie Borgnine, no small man, who had met us, came rushing forward, and they left hurriedly. The UA and airline representatives learned their identities, and we protested at the American consulate. There was some connection. Anyway, welcome to Munich!

As soon as we landed at the Bayerischer Hof Hotel, Anne, who had preceded us, called her doctor. Anne and Kirk Douglas were and are two special, rare friends, helpful beyond belief. Anne spoke fluent German, French, Italian, and knew the who—where—what —and—when of European cities. She was there with the doctor, two doctors, who concurred: the flu had settled in my liver, and I must rest and be careful or it could develop into jaundice. Swell! Anne instructed the company to rearrange the shooting calendar as I would be unavailable for two weeks. There was plenty to do without me, but still, it was just what they didn't need, another problem.

The baby developed eczema in her ear and was teething badly, so she was fitful and cranky. I was no gem. Bobby Schwartz arrived for a visit and with the help of Joan's boyfriend, Frank, we did manage to unpack every piece of luggage. Everything was at last under one roof. Slowly, too slowly for me, the penicillin and vitamin shots took effect and I regained strength. I just couldn't push myself so hard anymore. Would I ever learn?

We were in Munich from July 30 to October 5. The production prospered, thanks to its reservoir of talent. Everyone really worked well together, which yielded exciting results on screen.

Our picture family was harmonious and always interesting, but we all hailed wandering pilgrims from the States. Mrs. Ed Muhl (he was head of Universal), Goldie and Bob Arthur (a favorite producer), various United Artists officials, Stanley Kubrick, and—a distinct treat—Edie and Lew Wasserman and Teme Brenner.

Edie, Teme, and I journeyed to Dachau. Lew and Tony had taken Bobby to the airport. Thank God, because I don't believe Tony could have remained peacefully in Germany. My diary recorded this:

Our emotions were so strong, and such a mixture, that it is too difficult to articulate them. But I tell you this, if you are ever within range, it must be seen, it must be experienced. Not that you'll understand it even then, but you'll know that everything must be done to prevent it happening again. How it ever could have happened, I don't know. How this ever can be comprehended—oh God—I don't have the ability to sort out all my thoughts—I just know it can never be permitted to re-occur.

I can tell you the physical aspects of Dachau. It is about twenty minutes from Munich. It is a town and a huge Army base. The concentration camp has been kept as it was and is open to the public, a very wise move I think. To have it be observed by everyone, people were there from different parts of Germany, of Europe, people like me who were not very close to the war. A way of making us all convinced why IT COULD NEVER BE

ALLOWED AGAIN. NOT TO ANY PEOPLE—ANY-
WHERE—BY ANYONE.

Edie, Teme, and I were silent for the first time since their
arrival, it's such a personal reaction, we were absorbed with our
thoughts.

On the way back, in town, we passed by the building where
Hitler and Mussolini orated to the crowds below. No need to tell
you, I'm sure, my feelings when I saw that.

Mildred and Jerry Bresler, Mickey and Dick Fleischer, Anne and
Kirk, and Tony and I spent one wonderful weekend in Salzburg,
Austria. The tunnel into Salzburg was through sheer rock and then
we were in a fairyland. Especially done up in honor of the festival,
flags and decorations, hosts of celebrating guests. A huge castle on a
tall mountain with a funicular running up to it stood smack in the
center of town. The streets were narrow and cobblestoned. A river
flowed cozily alongside; there were many old-fashioned bridges,
and more tunnels and archways carved from rock.

About ten miles out of the city, down a side road, was the Schloss
Hotel at Fuschl am See. Anne and Kirk had been there previously
and made the arrangements for this stay. Enchanting! Big forests
surrounded a lovely lake; there were tennis courts, and a storybook
four-level structure tucked in rolling hills. I was greeted by an obse-
quious, hand-kissing count. This, we learned, had been Ribbentrop's summer home. Those guys lived well! The basement used to
be their own bowling alley and had been converted into an intimate
nightclub. The bar was on the first floor, the dining room on the
second. In one conference room on the third floor was an exquisite
checkerboard table where Hitler and Ribbentrop signed the pact
with Mussolini. After we spat on that, the ugly Americans walked
to the fourth floor, where Anne and Kirk ushered us into the most
lavish suite we had ever beheld. They were eager for our reaction,
this had been theirs before, but insisted we enjoy this time. The
entire hotel was richly appointed, impeccably furnished. Obviously,
those "leaders of the masses" thrived on tangible assets.

We had cocktails and hors d'oeuvres at the Goldenes Hirsch Hotel, known more for the "continental set" who frequented its premises than for decor. The aristocratic "old world society" was in full
dress. It was a trifle sad, really, for the dress suits were somewhat

worn and the gowns a little tatty. The eight of us walked to the opera house, which reminded us of a premiere at home, and Tony saw his first opera.

We met for breakfast on the terrace, under the cerulean sky, above the shimmering water, below the glowing mountains. Then we roamed about Salzburg before *Everyman* began. This English morality play was staged in the front courtyard of the cathedral. It was one of the most effective uses of the elements we had witnessed: the towers ringing the court, the organ and bells from the church, the choral group and orchestra secreted in the interior. Even the dusk contributed. As it grew darker, Everyman drew nearer to his end. And the cloudy dusk brushed the hushed air with a strange celestial aura. The content of the play was quite powerful, and the audience was very moved. There was no applause (this wasn't something you clap about); one just experiences it. But a great surge of passion swept the spectators at the finish, the artists knew they had reached the people.

Aristotle said, "If we touch only the minds, we are unlikely to move people to action, for motivation lies deep in the realm of the passions."

An accidental encounter validated this. I was in our suite, playing with the baby, waiting for the company car to take me to the studio. The call came that the driver was downstairs, so I quickly collected my things and left. As I turned right into the passageway, a couple coming from the opposite end turned left, just ahead of me. The woman walked behind the man and was rather nondescript. The man was something else; he looked as if he were a movie extra depicting a Storm Trooper in a World War II film: high black leather boots, black breeches, black leather coat, black riding whip, black hat. He was strutting slowly, and I was in a rush, so I attempted to ease past them. I went to the left, and the woman moved to prevent my passing. I went to the right, and again she maneuvered to block me. At first I paid no heed. But as the game stubbornly continued, a thunderbolt struck me. This was no casual shift of position. She was *malignantly prohibiting* me from walking in front of her husband.

Perhaps I would have reacted more calmly, even considered it droll, *if* I hadn't seen Dachau, *if* his outfit and aura hadn't conjured up such vile images. But I detonated like a grenade. I physically wrenched the two offenders out of my path and ran to the elevators. My rage frightened me, I was trembling like a vibrator, and I hated them for causing my reaction.

John von Kotze was a second-unit cameraman on *The Vikings*. He and his wife, Caroline, started with us in Norway, and we had become good friends. They were young, witty, attractive, and the four of us shared some good times. John's father had prophetically discerned Hitler's course and transferred his family from Germany to England, and thus to safety, in 1933. John spoke English with no accent but understood and conversed in German flawlessly.

The studio shut down at 2 P.M. on Saturdays. Usually we rehearsed upcoming scenes, but not always. On a free Saturday afternoon, John and Caroline took us for an outing. We motored on the Autobahn toward Salzburg, through peaceful farmland to the Chiemsee, and ferried to the island of Herrenworth. The manager of the Schloss Hotel had been notified and a horse and carriage were waiting to bring us to the castle. Herrenchiemsee Palace, built by Ludwig II, King of Bavaria, referred to as "the mad King Ludwig." Evidence shows he had been every inch a king, the embodiment of the late Romantic Movement, and worshiped by his subjects. The foundation of the German Empire in 1871 was the end of Bavaria as a kingdom. Embittered and disappointed, Ludwig withdrew from public life into the mountains and built three spectacular castles in rapid succession. Herrenchiemsee was to be an expression of his ideal of absolute unlimited monarchial power. Versailles, residence of Louis XIV, the "Sun King," was his inspiration and model. In 1885, the funds of the Treasury were exhausted and the palace only two-thirds finished. His contemporaries thought money had been extravagantly wasted on an eccentric's whim. Historians claimed later that he had stimulated craftsmanship in South Germany to an unforeseen renaissance, that the palace was more than a "copy"—it was an architectural monument, the last created by a sovereign. Ludwig was an enigma, a controversial figure. Had he actually been insane, or just a dreamer?

One fact I could guarantee: The palace was magnificent. Only about eighty years old, spared in both wars, in perfect condition. We saw the King's Guard Room, the First Antechamber, the Second Antechamber, the State Bedroom, the Conference Hall, the

Hall of Peace, the Hall of War, and the wonder work of the Great
Hall of Mirrors: 350 feet in length, with seventeen arched windows
corresponding to the same number of similar mirrors opposite,
thirty-three crystal chandeliers, forty-four candelabra. The State
Apartments on the second floor had over 6,000 candles, 2,188 of
which were in the Great Hall of Mirrors. It took fifty-eight people
eighteen minutes to light them all. The effect of the brilliance on
the gold and silver and crystal and gilt draperies was dazzling.

We had dinner at the hotel and the manager brought the guest
book for us to sign. He had quite a collection, accompanied by
some unpublished photos, including Hitler and his top aides.
Johnny conversed in German with the man and told us when he left
the table, "Obviously he was a Nazi. He is very proud of Hitler's
signature and holds these infamous leaders in great reverence, as
heroes."

Tony and I had weird vibrations putting our names in the same
book. Tony wrote, "I am a Jew, signing this book that Hitler also
signed, in a place owned by a Nazi. What does it mean? Are these
people not even true to their own disgusting beliefs?"

The five months were winding down. We had completed the
television short Stan Margulies produced on the making of the film.
We had chitchatted with the world's journalists. We had ransacked
the stores of all the visited countries, for ourselves and for presents.
We had gleaned museums and artifacts and landmarks. And we had
almost finished the actual shooting, dubbing, and stills of an epic
endeavor.

We had entertained a stream of transient friends, Buddy Rich,
Harry James, The Charlevilles, Edd Henry, and Laurie Evans, and
we had broken bread with numerous indigenous inhabitants.

The most memorable of the latter was the famed Hungarian
writer Bush Fekete. We spent an evening with Anne and Kirk in his
apartment, where his wife prepared a real Hungarian feast. They
were a fascinating couple, literate, cultured, displaying the unique
patience of those who have seen suffering and who have themselves
suffered and are able to maintain the compatible equilibrium. Much
of the evening's conversation was directed toward the Hungarian
Revolution. I had just read James Michener's *Bridge at Andau* and
was very much caught up in the tragic plight of these brave people.

Tony too was naturally concerned. *Beware,* I kept thinking. Were we tolerating another insidious movement? Were we again meandering passively along?

There were many social events, including the premiere of Kirk's picture *Paths of Glory,* and Jack Cardiff's party at a real rathskeller with a zither player, beer barrels, and wooden benches. The last event was the opening of Oktoberfest, a two-week annual celebration in Munich, observed by most of Germany. There was an all-day parade, a continuous carnival, a welcome excuse for fourteen days of robust reveling by an industrious nation—the German version of the New Orleans Mardi Gras.

The immense crates we had built were filled and shipped, the wild brawling "wrap" party made hangover history, and on October 5 we departed for Paris. Joan was going to California with us, to stay until we found another nurse. It was difficult to believe she had only come for a few days to help me with the mail in London.

Tony bought me my first Paris creation, at Jacques Heim. And he supervised my nervous haircut. I was back to my natural darker blond, and he believed I should have the new shorter look. We also assumed, since I was going to portray a WAC captain in my next picture, that long tresses would not be appropriate. (What a can of peas that bob opened later!) We played with Anne and Kirk, Jeanette and John Levee, and Hal Wallis took us to supposedly the best restaurant in Paris, Le Grand Véfour. Plaques adorned the spot where Napoleon had sat (and evidently took Josephine upstairs), and Colette, and many others.

On October 10, 1957, we went to Cherbourg and onto the *Queen Mary.* And on October 15, 1957, we had another "U.S.A. Appreciation Day": no matter where we went or what we saw or who we met, "There was no place like home!"

New York was the usual commotion; I dashed to interviews, fittings, and saw a steady flow of chums. Marge and Gower Champion were now among the New York contingent. We went to the thrilling *West Side Story,* and attended the "intimate" soiree given by Elizabeth Taylor and Mike Todd at Madison Square Garden. It was literally a three-ring circus. Thousands of people inside, and more outside. Mike was a showman for sure. He had garnered acts from all over the world, even the fabulous rectangle of fountains, "The

Dancing Waters." This was an affair to tell your children about. (We tried, but Kelly didn't seem too impressed.)

Tony left on the train, and Kelly, Joan, and I took the sleeper flight to California. It was a very Hollywood plane, with Sharman Douglas, Kurt Frings, Irving Lazar, and Ray Stark on board.

I had left Los Angeles with a baby, but I was bringing home a little person, one who walked, understood, talked, and was a durable source of joy and love and wonder. How quickly she was growing!

CHAPTER SEVENTEEN

Tony started *Kings Go Forth* in November, in the great company of Frank Sinatra, Natalie Wood, Leora Dana, and Carl Swenson, with Delmer Daves directing. Tony and Frank and Natalie got on well together, professionally and personally.

Frank had an aptitude for assembling assorted people and incubating and hatching friendships. He was then dating Lauren Bacall, known to chums as Betty. The word "broad" when applied to a female began as a derogatory description. 'Tain't necessarily so! "She was a good broad" could connote the most complimentary attributes. Which is exactly why I thought Betty to be a good broad. A no-nonsense, unpretentious, witty, caring woman whom I liked a lot.

Frank, Tony, I, and Peter Lawford were friends of long standing. Peter had married Pat Kennedy in April 1954. At the time I only knew of her as an eastern "socialite" whose family had a vague association with politics. When they set up housekeeping in California, and my exposure to her became frequent, I discovered her deeper values. I enjoyed her intellect, her awareness, her intense dedication to her family, her sense of humor.

Yes, relationships were still in fashion.

Years ago there had been a group who labeled themselves the Rat Pack. As Lauren Bacall, in her book *By Myself,* described: "Hjordis and David Niven, Gloria and Mike Romanoff, Swifty (Irving Lazar), Frank (Sinatra), Judy and Sid (Judy Garland and Sid Luft), Bogie (Humphrey Bogart) and I, formed the Rat Pack. In order to qualify, one had to be addicted to nonconformity, staying up late, drinking, laughing, and not caring what anyone thought or said about us. Spence (Spencer Tracy) was only an honorary rat because he lived a secluded life, but his heart was in the right place. We held a dinner in a private room at Romanoff's to elect officials and draw up rules—Bogie's way of thumbing his nose at Hollywood. I was voted Den Mother, Bogie was in charge of public relations. No one could join without unanimous approval of the charter members."

In 1958, when Frank and Betty (Lauren Bacall), Tony and I, Sammy Davis, Jr., Jeanne and Dean Martin, Edie Adams and Ernie Kovacs, Anne and Kirk Douglas, Pat and Peter Lawford, Gloria and Sammy Cahn, Ruth and Milton Berle began to appear inseparable, the media attached the same designation of Rat Pack to us. We never acknowledged the formal title, for the simple reason there wasn't one. We had fun, caroused together, and maybe kidded about the identification, but we never adopted bylaws or formed a club of any kind. But it didn't matter what we said, the name stuck. It seemed to please the press, to give them a hook on which to hang their coats of Hollywood tales. No harm came from it, just so the record reveals it was not sanctioned.

This period marked the sunrise of a glowing interlude, with high noon in 1960, and sunset at the end of 1961. We were beginning the climb to a higher plateau. Acceptance. Recognition. Status. Security. We only had to hold on and hope the thin air didn't make us dizzy and cause a tumble. We also needed to remember that the inside had to ascend together with the outside.

The Perfect Furlough was scheduled to begin in January for Universal, as one of our respective commitments. It was a delightful, amiable farce, written by Stanley Shapiro, produced by Bob Arthur, and directed by our bosom buddy Blake Edwards. Tony and I were looking forward to this; we always had extreme faith in Blake's talent. Elaine Stritch, Keenan Wynn, Troy Donahue, King Donovan, Linda Cristal rounded out the cast. I was a WAC captain in charge of a soldier selected for morale purposes to experience a perfect furlough which would be enjoyed vicariously by the remainder of his remote camp.

Unbeknownst to us, the studio had filmed second-unit footage in Paris using doubles, establishing long scenic shots of identifiable tourist attractions. All well and good—except that my double had long, very blond hair. So when I showed up in my chic natural coiffure, I thought the brass would have apoplexy. I couldn't believe it. I had seen Mr. Muhl in Europe. I had done an entire movie in my natural color. As for length, wasn't it customary to confer with a lady about a style? And didn't research show at that time women in the services were required to keep their hair trimmed? Apparently Mr. Muhl and Mr. Arthur had authorized a division already in Paris to photograph familiar sites for our project. Whoever supervised had an image of me and chose a double accordingly, not checking if his concept was current or acceptable.

They implored me to wear a wig, and I absolutely refused. That would have been wrong and I would rather have just bowed out. Blake actually solved the stand-off. When he saw what had been done, he was able to salvage the majority of the footage as background for "process,"* only losing a little where the model was too much in evidence.

Peace was restored and we could get on with the work. By this time Tony and I functioned smoothly as a screen team. I don't mean to imply there was no room for improvement. There was *always* space to go forward, always would be. But we knew each other so well, we were completely free and trusting, able to incorporate and expand suggestions from one another or a director easily. There were just some things you could do with a husband that you couldn't do with any other leading man and vice versa. Blake could never have asked me to do a certain stratagem with someone else. The straight-laced WAC fell in a wine vat and her uniform had to be dried before they could leave the French vintner's farm. She manufactured a Roman toga out of a sheet and appeared for dinner. This was the first time the soldier saw her as anything but an army manual. And Blake wanted a "wow!" reaction. I was off camera on Tony's close-up, and there were no prying eyes. As he casually glanced at me, I opened my robe, flashing nude as the day I was born, and the response was genuine surprise and a great expression.

Blake was, is, an innovative creative movie maker. His imagination knew no bounds and his wacky sense of humor fared him well.

---

* The "process" operation is rearview projection. A projector shows film on a screen, in front of which a scene is photographed by the camera, thus giving the illusion of simultaneous location and action. It is a tricky technical method, for the frames on each machine have to be synchronized, and complex for the editor as well, because any cuts have to perfectly match the front and the back.

Plus, he had the skill of his craft to back up his ingenuity. He was constantly inventing ways to get the desired effect. The now in love but still duty-driven WAC was nervously waiting for her absent ward, pacing up and down, waving her arms at her confidante, finally reaching for a smoke to calm herself. Blake put two broken cigarettes in the box, knowing when I tried to light one and couldn't, it would further the agitation. Only one hitch. I always checked my props before a take, so I found the broken cigs and replaced them. Then I realized what he had prepared, but I managed to make the scene move almost as well by accidently dropping the case with my shaky hands, causing the same result.

This may all sound trivial, but it's those minute touches that give a presentation the uniqueness, fullness, the special quality, and advance a performance or picture beyond the ordinary. Sometimes these extras are calculated, sometimes they just happen. It doesn't matter, as long as they work for the character and situation and overall effect.

Blake and I must have been related way back when we were swinging in the trees, because we were both charter members of the Klutz Club. Truthfully, he was as bad as I was. Early in his career he was at a swimming party, took a long running dive into the pool, overshot the water completely, and landed flat on his back on the cement. Not funny, but typical.

During *The Perfect Furlough* Tony and I were relaxing, gabbing with some visitors after rehearsing, while Blake was setting up the next shot with Phil Lathrop, the cameraman. Suddenly we heard a piercing scream and a lot of commotion.

"What's that?" the guests anxiously asked.

"Oh, probably Blake falling or something" was our casual reply, and we continued with our conversation. They must have thought us heartless, for Tony's stand-in, George, then informed the group that the heavy crane wheel had run over Blake's foot. "Par for the course," we said, but we checked to make certain no bones were broken.

One of us could often be found on crutches, or sporting a cane. On *My Sister Eileen,* at the end of the number "We're Great but No One Knows It," Betty Garrett and I marched bravely down the subway steps on our way to conquer New York. The steps had no backing, so naturally my foot went in between the slats up to my hip.

Fran and Ray Stark held a beautiful black-tie gala in their garden one summer evening. The pool was covered for dancing and the area was romantically dark. There were stone steps leading to the pool, obscured by bodies and dimness, and when I left the dance floor—no, I didn't fall in the pool—I stubbed my toe, resulting in a break.

I won't go on; take it from me, Blake and I were in a class by ourselves.

March 1958. Joy of joys, I was pregnant again! In the elevator on my way to see Dr. Leon (Red) Krohn, whom should I bump into but Anne Douglas and Quique Jourdan. No possibility of secrecy this time. No matter, Anne was enceinte also, and we effervesced together. Tony and Kirk were prancing around, the proud peacocks. Kirk had the upper hand as he had had two children prior to Peter; Tony had catching up to do. (He eventually did surpass Kirk.)

Fate worked in strange ways during this pregnancy. As my miracle was confirmed, word flashed through the community that Mike Todd had been killed in the crash of his airplane, *The Lucky Liz,* on his way to accept the Showman of the Year Award from the National Association of Theatre Owners. Elizabeth had been spared, she was home ill with a virus infection. "The Lord giveth, and the Lord taketh away." I shuddered when I tried to put myself in her place. What if it had been Tony! The sense of loss produced was too overpowering, too painful. How she must have anguished—again alone—her Goliath gone. I wished I could comfort her in some way.

Van and Evie Johnson had a dinner planned that evening, and a subdued group gathered. I remember this night so vividly, for the obvious reason, the paradox of elation and tragedy, but also for the cementing of two friendships. Leonard Gershe was a well-known writer in both films and television. He later expanded his horizons to theatre with the hit play *Butterflies Are Free.†* Roger Edens had

---

† Life is a spider web of crossed threads. When my daughter Jamie Lee auditioned for Monique James at Universal she chose a scene from *Butterflies.* Her godparents,

arranged music for Ethel Merman and numerous musical personalities, championed Judy Garland and countless others, and was a producer. Starting on Broadway, he moved to Hollywood in the late thirties, and during his tenure at MGM he received at least eight Academy Award nominations, either in the best song or best score category, and won three gold statues. Lennie wrote and Roger produced the wonderful *Funny Face,* starring Fred Astaire, Audrey Hepburn, Kay Thompson. We had met previously, and exchanged pleasantries, but this time we were drawn closer together. These two men proved to be among my most loyal, trusted, cherished friends.

Stanley Kramer cast Tony in *The Defiant Ones,* co-starring Sidney Poitier, and featuring Theodore Bikel, Charles McGraw, Lon Chaney, Jr., King Donovan, Claude Akins, Lawrence Dobkin, Whit Bissell, and Carl (Alfalfa) Switzer. I'm not sure if the company was aware of what they had during the filming of this picture, but the magnitude of the film was obvious at the conclusion. It was one of Kramer's most important achievements, with superb, trenchant performances by Tony and Sidney. It was around October at the Screen Directors Guild when we viewed the finished product. There was a hush at the end, and then the entire audience, composed of seasoned members of the movie colony, rose as one and cheered. I was so proud of my husband I could have burst. (Good thing I didn't—the ten pounds gained were once again sticking straight out in front.)

And, not to change the pattern, once again we moved. Oddly, to a house about a block and a half away, 1151 Summit Drive, and owned by relatives of Lennie's, Mildred and Sam Jaffe. It was a beautiful Mediterranean two-story home. The long driveway circled around a huge old tree; there was a big welcoming entrance, a wide hall, perfect for displaying art; a 30-by-40-foot living room; a den and bar; a study and dressing room for Tony; a sunny, airy master bed and sitting room; mirrored closets, and a huge bath area; a dining room to seat thirty; a breakfast room; a kitchen; and two servants' quarters. Upstairs had a large center spread flanked

Edie and Lew Wasserman, headed the studio, only they had no inkling of her contract. She called afterward and identified herself as their new employee.

by four bedrooms and a compact kitchen. Outside the lawn and trees led toward the good-size pool and changing rooms and kitchen. A dream house! And a *long* way from the Harvey Hotel. I was busy with painters, electricians, plumbers, and our tasteful, talented decorator Ruby Levitt. She was gratifying as a collaborator because she didn't overpower our identities to force her preferences. She suggested, guided, but allowed us the final choice, so the outcome reflected our personalities. I've never felt comfortable in a home done solely by a decorator, however stunning it might appear. Too impersonal, too sterile, too academic. And Ruby didn't object to a budget, a necessity in our case. All of this was very expensive.

Although I wouldn't chance working, I did attend several key openings of *The Vikings* around the country with Kirk and Tony. Fon designed three maternity evening gowns so I wouldn't feel or look too cumbersome. But I was oh so careful not to tire myself or overdo things.

Kelly was my main focus of attention, to prime her for the new addition to our family. She now had perfect control of speech and personal habits, and was a funny, gay, adorable companion. I explained about Mommy's tummy, how a baby was growing inside, how Mommy and Daddy's love had brought her to us and would now bring a sister or brother, how her position would remain intact and our love assured, how she would help Mommy care for the arrival. She adored emulating my actions, and the nurse's, so this especially appealed to her. The groundwork was simple, since our lives continued status quo. The test would be when there was actually another little body in the next room. I never could figure out which was more of a problem; to be the first child and have to learn to share the parents, or to be the second and arrive fighting for position. Each has advantages and disadvantages and certainly each produces completely individual personalities.

Kelly's second birthday party was quite an event. We went all out: pony and cart, merry-go-round, a new sandbox, gym unit, and roller coaster. The guest list was a who's who of the romper set. Amy and Vicky Kanter (Judy Balaban and Jay), Scott Shepherd (Judy Goetz and Dick), Peter Douglas, Michael Rudolph (Joan Benny and Buddy), Gregg Champion, Jenny Edwards (Pat and Blake), Casey and Tory Quine (Barbara and Richard), Casey

Kramer (Stanley), Joey and Lorna Luft (Judy Garland and Sid), Sydney and Christopher Lawford (Pat Kennedy and Peter), Gina Martin (Jeanne and Dean), Carrie Fisher (Eddie and Debbie Reynolds). Plus grandparents, nurses, friends, and most of the parents. The photographers were Daddy, Uncle George Sidney, Uncle Jerry Gershwin, and Pat Newcombe (a longtime chum who was then at Rogers and Cowan Public Relations firm). I do believe the adult contingent enjoyed it as much as the toddlers.

The friendship between Patti and Jerry Lewis and Tony and me had waned. As our dependence decreased and our security increased, our paths diverged.‡

Ironically our affinity with Jeanne and Dean was strengthened along the way. Jerry and Dean had split their partnership in 1955, causing heartache for both, I know. They did well, however, in solo acts. Dean's movie career began slowly as a single, until he was cast in the absorbing drama *The Young Lions,* released in 1958, opposite Marlon Brando and Montgomery Clift. From then on his reputation grew.

We were going to Jeanne and Dean's one night for a casual, thrown-together dinner. There were more autos than usual in the driveway, and I said to Tony, "Doggone it! I bet Jeannie forgot how many she invited. It's probably a party." It certainly was. When she opened the door about sixty voices yelled, "Surprise!" It was a shower for me. I was totally unprepared, it hadn't entered my mind, and I was very touched. Our second blessed event was to have the same grand layette as the first. I had passed on so much equipment and clothing as Kelly grew that I really lacked essentials.

‡ Jerry and I caught up with one another again around 1965 when I played opposite him in *Three on a Couch.* Our friendship resumed as if there hadn't been a hiatus. He directed as well, and I could understand why the French held him in such high esteem. His guidance in general and for one scene in particular was outstanding. I played a self-assured psychiatrist, about to be married, but only after I fulfilled my obligation to three confused girls. Jerry attempts to help by being each girl's ideal, just so we can wed. When I discover the subterfuge I quite naturally am burned and walk out in a huff. My interpretation was anger and attack, which worked all right. He said, "We have that, and it's fine. Let's do another take, and in this, still use the anger, but for the first time this woman is out of control, hurt, hesitant, even showing hints of uncurbed hysteria—in front of her patients—who do the turnaround and try to stabilize her." It was so much better, added another dimension, and it was such fun to do. I wouldn't have thought of that approach.

Precautions are compulsory, yet circumstances can still concoct unavoidable pitfalls. One night, two carloads of people drove to Pat and Peter Lawford's beach house for an evening of food and poker. This was a "ladies included" game, for small stakes. Sometimes the guys would play at their level of chance. Tony and I had arguments about that. A "boy's outing" never bothered me, but losing money bothered me a lot. I just couldn't reconcile myself to gambling with any substantial sum. It seemed stupid and wasteful. I had to work too hard earning those dollars to throw them away. We did not see eye to eye on that issue—ever.

We were coming home about 1 A.M. Tony drove, with me and Jeannie in the front seat and Dean, Glo and Sammy (Cahn) in the back. Frank was following behind us. Going east on Wilshire Boulevard, we noticed a car driving erratically a few autos ahead. The driver seemed to be looking back at us and weaving in and out of lanes. We assumed he was potted and tried to keep our distance. Suddenly he pulled out into oncoming traffic, looped a U turn, and appeared to head toward our left side. "My God, he's going to ram us broadside!" I screamed, just as the impact came. I kept yelling for Tony because I thought he was hurt. Somehow we scrambled out of the car, not sure if it would explode. Horns were honking, Frank was calling, "Mayday! Mayday!" on his phone and directing traffic around the collision. Soon sirens were added to the din, the police and an ambulance.

I was bundled into the ambulance, really just dazed, and taken on a wild ride to the house, which was as nerve-racking as the accident. Dr. Krohn met me there. I worried the commotion would wake up Kelly, but she stayed peacefully asleep. Miraculously, no serious damage was done to anyone. We were all shook up a little, and Dean sprained his back slightly. The car was the worst casualty. When we gathered at our place later, the bizarre event was sorted out. The man was drunk, and he thought he saw his wife in our car and wanted to punish her and whomever. He couldn't manage to get close enough to bump the tires and that prompted the swing around and the side butt. The dummy could have killed himself and us too!

Another day, a rainy morning, I was on my way to pick up Mom. I was worried about her; she was increasingly reluctant to initiate activity on her own. I did what I could during the day, brought her to the house to help with Kelly, took her with me on errands, anything to provide a purpose. Dad spent more and more time away from the apartment. Their building was on a hill. I had stopped with my turn-indicator blinking left, when *wham,* a jolt from the rear end spun me clear over the double line to face in the opposite direction. The poor guy felt awful, especially when he saw my condition. It wasn't his fault. The brakes didn't hold; they were wet from the downpour. Mom ran out, all upset, and the police quickly appeared. Again Dr. Krohn was called and met us at Jackie Gershwin's. And again I was lucky. My little tyke in there was tough, hanging on for dear life, and that was the truth.

In late summer, Tony started filming the classic comedy *Some Like It Hot,* a United Artists–Mirisch production, starring Jack Lemmon, Marilyn Monroe, with Joe E. Brown, George Raft, Pat O'Brien, Nehemiah Persoff, George E. Stone, and Joan Shawlee. Billy Wilder directed, and wrote with I. A. L. Diamond. What an opportunity to work with the very best! Jack and Tony played out-of-work musicians who were unintentional witnesses to the St. Valentine's Day Massacre and fled the wrath of the mob by posing as the last-minute replacements in an all-girl band headed for Miami. Joe E. Brown makes a play for Jack, and Tony makes a play for Marilyn, when he isn't being her best "girlfriend." The possibilities were endless, and under Billy's leadership, they all were searchingly explored. The two leads were hysterical, decked out in their ladies' wardrobe. They spent hours deciding on the voice to use, the walk to perfect, the feminine personality to project, while still maintaining their masculine characters under the disguise. Quite complicated. They soon discovered too that being a woman wasn't all peaches and cream. Those high heels were uncomfortable and it was difficult to keep on balance. The wigs were hot and itchy, and they had a heck of a time with the makeup and the five o'clock shadow. And not even *we* ever found consolation in stifling corsets or tight brassieres.

Marilyn was tortured by insecurity. This exquisite creature, so talented, so vulnerable, so irretrievable, labored just to come on the set. She was there at the studio, but was hard put to muster the courage to appear. It was not malicious game playing or status tactics but just plain terror that forced her to retreat. This was very trying, especially for the boys. They would report for makeup and wardrobe, and then wait. And wait. The more intolerable their position, the more intolerant their attitude. Of course they were sympathetic to her plight; it was an unfortunate situation. But, oh boy, when she *did* make it, when Billy *did* get it out of her, the screen sizzled. What a high price to pay!

In late August the company located near San Diego at the wonderful turn-of-the-century hotel Del Coronado. I packed Kelly and the nurse and my maternity bathing suit to enjoy the lovely wide oak hallways, high ceilings, paneled dining room, solid wood carved staircases, encircling verandas. It was a pleasant two weeks, in the company of Audrey Wilder (Mrs. Billy), Lottie Mirisch (Mrs. Harold), visiting Pat Newcombe, Warren Cowan, and others. This was where the famous last line was filmed, when Jack confesses to Joe E. Brown he really is a man, not a woman. Joe E. Brown looks and says, "Well, nobody's perfect!"

The baby was due November 19. But that was the day Papeleh was buried. He didn't live to see his second grandchild. Momeleh had called about ten o'clock, two nights before. We rushed to their apartment; Jackie and Jerry met us there for support. It was over. Mercifully, he hadn't lingered to suffer. We knew Manny's heart wasn't strong, but, fortunately, he hadn't lived the last years enduring constant pain. However we rationalized, though, the loss was devastating. Momeleh was a total wreck, and Bobby was absolutely lost. The strength had to come from us. Tony and Jerry took care of the arrangements. Jackie and I cleaned up, ordered food, handled relatives and friends, and were handy shoulders for Momeleh.

Edie had an extra limousine at the services in case my time came and I had to be whisked away, but I held off for three more days. The evening of the twenty-first we drove home from Momeleh's. I was very tired and not feeling up to snuff, but I had no definite signs. Dr. Krohn decided I should go to the hospital in any case. I was close, he was sure, and I needed the rest. The nurse gave me some sort of calming shot despite my protests. I was afraid I wouldn't know when labor began, which was silly. There was no sleeping through that sensation.

Within my daze, a gnawing thought tried to push to the surface from the recesses of my mind and finally wouldn't be submerged. I was jealous. I was jealous of Tony's devotion to his mother and brother at this time. I wanted all of his attention for me and the child I would soon bear. I didn't want a proxy in the waiting room, I wanted the real thing and all of it. I knew the situation—Manny hadn't chosen to die, Momeleh hadn't planned to usurp Tony's attention, Bobby couldn't change being helpless, Tony couldn't shirk obligations. Oh God, I had loved Papeleh and had no wish to deny the mourning. The needs of his family usually took precedence in our lives. I had acknowledged and sustained this during the seven and a half years, until now. But I yearned for an unconditional welcome to our secondborn too, and I knew it was impossible. And I was resentful. And guilt-ridden. And irrational. I couldn't compel an exact reproduction of the emotions we had experienced with the first baby. They could be equally intense, but they had to be different. How many times had I said something similar? Understood? And here I was in contradiction; I didn't make any sense. I was too ashamed of my selfishness to ever share my distress with anyone.

Jamie Lee Curtis arrived at 8:37 A.M., November 22, 1958, weighing six pounds twelve ounces and measuring twenty and a half inches. There was no lack of excitement or joy or love surrounding the event. On the contrary, the poignant circumstances made her birth especially dear and valued to everyone. I throbbed with anticipation to again hold the tiny blanket with its precious gift. Even though I knew better, I could have sworn she focused on me with those big beautiful eyes and shot a Cupid's dart straight to my heart. I couldn't get enough of just staring at her perfection. God had chosen to overlook my anxiety transgression and had blessed us once more.

Kelly was curious and eager to have this apparition become visible, to judge for herself how the newcomer would affect her world. We tried not to rock her boat with too many waves. The visitors took our cue and fussed over Kelly before asking her to introduce them to Jamie. The smart ones also brought along a small remembrance for her in addition to the baby gift. It was such a kick to see them together, to look at our busy two-and-a-half-year-old and then at this little doll and realize I was going to have that experience again of watching and guiding a being develop. The wonder of it all!

The situation seemed to be under control, and then the nurse asked me to come upstairs immediately. I became suspicious, because I wasn't supposed to climb stairs for four weeks. She had noticed during the bath that Jamie had a swelling on her right side that was tender as well. I sent for the pediatrician, Dr. Zall, who came right over. He wanted a second opinion and called a specialist, Dr. Gans, who concurred. A tear or weakness in the wall of the intestine had caused a hernia and they would have to operate to repair the damage. Neither could explain why; it was a congenital frailty. Not unusual. Not dangerous, except that she was only two weeks old.

Oh my Jesus, help me not to panic! To have faith! I reached Tony, who met us at the hospital with Edie and Lew and Jerry. Jackie drove us to Cedars-Sinai. I cradled and hugged and rocked and wouldn't let Jamie out of my arms; they could do any preparations right there, until Dr. Gans, Dr. Krohn, Dr. Zall had to take her. So petite, so fragile, so innocent! And then I prayed.

No doubt about it, Jamie was conceived tenacious. She was determined, despite auto mishaps, tragedy, and an operation, that she would survive. Her recuperation was speedy, the elasticity of her infant body made healing easy. The days at the hospital were lessons in humility for me. When she was asleep, I walked around the children's wing, talked with some of the parents, played with the minute patients when allowed. I was humbled by their behavior, their courage, their belief, sometimes in the face of unacceptable conclusions and consequences. It was almost more than one could stand. And yet *they* could, and did. Again the brand was seared into my brain, in case I might forget or ignore, how lucky we were.

Tony was about to reap an ultimate reward. He was going to co-star with his idol and everyone else's, Cary Grant. He was a gibbering mass of mush. At least one of us was going to have the opportunity to work with this "star among stars." The magic prevailed under closer inspection. Cary's urbanity alchemized ordinary daily routine, and yet he never seemed unreachable. I repeat, quite a man! The picture was *Operation Petticoat* for Universal, with Robert Arthur producing, Stanley Shapiro writing, and Blake Edwards directing, with Joan O'Brien, Dina Merrill, Gene Evans, Arthur O'Connell, and Richard Sargent. Funny idea—nurses are rescued from a besieged island and taken aboard a crippled but plucky submarine.*

The location was in Key West. In January 1959, I joined Tony for two of the three weeks. Jamie and Kelly were fine, and we required some time alone. There hadn't been much privacy for us recently, and the epidemic of traumas had left us a trifle limp. It was a glorious second honeymoon. We replenished our spring of romantic waters with impulsiveness and spontaneity. Our batteries were recharged and the electricity flowed anew with each look or touch.

I wasn't filming, but I ended up being the public relation representative for the company. I was "Miss—You Name It!" Goldie (Mrs. Robert Arthur) and Bob were influential Republicans with an inside track to the armed services, which was obviously helpful in this particular movie. The various branches contacted Goldie for any requests, and she utilized me. What a time we had!

I actually flew with the "Blue Angels." They were the Navy jet pilots who performed aerobatics in tight formation across the country for recruitment purposes and public awareness. I donned the whole paraphernalia and sat in the second seat of the lead plane. I was terrified, felt like Abner Dean's "What Am I Doing Here?" but couldn't renege. We broke the sound barrier, we flew upside down, all together. When I permitted myself to peek, the other planes seemed near enough to nudge. How exhilarating, how frightening! My cherished prize, later, was a large portrait, inscribed and signed by every member of the team, with me in the midst. A few years afterward, some of the men were killed in an accident caused by flying too closely together.

I had a trip in a Navy helicopter, and I became an honorary submariner. The initiation for the latter necessitated a one-two-three heave into the ocean, which brought back my terror of the ocean depths. But the sailors jumped in with me, so I couldn't very well let on how scared I was.

Batista had been ousted, and Fidel Castro was about to make his triumphant march into Havana. Key West was a mere ninety miles away, and the studio had a promotional brainstorm. Why didn't

---

* Another thread in that spider web of coincidence. Jamie Lee's first part under her contract at Universal was as one of those nurses in the ABC series "Operation Petticoat," eighteen years later.

Cary and Tony and Janet go over and greet the conquering hero? It would be the biggest publicity coup—make every newspaper headline and magazine cover worldwide. Preparations were actually under way, and excitement mounted. Thank our lucky stars there was *one* thinking prophet in the vicinity. This small voice quietly posed a question, "But what if he isn't quite what we think he is? What if it turns out he isn't one of us? And there are the documented pictures linking Cary and Tony and Janet to Castro?" Mouths gaped, heads scratched, and the wheels in motion came to a screeching halt.

By 1959, our "Tinsel Town Trolley" was well on its journey. We moved in all circles. We saw the latest movies at various private projection rooms, mainly at Lottie and Harold Mirisch's. We played team gin rummy with Anne and Kirk, Glo and Sammy Cahn, Edie Adams and Ernie Kovacs, Audrey and Billy Wilder, Lottie and Harold. We attended the intimate dinners at Swifty's (Irving Lazar), Frank Sinatra's, Joan and George Axelrod's, Edie and Lew's, Edie and Bill Goetz's, Roger Edens's, Pat and Peter Lawford's. And the big affairs. We spent weekends and weeks in Palm Springs with Anne and Kirk or Lottie and Harold or Jeanne and Dean, and soon bought our own desert refuge. We entertained, and Camp Curtis was founded. On weekends, chums and children would gather for fun and games and we had Camp Curtis T-shirts made. And there were constantly new acquisitions. One birthday we had a party and Tony hired a plane to fly overhead with a banner, "Happy Birthday Janet." On another, I found a rack of Jax dresses (Jax clothes were almost a uniform then) in the living room. Heady stuff!

In February, the list of Academy Award nominations was announced. Best Actor category included David Niven for *Separate Tables,* Spencer Tracy for *The Old Man and the Sea,* Paul Newman for *Cat on a Hot Tin Roof,* Sidney Poitier for *The Defiant Ones,* and TONY CURTIS for *The Defiant Ones. The Defiant Ones* also received the nod for Best Picture, Stanley Kramer for Best Director, Theodore Bikel for Best Supporting Actor, Cara Williams for Best Supporting Actress, Nathan E. Douglas and Harold Jacob Smith for Best Screenplay Written Directly for the Screen.

Such a high spot! We were thrilled. It was nice the nominees had some weeks to bask in glory, to savor the honor, to acknowledge

TOP: our tub scene, 1961. BOTTOM: left, a delightful respite, after the Inauguration, in Palm Beach. Top row: Peter Lawford, Ambassador Kennedy, Roger Edens; middle: Pat Kennedy Lawford, Janet; bottom: Tony, Leonard Gershe. Right, Danny Kaye, Tony, and I performing the song "Triplets" for the Academy Awards show, 1961.

TOP: with Eleanor Roosevelt prior to the Madison Square Garden Event, 1961. BOTTOM: with Dick Van Dyke on the set of *Bye Bye Birdie,* 1962.

To Mr. & Mrs. Robert Brandt
with appreciation for a most enjoyable visit
Lyndon B. Johnson

TOP: our wedding celebration hosted by Dean Martin at the Sands Hotel in Las Vegas, Nevada, 1962. BOTTOM: Bob and I at the White House with Vice President Johnson, 1963.

TOP: left, with Rock Hudson, receiving an award from Mayor Yorty, 1967. Right, Bob and I with Ted Kennedy, 1963. BOTTOM: on the set of *Wives and Lovers,* with Van Johnson and two little onlookers — Jamie and Kelly, 1963.

With Bette Davis at a benefit performance for the Variety Club, 1970.

Jamie and Kelly in my dressing room on the set of *Three on a Couch*, 1965.

TOP: a family ski trip in Aspen pleasantly interrupted by President Johnson's invitation to me to become Ambassador to Finland. BOTTOM: on location for *The Fog* with Adrienne Barbeau, director John Carpenter and my daughter Jamie Lee Curtis.

TOP: left, learning my part — the swinging ladder — for the SHARE Show, 1978. Right, Kelly, 1982. BOTTOM: left, with my daughter Kelly at Triangle X Ranch, Moose, Wyoming, 1971. Right, success at Snake River, Wyoming, 1972.

the earned adulation, because the Academy Award night itself was nerve-racking suspense. The only calm people in our family were the girls. Jamie just gave us her little "gas smile," and Kelly attached no importance whatsoever to "Daddy's nom-a-shun." It was almost impossible to mask the mental anguish as we walked the long path to the theatre. Especially for Tony. The hand in mine was cold and clammy and his face was pinched tight. He had said he didn't hold much hope, probably Sidney and he would cancel each other's chances, but just like that day for me long ago in Miss Burns's office, one can't strangle that bud of promise. As the evening wore on, our tension intensified. Nathan and Harold won for their screenplay, maybe that was a good omen! And then the boom lowered. Cara lost to Wendy Hiller *(Separate Tables)*, Theodore lost to Burl Ives *(The Big Country)*, Stanley lost to Vincent Minnelli *(Gigi)*, the picture lost to *Gigi*, and Sidney and Tony lost to David Niven *(Separate Tables)*. This had been a highly competitive year, every nomination worthy of the distinction, every winner deserving of the award.

Of course Tony had to be disappointed. But he had made his mark, and in impeccable company.

I returned to work in late spring in a delightful comedy from Columbia, *Who Was That Lady?* with Tony and Dean, and James Whitmore, John McIntire, Barbara Nichols, Larry Keating, and an early friend, Larry Storch. Norman Krasna adapted from his original play, and George Sidney produced and directed. This was a romp from start to finish; I hope the audience had as much fun as we did. The basic premise: a professor (Tony) is seen by his wife (me) embracing a beautiful student; his buddy (Dean) invents the excuse that they are both FBI agents on duty, the professor was after information; the only problem develops when legitimate foreign spies believe their story. We really rolled with this one. The personal familiarity of the three of us allowed absolute freedom, and the interplay was wild and woolly and inventive. There was one close-up of Tony by the fireplace, listening to his friend rave about his unselfish devotion to the cause, where you could see the struggle not to break up. Dean carried on with such nonsense off camera, and the result was perfect, and different.

Possibly the worst, or best, water war happened on this film.

Again it started innocently and quietly. A paper cup here, a flick there. It grew to water guns, first casually, then ambush. We would wait on top of our dressing rooms for one unsuspecting victim to return from lunch or the restroom and attacked from above with one or two weapons.

The climax of the combat and the picture coincided. The two pseudosleuths believed they were in a sinking submarine, dying for their country, clutching each other, patriotically singing "The Star-Spangled Banner." Actually they had been locked in the basement of the Empire State Building and a pipe had broken. The water gushed from the pumps and began rising around them. I was through for the day and had said my good-byes. Only I hid. When George had all the footage he needed for the shot, he gave me the signal and kept the camera rolling. I let myself be caught in the stream and then blithely swam by them, nonchalantly waving hello. Their reaction was unintelligible, unrepeatable, and unmatchable. I was victorious!

Kelly was to start nursery school in September. Anne Douglas, Judy Goetz Shepherd, and I had scouted all the existing schools and had settled on the John Thomas Dye School. A small, peaceful, highly recommended private institution on Chalon Road in Bel Air, offering nursery, kindergarten, primary, first through eighth grades. The car-pool days were about to begin, and wouldn't end for sixteen years. And I wouldn't trade those times for anything. Sleepy little faces (and one big sleepy face), scared little faces, eager little faces, rebellious little faces, loving little faces. Special, indelible hours for a mother.

One hurdle before this commenced, however. In late August the girls and I were having our bath together, a treat we shared often, and I noticed a swelling on Kelly's side. Alarmed and already wary I called for Dr. Zall who called for Dr. Gans who sent us packing to the hospital. It was one of those unaccountable quirks of nature that both children would have the same problem! Handling Kelly, however, presented a different challenge than with Jamie. She had been to the doctor's office for checkups and shots and had already expressed her dislike for this treatment quite vehemently. Getting her to sit still for the necessary examinations and preparations was nearly hopeless. We tried games, we tried everything, but I couldn't lie to her and say, "This won't hurt, honey." Finally, we hit upon the right ingredients for a solution. The nurse did the procedure with me first, and I gave an honest reaction. Then it was her turn, and we compared notes. She was old enough to be insecure with this irregular incarceration, and I wanted her to understand and cooperate as much as she was able. We were moderately successful. But the surgery was totally successful. Kelly's recuperation period forced her to delay starting in school, but at that level it didn't really matter.

Another member of the family developed a health problem. Tony was in the middle of *Spartacus,* an extremely well-made Roman versus slave epic produced by Universal and Bryna, and boasting weighty professionals. Dalton Trumbo wrote, and Stanley Kubrick directed Kirk Douglas, Laurence Olivier, Charles Laughton, Jean Simmons, Peter Ustinov, John Gavin, Nina Foch, Herbert Lom, John Ireland, John Dall, Charles McGraw, and Woody Strode.

One night at a tennis party given by Anne and Kirk, Tony, who never played, decided to try hitting the ball. He was a good athlete and well coordinated and was doing quite well, running all over the court, when he lunged and heard a snap. He hurt and stopped, but it wasn't until the next day that the full extent of his injury was known. The pain increased, and the diagnosis was a severed Achilles tendon. The A.D. called me from the set, and I rushed to Cedars-Sinai. The doctors had to go all the way up the leg to pull the tendon back down and secure it. Tony would be in a cast from four to six weeks. He was fit to be tied. The company adjusted the schedule. Fortunately there was plenty to film without him, and he fidgeted. It was harder to keep him under control than Kelly.

CHAPTER EIGHTEEN

Alfred Hitchcock. My mind kaleidoscoped stars and scenes of his movies, interlaced with people and places of my life. Laurence Olivier and Joan Fontaine in *Rebecca,* Joel McCrea and Laraine Day in *Foreign Correspondent*—Stockton and Dick Doane. Cary Grant, Joan Fontaine in *Suspicion*—Merced and Kenny. Gregory Peck, Ingrid Bergman in *Spellbound*—Stockton and Stan. Cary Grant, Ingrid Bergman in *Notorious*—Hollywood and Stan. James Stewart, Farley Granger in *Rope*—Hollywood and Barry. Marlene Dietrich, Jane Wyman, Michael Wilding in *Stage Fright*—Hollywood and Arthur. *Strangers on a Train, Dial "M" for Murder, Rear Window, To Catch a Thief, The Man Who Knew Too Much, Vertigo, North by Northwest*—Hollywood and Tony.

Alfred Hitchcock! Descriptions and depictions skirmished for admittance to my head. Genius. Suspense. Girth. Clever. Witty. Master. Naughty. Cameo. Mystery. Pretty ladies. Debonair men. Evil. Controversial.

Alfred Hitchcock sent me a book to peruse, a novel entitled *Psycho* by Robert Bloch, that was to be his next film. I was to consider the role of Marion. I would have said yes without reading the manuscript or without his assurance that Marion would be improved and upgraded. The size of the part had no bearing. Alfred Hitchcock was enough incentive for me.

The first in-person encounter was tea in Hitchcock's home on Bellagio Road, in November 1959. His deportment was cordial, matter-of-fact and academic. He outlined his modus operandi. The angles and shots of each scene were predetermined, carefully charted before the picture began. There could be no deviations. His camera was absolute. Within the boundary of the lens circumference, the player was given freedom, as long as the performance didn't interfere with the already designed move. "I hired you because you are an actress! I will only direct you if A, you attempt to take more than your share of the pie, or B, if you don't take enough, or C, if you are having trouble motivating the necessary timed motion."

I could see how this method might incur the indignation of some actors, be considered too set, hindering, confining. But I thought of it in a different light. This was the way the man worked. And since I had profound respect for his results, I would earnestly comply. As I reflected, I realized he was in actuality complimenting our profession, giving credit to our ability to inspire our own reasons behind a given movement. He was proposing a challenge, throwing down the gauntlet to our ingenuity. And I intended to be a contestant. Marion was on the screen only a short time, but she was a focal point and offered unlimited potentials in characterization.

Much has been written about Hitchcock, pro and con. I am in accord with some documents and take exception to others. The basis for my opinions rests solely on my individual exposure and observation. I've had no inside tunnel to the mine of facts and figures of others. I hope biographers of Hitchcock and *any* late personages who chose a negative approach *did* have access to pertinent information, or they would be guilty of grave injustice to the memory of the dignitary in question, and to the legion of admirers whose hero they have tarnished.

Days on the set with Hitch were surprisingly calm, pleasant, swift. Because the work was already delineated, he was relatively relaxed. The crew functioned quickly because he was prepared. Once he knew my sense of humor, he enjoyed being the raconteur. Sometimes I would still be laughing from a story (usually risqué), and the A.D. would inform him the camera was ready, he would give the signal to roll, and I would have to call a halt, to get my head straight for Marion.

He relished scaring me. He experimented with the mother's corpse, using me as his gauge. I would return from lunch, open the door to the dressing room, and propped in my chair would be this hideous monstrosity. The horror in my scream, registered on his Richter scale, decided his choice of the Madame.

He was very thoughtful in regard to comfort and safety. His first impulse was to have me wear contact lenses for the close shot of the dead eye. When we went to the optometrist to select the lens and be fitted, the doctor explained he would need a few weeks with me to demonstrate the insertion procedure and accustom my organs to the foreign objects, or else my eye surface could be damaged. We didn't have the time, and Hitch wouldn't permit the risk, so he scrapped that idea. "You'll just have to go it alone, ole girl." And he was adamant about the temperature of the shower water, tested it himself to insure its warmth. Which caused me a slight embarrassment.

What I was to wear in the shower gave the wardrobe supervisor migraines. I had to appear nude, without being nude. She and I pored over striptease magazines, hoping one of their costumes would be the answer. Every male on the set tried to donate his services in the search. We had popular literature. There was an impressive display of pinwheels, feathers, sequins, toy propellers, balloons, etc., but nothing suitable for our needs. Finally the supervisor came up with a simple solution: flesh-colored moleskin. Perfect! So each morning for seven shooting days and seventy-one setups, we covered my private parts, and we were in business.

The lengthy shot, starting with the eye in full frame and gradually easing back to disclose the draped body still clutching the torn curtain, the running water, the entire bathroom, was a thorny intricacy, from the technical side and from my side. I had to fix and maintain that empty glazed stare. Hitch found the spot where the camera wouldn't pick up a blink and snapped his fingers to let me know. (Mrs. Hitchcock always claimed, "I saw Janet blink in the film." I didn't see anything, but I couldn't be positive it wasn't there.) For sundry reasons we had to do it over and over. At long last a take was near completion without a mishap. Abruptly I felt something strange happening around my breasts. The steam from the hot water had melted the adhesive on the moleskin, and I sensed the napped cotton fabric peeling away from my skin. What to do? Decisions, decisions! To spoil the so far successful shot and be modest? Or get it over with and be immodest? I opted for immodesty. No one there would see anything they hadn't seen before—it was below the edge of the tub and out of the camera's view—and I had had enough of that gauche position. I made the correct judgment. That was the printed take, and no one noticed my bareness before I could cover up. I think!

Brilliant artist Saul Bass designed the titles, and also did a thorough storyboard for the shower-scene montage. Hitchcock diligently adhered to Bass's blueprint. Some of the prescribed angles required the construction of elaborate scaffolding, just for a few seconds' flash on the screen. But there was no compromising. Certainly that is one reason why the sequence had such impact. The combined endowments of these two gave us a course in fantasy. Did we see the knife penetrate? Or didn't we? Did we see complete nudity? Or didn't we? Our mind's fantasy will swear we saw both. That demonstrated their skill and our entrapment. I believe that class of film making was more effective than the current standard. The censorship obliged creators to find a way to show, without showing, thus giving the viewers liberal range for their imaginations. This was much more demanding for the architects. It's fairly uncomplicated to take a picture of the lethal weapon apparently slashing an obviously naked body with blood gushing in full view, which is tolerated today, but far more complex to present the *illusion* of that happening.

Even with the existent strict code, Hitchcock was cunning in getting certain heretofore taboo images on the screen. He traded. He deliberately inserted more questionable shots in the script, knowing quite well they would be unacceptable, but with each disallowed one, he gained leverage in his bargaining for the ones he had really wanted all along. He argued that the unprecedented shot and sound of a toilet flushing was a vital component of the plot. Lila Crane (Vera Miles) found the scrap of paper that had refused to go down and substantiated that her sister, Marion, had been in the motel. Marion's half-clad appearance in the opening shot with her lover Sam (John Gavin) was necessary to prove the furtiveness and futility of the affair, which prompted her theft. The mixed blood and water gurgling down the drain was the necessary chilling substitute for any blood spurting or bloodstains.

There have been conjectures for two decades about the use or nonuse of a nude model in the shower sequence. This is what I know:

When Norman Bates (Anthony Perkins) cleaned the bathroom after the murder and put the body in a sheet and dragged it to the car, that was a model. Hitch told me there was no reason to subject me to the discomfort since it was a distant high angle anyway. He also told me his original intent, as discussed with the writer Joseph Stefano and whomever, had been to employ a professional model for some of the shower shots. But he said he abandoned that thought because we had already accomplished what was essential. I have observed the film many times, and I can't find any glimpse of an unfamiliar shot in that montage.

Hitchcock made films for us to enjoy on varying levels of insight. You might see one the first time and appreciate just the entertainment, enough in itself of course. Then you might see the same picture a second time and discover a sublayer of meaning. The third time could uncover even deeper values. Donald Spoto, professor, lecturer, writer, and authority on Hitchcock, wrote a fascinating book, *The Art of Alfred Hitchcock,* in which he detailed in depth this multitiered perception. An abbreviated illustration in *Psycho:*

> Hitchcock directs the audience . . . It is *our* psyche that is being opened up, analyzed, searched. "Psycho" is a film that really takes place in the mind of the viewer . . . The camera lens becomes the eye of the viewer . . . waiting to be shocked and willing to indulge in the crassest kind of voyeurism . . . A further indication . . . is the constant use of mirrors . . . no accident. The story concerns a pathologically split personality, and the constant presence of mirrors suggests that the other characters are similarly split. What we are really frightened by is the alarming suggestion that we all have split personalities to some degree . . . Because the camera forces our identification first with Marion and then with Norman, and because the ubiquitous mirrors reflect them out, towards us, it becomes impossible to separate ourselves emotionally or psychologically from their moral descent . . .
>
> . . . the "cutting" imagery . . . the bisecting horizontals and verticals (in many shots) . . . and other suggestions of slashing . . .
>
> The double meanings denoted in - bird - ! In English slang - a bird - is a young girl. What did Norman Bates do for a hobby? - he stuffed birds. What was Marion's last name? - Crane. Where did Marion Crane live? - in Phoenix (a city

named for the mythic bird that returns from the dead). Where did Marion sit in Norman's parlor? - on a couch in front of a wall of stuffed birds. What did Norman say when Marion left her sandwich? - "You eat like a bird." What was Norman's last name? - Bates. And don't you "bait" birds?

There are endless examples of what can be discerned in Hitchcock's movies, and they are all there, waiting to surprise us.

Psycho was an enormously commercial success, but oddly not critically acclaimed in the beginning. It is interesting, and gratifying, that over twenty years later, the imprint of that film is still vividly etched in most minds. And, for the record, *no, I do not take showers.*

Psycho was written by Joseph Stefano from a novel by Robert Bloch, the photographer was John L. Russell, and the music was by Bernard Herrmann. The cast included Anthony Perkins, Vera Miles, John Gavin, John McIntire, Martin Balsam, and Simon Oakland.

Nineteen-sixty was a year of increased political awareness and involvement. Our family had always been Democrats, and when I was of age, I followed the tradition. I voted religiously, rooted for my candidates, was disappointed if they didn't win, and that was about the extent of it.

When I first arrived in Hollywood, Selena Royle took me to a Screen Actors Guild meeting, but I wasn't enticed enough to be anything more than a passive member. I was too busy with the demands of my life, trying to make a living in my new profession. In the fall of 1947, Congressman J. Parnell Thomas, head of the House Un-American Activities Committee, began investigating Hollywood. Fear ran through the creative community, and a blacklist circulated in the high echelons of the studios. A contingent of the brightest luminaries in show business made a pilgrimage to Washington, D.C., to protest the scare tactics employed by the Committee. It seemed in this case, anyone questioned was guilty until proven innocent, rather than what our law really states, innocent until proven guilty. I read about these proceedings; it was the first time I had heard the phrase "taking the Fifth," meaning a person cannot be forced to testify against himself. I abhorred any injustice or infringement on human rights, but I didn't align with any organization. I really couldn't see how my small voice would carry any weight or tip any balance.

In 1950 the Republican senator from Wisconsin, Joseph McCarthy, began his tirade, accusing the State Department of harboring Communists, charging Communist infiltration into government, education, defense industries, and other fields. Highly publicized congressional hearings were the order of the day. Again, I deplored vague innuendos, but felt no urge to join an attack group. At twenty-three, my head had no room for extracurricular activities; my work and my love commanded my attention. And participation by me wouldn't have altered the course of events. Amends were made when the Senate censured McCarthy in 1954, but not before irreparable damage was done to countless lives.

The Korean War, 1950 to 1953, brought my patriotic response and sympathy for the brave men lost. For the average citizenry, of which I was one, there wasn't much more we could do.

Far away in Vietnam, too far away in distance and scope for most of us to acknowledge, the Vietnamese Communists defeated the French in 1954; 1959 saw the Communist-supported guerrilla forces from North Vietnam (Vietcong) invade South Vietnam, and in 1960 the United States sent more military advisers to South Vietnam.

There lay the history of my political sophistication. I had backed Adlai Stevenson in 1952 and 1956. I believed, and believe, he was a great man. But one could not dislike Dwight Eisenhower, and once he was President, he deserved loyalty. In 1960, however, I was looking for a sun to rise on the Democratic horizon.

In early March 1960, the Screen Actors Guild announced that negotiations for a new contract with the Motion Picture Producers Association of America were at a stalemate. On March 7 a strike was declared. When we were asked at dinner parties by a producer or a head of a studio why the actors were still striking after so many concessions had been made and problems reconciled, our foolish answer was, "We're not sure!"

We were not in a precarious personal situation. Tony had just done *Rat Race* with Debbie Reynolds, I had finished *Pepe* with the wonderful Cantinflas from Mexico and a "cast of thousands," and Tony was on a holding salary for his next. But a shutdown threw thousands out of work in an already shaky industry, and we were concerned. We wondered how many of the membership were as confused as we. With T's blessing, I organized an open meeting at our home. I called and asked the board to speak to us. I alerted the trade papers, inviting the rank and file, only stipulation being they had to call to give their guild card number and put their names on a list as attendees—so we wouldn't have any crackpots causing chaos. I enlisted the aid of the Beverly Hills Police Department, who were instrumental in maintaining order and keeping out crashers. I rented chairs for the emptied dining room. I was ready. What I hadn't anticipated was the media reaction. This was construed as an antistrike move, as a threat to the unity of the union, and played to the hilt in every publication. And all we wanted was information!

No wonder a curt, grim Ronald Reagan, president of SAG, and his executive committee strode sternly to the setup head table and wasted no time in addressing the audience. The turnout was imposing, representing both sides of the issues. The salient point of contention was over the handling of the residuals of motion pictures going to television covering the period from 1948 to 1960. When Mr. Reagan explained the union's position and answered questions from the floor, the majority present agreed with the course of action and endorsed the leaders. Afterward, when everyone was at ease, Reagan appointed David Niven and me as liaisons to the producers. David and I looked at each other in disbelief. *Us?* What could *we* do? We did eventually meet with some people but I don't think accomplished much toward ending the strike. Nancy Davis Reagan and Ron were in close contact with Tony and me for the duration. Emotions were inflamed, especially as financial pressures increased and funds decreased. Then one glorious day, April 18, 1960, a news bulletin flashed—settlement had been reached. The compromise was the producers established a lump-sum welfare plan. The joy was the return to work and paychecks. We didn't hear from the Reagans again; he resigned from the SAG presidency soon after. The noticeable result for me exclusively was my unbidden involvement.

In the summer, at the Lawfords' Santa Monica home, Pat asked if we would host the September kickoff luncheon for her brother's campaign to be President of the United States.

John Fitzgerald Kennedy. On television at the 1956 Democratic Party Convention in Chicago, I had seen his struggle with Senator

Kefauver for the vice presidency. He withdrew, but he had made a mark. I had heard about the young congressman who became the young senator who became the young author (of *Profiles in Courage*). I learned more about the Kennedy family as our friendship with Pat and Peter ripened. I had just witnessed his debate with Lyndon Johnson at the Los Angeles Democratic Convention and his unanimous first-ballot nomination. And I unhesitatingly answered in the affirmative to Pat's request. I had found my sun.

I believed in that man. He didn't seem to make speeches, he *talked* to the people. And he cared for the people he talked to. He was a human being—not a perfect human being, but one whose ego could accept that, and then press on toward his goals for the country. He was courageous, able to admit and take blame for a failure, undaunted by awesome power, strong against aggression, vengeful against prejudice, unafraid to explore the unknown outer space, and valiant enough "to show friends and foe alike the suicidal futility of nuclear war and the enduring possibilities of peace." He had compassion for the ill, for the old, for the young, for human dignity, for human rights. He had the capacity to bring the American people to a realization of their responsibilities, to indeed "ask not what your country can do for you, ask what you can do for your country."

I went to work with an impassioned dedication. Once I was committed, I didn't do things by halves—it was gung ho! I discovered I was not alone, most of Kennedy's disciples had the same zeal. I met scores of new friends in my adopted venture. Two in particular, Rosalind and Eugene Wyman. Ros was then a Los Angeles councilwoman and Gene a prominent lawyer. She was in charge of the opening luncheon, among numerous other duties. The affair was an unequivocal bonanza. When Ros saw the numbers mount, she approached our next-door neighbor, Joe von Ronkle, to ask if he would accommodate the overflow. He went one better. He offered to put a gate in the fence separating our properties so passage between would be simplified. Another relationship bloomed.

The day was gorgeous, but Beverly Hills was never the same again. Hundreds of buses, filled to the brim, came from every district of the county. Traffic was backed up all the way down the hill south of Sunset and the Beverly Hills Hotel. The battered policemen were lost in the sea of cars and vans and buses. Thank God

Edward Kennedy, our speaker, and Frank and Dean and Sammy, our entertainment, had arrived early at the house. There were no more tidbits, nothing left to sip, the hubbub was deafening, and a riot imminent, when at long last the final unloaded guests straggled in and we could begin. The sound had been piped to both areas, but since the second yard was also crowded, we did two shows. Once we started, the audience couldn't have cared less about the arrival inconvenience or the insufficient food and beverage. They were mesmerized by Frank and Dean and Sammy and Ted—and 100 percent for J.F.K. Quite a day!

That may have been our first political rally, but it definitely was not our last. Tony was shooting *The Great Imposter,* so I was mainly designated as the recruiter. I became a deputy registrar and traveled to every nook and cranny to encourage registration. One time, at a shopping center, there was a long line waiting, and after a while a little lady was standing before me.

"Hello there!" I greeted. "I'll just start right off. Party preference?" Pause. "Name?"

A blank look. "What do you mean?"

Now my blank look. "Well, aren't you here to register to vote?"

Panic. "Oh, dear me, I saw the queue and I just joined. I, uh, I thought you were giving something away."

"As long as you're here, are you registered, or may I help you?"

More panic. "No. Oh, I mean, my husband takes care of all that!" And the poor woman fled.

I made appearances all over the state, and penetrated other states as well. In Arizona, Goldwater territory, we had a lukewarm reception; we were considered iconoclasts, I guess.

I was with Tony on the first location for *The Outsider.* What a heartbreaking true story that was. Ira Hayes, an unassuming American Indian, accidently became a war hero when he was asked to assist in the flag raising on Iwo Jima. (In 1945 photographer Jack Rosenthal won the Pulitzer prize for his historic still of World War II, used on posters for war-loan drives.) Unfortunately Hayes couldn't cope with the fame or comprehend the responsibility; which resulted in the waste of a good man. The producer was Sy Bartlett, the director Delbert Mann, and James Franciscus, Bruce Bennett, Gregory Walcott, and Vivian Nathan were featured.

While in Arizona, we visited Ira Hayes's real-life family on the reservation, and we were unprepared for the conditions. A two-room hut housed several occupants; there was a dirt floor and barren wasteland outside. No water. Beyond the border dividing the settlement from other property we saw lush irrigated green fields waving healthily in the breeze. We didn't understand the disparity.

Frank, Peter, Tony, and I joined Senator Kennedy at the podium in a New Jersey speech. This was Frank's home stamping ground, and there wasn't a place big enough to hold the gathered crowds.

In Los Angeles, at the Shrine Auditorium, Kennedy broke all records. Thousands couldn't fit inside and chanted in the streets, "All the way with J.F.K.! All the way with J.F.K.!"

I believed those outside should also have personal contact, so I prevailed upon Ros, the reluctant harassed security officers, and a few other performers backstage to brave the crush and go on out. It was almost a disastrous endeavor, however well meant. Funny thing though, once the mobs realized we weren't trying to get away, that we were moving toward and in the midst of them, we had safe passage, and the improvised show and sing-along confirmed their endorsement. I recalled and used that crowd psychology often.

We met the remainder of the Kennedy ensemble: Eunice and Sargent Shriver, Ethel and Robert Kennedy, Jean and Stephen Smith, Ambassador and Mrs. Joseph Kennedy, plus Governor and Mrs. "Pat" Brown, Pierre Salinger, Theodore Sorensen, Theodore H. White, and on and on.

The four debates between then Vice President Nixon, the Republican candidate for President, and Senator John F. Kennedy took place on September 26, October 7, October 13, October 21. They escalated in rancor, and the proposed fifth debate was scuttled by the Nixon camp. Undoubtedly the Kennedy image had been substantially strengthened. Political observers and laymen alike were increasingly impressed with Kennedy's command of facts and his ability to push Nixon into generalization. He appeared cool, collected, nerveless. And he spoke directly to the television audience. The experiment itself succeeded beyond the wildest dreams. It was estimated that 120,000,000 Americans had seen at least one of the four meetings. Never before had so many seen and heard the two men between whom they had to choose.

The big day, November 8, 1960. We had a large group over to watch the returns; no one wanted to be alone, either in victory or

defeat. Ros and Gene, Ruth and Milton, Frank, Sammy, Glo and
Sammy, Lennie and Roger, Barbara Rush and Warren Cowan, Pat
Newcomb, Lottie and Harold, Gwen Davis (author), and more that
I forget. All eyes glued to the set, fingernails gone along with
nerves. Cheers—then groans—cheers—groans—cheers—cheers—
cheers! The Kennedy electoral vote was 258 to 269 needed. Nixon
couldn't win, but because of a few unpledged elector states, the
election could be thrown into the House of Representatives. Nixon
did not concede that night. I remember someone, in frustration,
yelling at the television, "Concede, damn it, concede!"

Bleary-eyed people stumbled home about 4 A.M., tentatively jubilant. The next morning we learned Minnesota had definitely gone
Democratic, and the suspense was over. John Fitzgerald Kennedy
would be the thirty-fifth President of the United States. We had
won!

Some other things happened in 1960, of course. The girls continued to grow and learn and be bottomless wells of delectability.

Alex Illes, a member of the Hungarian Olympic Soccer Team,
was interviewed on radio in his native land, and made the mistake
of saying, "I am going to Hollywood and marry Janet Leigh." He
was suspended from the team, and the newspaper headlines read,
"How the U.S.A. uses movie stars to lure our citizens!"

And the long-held, tightly guarded secret of my teenage indiscre-
tion became public knowledge. I had done an in-depth interview
for a credited national publication with a trusted writer, who had
done his homework but who also had the sensitivity and ability to
handle a delicate subject. I bit the bullet. I felt this was the time and
the circumstances for divulging my first "marriage," before an irresponsible and inaccurate report surfaced. The irony was no one
gave a damn. All the pain, the fear, the worry, and no one gave it a
passing thought. All except Kenny, who objected through a lawyer
to the use of the word "dark." Nothing came of it because I had
only described him, and he did have dark hair and dark eyes. I was
still convinced, however, that an earlier disclosure could have had
quite a different result. In any case, it was a relief to have the
episode over and out. The damage had already been done to my
soul, but maybe one day that would be over and out too.

Tony was again on location for *The Outsider* at the Marine base

Camp Pendleton. The girls and I were with him in nearby Ocean-side. Warren Cowan made a trip down, to urge me to make a bid for an Academy Award nomination for *Psycho,* in the Best Actress category. "Are you crazy? I am only in the first third of the picture. No possible way! Anyhow, I'm too scared."

He kept insisting, "At least for Best Supporting Actress." I said I'd think about it. When I returned to Los Angeles, Lew, Edd, Herb, Warren, and I had a confab.

Normally Lew was taciturn about anything promotional, but this time he was vocal. "I think you should. Hitch thinks you should. The picture is an undisputed box-office champ, and your contribution certainly warrants recognition." Hitchcock, whose parsimoniousness was well known, offered to foot the bill for the ads in the trade papers. Well, what did I have to lose? Besides a little security, a little pride, a little dent in my protective armor! Okay, I agreed, Rogers and Cowan could go ahead with the advertisements.

CHAPTER NINETEEN

Nineteen sixty-one had all the elements of being one of the best years of our lives. We shall see.

It sure started off on the right foot. Plans and preparations for the January 19 Gala, the January 20 Inauguration, the inaugural balls were hot and heavy. Edith Head made me two stunning gowns and a cocktail dress. Frank was to produce the Gala, Roger Edens to be associate producer, Lennie Gershe was to write the book and Sammy Cahn the special lyrics, and scores of the famous in all fields were to participate.

The huge chartered plane was loaded with merrymaking moviemakers. Someone cracked, "If this plane crashes, the entertainment business is through!" Not funny. Not funny either was the novel I couldn't put down, Richard Condon's *The Manchurian Candidate*. I finished it on the flight and was so agitated I hurled it down the aisle. Luckily, it was a paperback. I couldn't shake this sinister shadowy feeling about that book. I didn't know then I would do the picture version. And I didn't know then about future assassination plots that would be successful and change the very core of our existence.

Ethel and Bobby had a dinner party the first night at their Virginia estate. And the next day was the rehearsal at the National Guard Armory, the site for the Gala. Leonard Bernstein conducted Gene Kelly, Milton Berle, Nat King Cole, Harry Belafonte, Fredric March, Juliet Prowse, Ethel Merman, Jimmy Durante, Alan King, Keely Smith, Louis Prima, Bette Davis, Joey Bishop, Helen Traubel, Ella Fitzgerald, Frank Sinatra, Peter Lawford, Tony, and me. The album of photographs from the rehearsal and performance belongs in a museum, except I wouldn't part with it. It is priceless.

Those photos captured the spirit, the idealism, the unabashed devotion we all felt toward the President. We were all for one, and he was one for all.

A snowstorm nearly ruined the evening. Traffic was almost at a standstill. We had no chance to return to the hotel to change. Some of the performers went onstage in their rehearsal clothes. My plucky hair stylist, Fred, who had come from New York, brought as many outfits as he could carry and find from the rooms, so a few of us were able to glitter. The talent glowed regardless.

The show was two hours late starting; half the symphony orchestra still missed the opening. But as soon as President and Mrs. Kennedy with family arrived, it began. And I think was enjoyed, despite the fact that some of the audience never did get through the blizzard.

Ambassador Kennedy gave a party at a Washington restaurant afterward, attended by the President, and the exhilarated gathering celebrated most of the night.

The day of the Inauguration was bitterly cold. We had chosen to watch it on television in the suite. It would have been impossible to see well, even with reserved seats. So, comfortable and warm, our group listened to Marian Anderson sing "The Star-Spangled Banner," a prayer, and Robert Frost recite his poem "The Gift Outright." We applauded Lyndon Baines Johnson of Texas as Vice President. And we sat spellbound as Kennedy took the oath and delivered his inaugural address. His text was brilliant, relatively short, and hailed by Republicans and diplomats as well as by Democrats. We cried when the band played "Hail to the Chief" for the first time for President Kennedy.

The inaugural balls, many in number, were held that evening. The President and his First Lady were present at each one, ending with Frank's forces at the Statler Hotel. Frank had gifts for everyone, on which the invitation to the Inauguration was engraved. These events would live forever in the minds and hearts of the participants.

We weren't through! January 21, we witnessed the investiture of Robert Kennedy as Attorney General of the United States, which was followed by a luncheon at Hickory Hill (Ethel and Bobby's home). Directly from there, we whizzed to the airport and the family plane, *The Caroline.* Ambassador and Mrs. Kennedy had invited us to Palm Beach. Jean Kennedy and Steve Smith, the Ambassador, Pat and Peter, Lennie, Roger, Tony, and I boarded the plush craft and headed for fun and games. Frank had to return to California for work and wasn't able to make this section of the trip.

It was a revealing experience. Amid the elegant manor, the expansive gardens extending to the ocean, children and grandchildren frolicked freely. There was a casual air but all the accouterments of formality. The President could call to speak with his father who might be bouncing a tot or two on his lap. We thoroughly enjoyed the hospitable visit and the insight into a remarkable family.

"Don't let it be forgot, that once there was a spot, for one brief shining moment that was known as Camelot."

February 27, 1961.

The sound of the telephone jarred the quiet of our Palm Springs house and I involuntarily jumped. The servants were off; no one but me to answer. The girls were napping in their rooms, so I ran to get it.

"Hello?" I said in a tiny voice.

"Janet?"

"Uh-huh."

The voice on the other end spoke each word very slowly, carefully, deliberately. "You have just been nominated for an Academy Award."

I silently screamed and yelled so I wouldn't wake the children.

"Oh my God. Tell me when did they announce it. Tell me, who else? Tell me, what did they say? Are you pleased?"

John Forman, of Rogers and Cowan, stopped my jabbering by answering as many questions as he could.

I wanted to run in and wake the girls, but they were two and four, so that would only have resulted in two cranky toddlers for the rest of the day. I knew Tony was playing golf with Frank, but I called the country club anyway.

"Please send someone to find Mr. Curtis and Mr. Sinatra. Tell Mr. Curtis that his wife has just been nominated for an Academy Award. Yes, this is Janet. Oh, thank you, thank you very much."

"Hello, Mom? I—oh, you heard it on the news?"

"Hello, Aunt Pope?"

"Hello, Grandma?"

"Hello, uh, may I speak with Miss Norma Shearer, please?"

"Hello, may I speak with Lillian Burns, please?"

"Hello, may I speak with Mr. Lew Wasserman, please?"

Even when there were no more people to call, I was still floating on cloud nine. I waltzed around the living room and out onto the terrazo floors of the patio, past the pool and into the garden, *all very quietly.* Finally, I lighted on a deck chair and gazed up at the gorgeous desert sky. I wanted to share this glorious feeling with the whole world, to share the wonder of it all.

Me! Fred and Helen's kid, little Jeanette.

> Glynis Johns, "Sundowners"
> Shirley Jones, "Elmer Gantry"
> Shirley Knight, "Dark at the Top of the Stairs"
> Janet Leigh, "Psycho"
> Mary Ure, "Sons and Lovers"

When I saw it in print, I still couldn't believe it. But it was real, it was true. The telegrams and notes of congratulations astounded me, because they weren't only from close associates or bosom buddies, they came from unexpected sources, people whom I knew on a limited basis—Larry Olivier, Greer Garson, Larry Lincoln (a clerk at the Canon branch of Western Union), Spencer Tracy—and my friends. I treasured their good wishes. Joseph Stefano, *Psycho's* writer, sent a beautiful tribute that still gives me chills. "My congratulations on your nomination. It was so right and so deserved. As I told you when I first saw the finished picture, your performance caught my breath and gave me the satisfaction a writer knows only when a deep, fine and thinking actor plays a role he has written. I hope you win the award; it could go to no finer example of expert and exciting picture acting. And I hope we'll be associated again, soon." An actress could ask for nothing more.

Tony, Jack Lemmon, and I did a couple of skits for the Writers Guild Award Dinner. These functions were always a highlight, the writers went all out and the show was a plethora of wit, satire, and virtuosity. Burt Lancaster, nominated for *Elmer Gantry,* did a hilarious parody on *The Music Man.*

Charles (Chuck) Walters, director and choreographer, asked Danny Kaye, Tony, and me to do an updated rendition of "Triplets'' on the Award show. God it was fun to expand and experiment with these achievers.

On March 16, the Foreign Press Golden Globes held their annual award dinner. I had been nominated in the same category. When my name was announced as the winner, my feet turned to lead, my knees to jelly, my head to empty. I was so nervous I forgot to thank Mr. Hitchcock, I don't remember whom I did thank or exactly what I said. What a thrill to win, to be rewarded for the work you love. Maybe it was number three in my life's priority, but it still was my profession.

April 17 was an endless day. We were at the theatre all the time. Rehearsals for "Triplets," and also as presenters, made it necessary for us to dress there. At least I didn't have that arriving long walk down the red carpet. The minutes seemed like hours. Finally, finally, it was under way. Our first appearance was as presenters. Then we scurried circuitously to our assigned seats to await the verdicts. Joseph Hurley and Robert Clatworthy, Art Direction in black and white; George Milo, Set Decoration; John L. Russell, Cinematography black and white, all nominated for *Psycho,* all had already been eliminated. Not an encouraging trend. As each name was read the camera panned to the nominee. I tried to be relaxed and cool, but it just wasn't in me. I was obviously strained, they said my little face almost disappeared. When the envelope was opened, the words rang out: "And the winner is, Shirley Jones for *Elmer Gantry.*" An electric shock ran through my body, and then weirdly, a flood of relief. The letdown would come later. Right then I didn't have time. After applauding Shirley and her acceptance speech, Tony and I were quickly escorted back through the maze of corridors, to prepare for our number. Then I was onstage again, cavorting with Danny and Tony in the zany athletic "Triplets."

Judy Garland Luft, in New York for her Carnegie Hall concerts, called me later that night, and said, "I couldn't believe I was watching someone who had just lost the Oscar."

When I was getting out of my costume and back into my finery, the Best Director winner was proclaimed: "Billy Wilder for *The Apartment.*" *Now* came the tears. I adored Billy, but I so wanted Hitchcock to have the gold statue for *Psycho.* This was his fifth nomination *(Rebecca* in 1940, *Lifeboat* in 1944, *Spellbound* in 1945— when again he lost to Wilder for *The Lost Weekend—Rear Window* in

1954, and now *Psycho* in 1960) and the Oscar had eluded him once more. What a shame!

Of course I was disappointed. Of course I wanted to be victorious. I would be a liar if I said otherwise. But the votes were cast fair and square. It was not my turn. And I *had* been nominated by my peers, and that daylight I would have always.

An emotional tumor was growing, infecting the tissue of our marriage. It was not malignant as yet, but without preventive treatment, it could mushroom at any time. We were beginning to look at our life through different sets of mirrors. There was a stratum of unshared delusion in our atmosphere, as if we should live by separate rules from the rest of the world.

Tony wanted a Rolls-Royce convertible. From what I could determine about our finances, we were already overextended. Not in dire straits by any means—a lot of money was coming in, and earning potential was very strong—but we still had huge expenses and payments and high taxes. I said I thought we should wait, clear up some matters before making new major purchases, be safe and secure. I didn't anticipate his burst of anger and resentment. His attitude was, what good was it to work if you couldn't reap the rewards? And I couldn't agree with the philosophy, buy everything just because you want it. I didn't relish a scene either. I called our lawyer, our business manager, our agent, and said, "You handle this, I want no part in the decision." Tony bought the car; they finagled to accommodate the added credit line. What the hell, I guess I didn't understand high finance. But I did understand the value of reality.

Our tenth-anniversary party was the biggest bash we ever gave, with over 250 guests. I had learned a great deal about entertaining by then; I even received an award as "Hostess of the Year." And as money seemed to be no deterrent, it was an extravagant ball. A dance floor was built over the pool, the orchestra played on an elevated dais in front of the changing rooms, a level platform was built and covered with artificial lawn to hold the tables, the color scheme reflected every shade in my Edith Head original. The guest list read like the Blue Book of the Movie Industry. Ranging in diversity from the rare presence of Norma Shearer and Marty Arrougé to the electric newer arrivals of the colony, Neile and Steve

McQueen. The Jimmy Stewarts, the Dean Martins, Shirley Mac-Laine, the Jerry Walds, the Marty Melchers (Doris Day), the Gene Kellys, the R. J. Wagners, Rock Hudson, the Jack Lemmons, the Lew Wassermans, the Mirisches, Frank Sinatra, Lennie Gershe, Roger Edens, the Peter Lawfords, the Kirk Douglases, the Warren Cowans, the Henry Rogers, the Milton Berles, the Sammy Cahns, and on and on, and the friends who perhaps weren't recognizable "names" to anyone but us. It was a beautiful affair. An ultimate statement. Does whatever goes up inevitably have to come down? Only if we let it!

I made good use of the constructions. The following Monday the Cedars-Sinai Women's Guild Annual Luncheon and Fashion Show was held in the backyard, amid the same decor. That amount of energy and investment might as well see full service.

Ambassador and Mrs. Kennedy asked us to attend Princess Grace of Monaco's International Red Cross Ball. Sammy would be the headliner. Tony couldn't go, Dean couldn't either, but Jeannie and I could. Pat was planning to meet Peter and Frank, who were already in Europe, so the three of us made our reservations to leave Monday, August 7, a few days before the August 12 gala.

On Sunday I was playing with the girls and packing a little, when Mom and Dad came over. I knew immediately they had been fighting, and my stomach tightened, just as Jeanette's did so long ago when they picked her up from the movies during a row. Could I still intervene? I put the children down for their naps, and tried to tiptoe into the fray. Only this time it had something to do with me and Tony. Daddy needed to borrow some money and Mom didn't want him to ask. But the urgency was strong enough to overcome restraint.

Oh boy! The muddle about finances had not completely cleared around our house, so Tony was in no mood to talk about loans, never mind for how short a time. There was no redeeming act that afternoon and no retractable words. I yelled at Tony, "These are my folks! If it was your family, you damn well would help!"

He yelled at me, "Oh, *now* it's okay to spend money! Not if I want something, but if your dad does, that's all right."

"Go to hell."

Mom yelled at Dad, "See what you've done? You're making Jeanette cry."

Dad yelled at Mom, "Stay out of this. I warn you, stay out of it!"
I yelled at Dad, "Why, Daddy? Why now? What happened?"

Dad yelled at all of us, "It just went wrong right now. I can't
help it! Jesus, do you think I like coming here and asking for a
loan?"

Nothing was absolutely resolved. Mom left crying, Dad left upset, Tony was furious, I was hysterical. I can't be sure, but somewhere in my head, I think a vague arrangement was suggested, an
"I'll think about it." Or, "I'll see what I can do; we can work
something out." The whole mucked-up afternoon was such a hideous blur, I can't be positive about anything, except the destruction.

I picked up Jeannie early the next morning, my faculties benumbed by the previous day's explosion. She wasn't in a great
frame of mind either; her path wasn't always smooth. (Whose is?) I
wonder if we should have known the trip to Nice was doomed
from the start. When we were at the airport, Jeannie discovered she
had forgotten her tickets. The representative had to write a new
series and void the others after Jeannie called home for the numbers. Then we met Pat at the New York stop, and *she* was in a bad
humor. At this point we had to shrug our shoulders and bully ourselves out of the dumps. By the time we reached Paris we had
rallied, put our troubles behind us, and set our course for a good
time.

Ambassador Kennedy met us in Nice with his niece-secretary,
who drove us to Cap d'Antibes, situated between Cannes and Nice.
The Hotel du Cap was full, but he had reserved rooms for us at the
nearby quiet Racquet Club. The Kennedy villa was close too. It
really was serene and lovely, with perfect weather, and just what we
needed. We paddled in the sparkling sea, attempted to play some
tennis, dined in the numerous excellent restaurants, and shopped.
We were compatible traveling companions.

One of the lighter moments was our encounter with a bikini
salesman. I always had trouble buying bathing suits; if it fit on the
top, the bottom was too big; if it fit on the bottom, the top was too
small. A friend of Pat's took us to a shop where suits were custom-
made. I chose some fabrics and then came measurement time. I
undressed down to my panties in the restrictive cubicle, and waited
for the fitter. The sales*man* unceremoniously pushed the curtain

aside, exposing me to the store. I screamed and tried to cover up, and he was totally perplexed. Topless was considered commonplace in St. Tropez. Jeannie laughed so hard she cried during my uncomfortable measuring moments.

I had spoken to Tony on the telephone and we patched things up. The girls were adorable and eagerly awaiting their surprise from Mommy.

Jeannie and I gussied up for the gala and left in our hired coach, two Cinderellas on their way to the jet-set ball. In a summer downpour. In a long stream of limousine traffic. The tiny principality of Monaco lies between the Alps and the Mediterranean, just north of Nice. It was usually a short drive, but not that night. Each arriving car at the Monte Carlo resort deposited its fancy cargo at the top of an elongated stairway, in a blaze of lights and a convoy of photographers. A very grand entrance. The Kennedys, Pat and Peter, and their other guests were already assembled and we were led to the table. I looked around in amazement; the entire scene looked like a fairyland. They really were "the Beautiful People" in a magical kingdom.

Prince Rainier and Princess Grace welcomed the convivial gathering, and introduced the show. Sammy was spectacular, sang his heart out, giving the audience his full 1,000 percent. At his finale, I was wildly applauding, and as I glanced about, I had the impression he was not receiving the enthusiastic response he was due. I could feel an anger rising and my eyes welling, so I excused myself and tried to find the powder room. It was on the second floor of the Casino. And there I went completely to pieces. Uncontrollable sobs, deep wretched heaving sobs, racked my body. A sense of inconsolable desolateness engulfed me that I was powerless to control. I was drowning in an ocean of tears, and I couldn't breathe. And I didn't know why. Any reaction, or nonreaction, to Sammy didn't justify this.

Peter found me, he said, two hours later, curled up in a shrunken heap in a big window alcove. I apologized for my unaccountable behavior, and asked him to give my regrets to the table and to tell Jeannie I would send the car back to her as soon as I reached the hotel. Making my exit appear casual and normal was a challenge, because the partying had barely begun. I sat alone with my thoughts in the back seat and in my room. My thoughts about what?

I had no thoughts. Only despair. *Despair about what?* I had no answers.

A fitful night. Dozed some, I guess. When I heard Jeannie stirring next door, I went in to hear about her evening; maybe company and distraction would jar me out of the slump.

The Ambassador telephoned. I was embarrassed. He said he wanted to make sure I was all right and that I was in the hotel because Tony was going to call. How strange. I attempted to thank him and explain last night's sudden departure, but he cut me short, "Leave the line open for Tony." Even stranger.

A ring, and Tony was on the phone. "Is Jeannie there with you? Good." A pause. "Janet, your dad died last night. He committed suicide." That was all I heard; I don't know what happened then. The waves of the ocean relentlessly washed over me and I let myself be swept away. To where? To a foreign land where there was no Daddy. How could I find him to tell him I loved him? To tell him I was sorry? To tell him I would do anything to help? Ah, but I didn't, did I?

How could I stop him if I couldn't find him? How could I tell him everything would be all right, if I couldn't find him? How could he see the children grow if I couldn't find him to stop him? How could he go away from me?

O my dear Lord in Heaven, help me to understand, help me to do what I have to do. Let me be strong for Mom.

Mercifully, the waves stopped. And I focused on Jeannie's concerned face. What a friend she was—is. She never uttered a word about her ruined vacation, never a reproach or a reminder; she was only helpful. From then on, at least for a while, I functioned. Automatic, perfunctory, but a working mechanism. Jeannie and the Ambassador had already booked us on an early flight the next morning; we had missed any chance that day, Sunday. She took all the incoming calls, because by then the news had reached the wire services. She helped me pack. And she was the one who had the task of telling me the tragic story, as much as she knew from Tony.

O God, I do believe You have the power to heal our wounds, the inner and the outer. Mine are not raw any more, but the tenderness lingers. Over twenty years have gone by, and I still find it difficult to dwell on that time.

On August 12, in the late afternoon of that fateful Saturday, a friend of Daddy's had evidently been talking to him at his office. When he couldn't make contact again, he became alarmed and went to the office . . . He panicked, called the police, and eventually Tony. There was an empty bottle of sleeping pills. And there were notes, taken by the authorities for evidence, subsequently released to the media. A scathing, vitriolic letter to my poor mom was reproduced for all to see. Aunt Pope and my Uncle George swore that Mom never saw it; the doctor sedated her, and they had destroyed any publication that ran it and kept the radio and television off. I never saw the papers either, but I heard. Oh yes, *I heard.*

Even now, so many years later, I think, *Dear God, why didn't I get a note, why didn't he leave a message for me?* Did I mean too little, or too much? Or wasn't there time?

So many lights have gone out. It's so hard sometimes to keep a beam shining. Yet I know I must, and should, and can. But I feel so little sometimes.

Mommy, you finally did what you wanted to do, ever since Daddy left. You joined him. Almost to the day thirteen years later. Are you happier now? I keep thinking, hoping, that maybe you found each other again. That maybe you found yourselves too; that maybe the two of you are even near me, and there's no reason to feel so alone sometimes.

God, please tell me they know about their beautiful grandchildren. That they know about my life as it is now with my Bob. That they are peaceful. That they have water fights like they used to in that other life.

In Cap d'Antibes, an unspoken truce sprang up between Jeannie and me and the rest of society. We sort of put up shields and existed behind those barriers, a holding pattern, a respite, until the onslaught would hit us full force in Los Angeles.

The farewells at the Kennedy villa were awkward. Ambassador and Mrs. Kennedy were gracious and conciliatory and sympathetic, but I felt strained. I was aware that the Catholic faith considered suicide a mortal sin, so I knew they had to be troubled by the situation.

Jeannie and I had time to meditate about the connection between my erratic conduct on that hateful night and the catastrophic occurrence over seven thousand miles away. I must have had a flash of clairvoyance; some power or current must have been reaching out across that distance trying to penetrate my consciousness or send a warning. There wasn't any logical, scientific explanation. I guess some things in life never have an answer or conclusion.

The airline personnel were extremely thoughtful and protective. They insured our privacy on the plane, and on the London stop would not allow any press near us. That's the only time I can recall that I deliberately avoided an open discussion with the media. I just wasn't ready to handle them.

The airline company also made arrangements for two limousines to meet us on the field after we landed. Jeannie and I were sneaked off before the craft taxied to the gate and we were met by Tony and Lennie and Warren. Any hint of past grievances was dissolved and Tony just held me and comforted me. He was tender and compassionate.

I was nervous about the encounter with Mom, hoping I could hold on and offer strength. She was, typically, more worried about me than herself and bore up admirably. The house was filled with relatives and friends and we could hide among them. Aunt Pope and my uncles had organized the necessary plans for the next day's services.

To kiss and hug my girls was the best therapy I could have had. Of course they didn't comprehend what the commotion was all about, although at five Kelly could tell it was something momentous. "Grandpa going to Heaven" didn't yet register though. Why should it? They had time for all that, plenty of time. Right then was the time for loving, and opening surprises, of being cuddled and squeezed.

The funeral was held on Tuesday, August 15, 1961. Odd what endures in one's mind about such a day. I went through all the motions, was aware of all the proceedings, but my lasting, clearest memory was the music. All the songs and melodies he loved so much. I lost control with those passages of musical expression.

Oh, Daddy, I think of you every time they play one of your favorites. There is an FM station now that only airs the oldies; you and Mom would like that. When the sound fills the room, you seem close to me, not so far away.

CHAPTER TWENTY

The vagabond Curtises were off again, sailing away to South America, not knowing yet it would be the last journey with this particular cast of characters. Kelly and Jamie, nurse Ginny, indispensable secretary Joe Warren, Tony, and me.

Tony was scheduled to make *Taras Bulba* for United Artists and Harold Hecht in Salta, Argentina. Directed by J. Lee Thompson, it starred Yul Brynner, Tony, Christine Kaufmann, Sam Wanamaker, Guy Rolfe, George Macready, and hundreds of gaucho cossacks. It was, not so surprisingly, about a cossack leader and his insurgent son.

When Bobby Kennedy heard about the trip at a luncheon at the Lawfords', he asked if I would be willing to do some work for the United States Information Services while I was there. "What do I look like, a spy?" I joked, having no idea of the agency's function. From the explanation, however, it seemed I just had to be myself; meet people, talk to them, get to know them and become better known to them, and maybe promote better understanding between our countries. So, I had my project laid out.

We left from New York on the SS *Argentina* on September 15, 1961, old hands at shipboard protocol by now. Tony didn't seem himself though. He was preoccupied, edgy, and restless—not continually, but spasmodically, joining in the activities once in a while. The rest of us had a good voyage. Ginny and I submitted to the indignities heaped on polliwogs (those who cross the equator by sea for the first time), as ordered by the Royal Court of Neptunus Rex. We were smothered in shaving cream, then dunked in cold spaghetti. An extra dose for us because we tried to escape. The girls giggled and shrieked and loved their funny-looking mommy and Ginny.

The liner stopped briefly in Barbados, then at industrial Recife, Brazil. We disembarked at Santos, Brazil. Mobs greeted us. They were so enthusiastic we were nearly pushed into the ocean. We grabbed the little ones with one hand, signed autographs with the other, and tried to dash for safety. People swarmed up the gang-plank, even climbed up the mooring ropes. His Excellency Governor Carvalho Pinto had sent his car to meet us, but when we reached the dock we dived into the first available vehicle. It was the wrong one; it was a rickety, beat-up taxi, but we couldn't get out because of the crush. Fortunately the police escort ringing the governor's auto realized what had happened, immediately took a position around us, and we sped off.

On the way to São Paulo, we had a flat. That poor driver was so embarrassed he was close to tears. I felt sorry for him, but Tony took a look and saw the other tires were in worse shape, so we decided we'd better change conveyances. Just then some press photographers hurtled up in a jeep, and we piled in—Kelly, Jamie, Ginny, Tony, and me. The girls thought this was a great game. I had my reservations. That was only the first of many South American madcap rides.

Tony trained it from São Paulo, Brazil, to Buenos Aires, Argentina—the five of us flew. A beautiful city, modeled after Paris, but with its own charm. Doris and Yul Brynner had already arrived and the wheels were in motion for the P.R. work. We were received by President Arturo Frondizi; there were the tumultuous press conferences; I made appearances for the USIS. These weren't difficult assignments at all. I liked meeting people, and they were absolutely delicious to me. Overall I sensed a subdued demeanor, a residue from the tug-of-war of Perón. The country was in the throes of an austerity program to combat inflation and debt, which accounted for part of its reserved attitude, I'm sure.

Northwest of Buenos Aires, near the borders of Bolivia on the north and Chile on the west, was the town of Salta, our new home for a few weeks. The company had rented a cottage for us, with a majordomo, maid, and guards. The Brynners were next door, and a company carpenter built stairs over the separating wall for easy access.

This should have been a fun adventure, but it really wasn't the best of times, for a lot of reasons, I guess. The film was rough to shoot because of the unfamiliar territory and the many people to be organized. Management of the house proved a formidable task; the language barrier, the routine needed for the children involving meals and laundry and rest, plus again the alien territory. The quarters were small for all of us; we were on top of each other wherever we turned. The old nemesis, my stomach, misbehaved. And the worst, Tony and his driver took Jamie to the park and while playing, throwing her up in the air, one of them dropped her accidently, and she broke her clavicle, a bone in the shoulder. I knew Tony felt responsible, and that was upsetting. Finding a doctor, trying to communicate, understanding the X rays, keeping Jamie still and entertained was very difficult.

There were some good moments. Kelly attended a nursery school, and the children took her in like a long-lost friend. In no time Kelly absorbed some Spanish and her classmates some English. When she left, these budding envoys carefully printed on the blackboard, GOOD BYE DEAR KELLY. A perfect example of constructive reciprocity. We entered into the local social life somewhat. Kelly and I participated in a charity fashion show sponsored by the school. Because of her sling, Jamie could only be in the audience, which didn't thrill my little ham one iota.

I had my usual close call during an afternoon outing on horseback with a few generals. The Argentinian saddle was higher, but similar enough to a western model that I quickly adjusted. Once I was on the trail, the trot accelerated to a gallop. I kept a tight rein, by our standards, and should have been in command, but I couldn't hold the horse. My spirited stallion was gone with the wind. What I didn't understand was that South American horses are broken to have a tough mouth, so my gentle lead couldn't mean a thing to the animal. He thought he was on his own, and he was right. The others did catch up and they were impressed by my daring. Little did they know . . .

Tony had two weeks or so remaining when it was time for the girls and me to leave for a week in Rio de Janeiro for the USIS, and then the good old U.S.A. He was relieved we were going, I could feel it. Nothing to do with his love for the children, it was more a yearning for a release from regimen and freedom from a time clock and the one (me) to whom he was answerable.

I probably should have realized—but I don't think it would have changed anything—that the time was right, and Tony was ripe for the picking.

Rio was the vacation spot of the world, with dazzling white beaches, a bay sparkling like diamonds with the famed Sugar Loaf Mountain jutting toward the blazing sun, and the towering majestic concrete statue Christ the Redeemer atop Corcovado Mountain. It was a playground paradise for young and old. Ginny and the girls were happily based at the Copacabana under the protective wing of owner Jorge Guinle while I toiled. But it was a labor of love. On the whole, the people in the small towns as well as the larger cities were warmly receptive and insatiable in their interest in North America. I spoke at binational centers, in school auditoriums, government houses, on radio, and appeared on television, always to huge numbers. I found in most of the questions a high level of intelligence and obvious knowledge of world affairs.

The central coordinator, Harry Stone, accompanied me on these trips, and was a very capable liaison with each local entourage. Harry would brief me about the next locale, so I could comment on the new skyscrapers and wider streets in Belo Horizonte, or the growth of Anápolis from 45,000 to a population of 180,000 in a few short years. In Goiania, a hotbed of rebellion, I was addressing a standing-room-only hall, and there was a "plant" in the audience, hoping to raise a little hell.

"U.S.A. isn't so great. You have race problems all the time. We saw *Blackboard Jungle!*" he yelled.

Gulp. "Of course we have problems. But I see one big difference between us and some other countries or ideologies. We are not afraid to talk about our sore spots, to show our citizens the mistakes and areas that need correcting. Not only to show, but to document. No one was punished for making that movie. On the contrary, the film was honored for its quality. Only by airing an issue, having open discussions, like we are now, can there be a healthy solution. Meanwhile, you and I can hope to know each other better, and through knowing, understand. For instance, you and I have given to each other already—oh yes we have! I love to samba, and I bet you like to jitterbug—come on up here and let's dance!"

The crowd clapped and sang as my antagonist became an ally. Thank God I hadn't forgotten the samba number from *My Sister Eileen.*

In the new capital, Brasília, we were invited to the Palacio da Alvorado to see President and Mrs. Goulart. When we arrived, however, there was an emergency meeting with the mayors from all of Brazil's major cities. We couldn't wait long enough for our conference with the President, but we felt it was quite an accomplishment to shake hands and chat with the main representatives of the leading cities. We exhausted the supply of two hundred photographs Harry was carrying.

On our way to the American Cultural Center in Cascadura, a working-class suburb on the northern outskirts of Rio, our motor caravan passed a roped-off side street where a lot of people were gathered. Harry explained that the different sections had started practicing for the Mardi Gras. "Oh, I want to watch," I said, and the driver obliged my whim. The other cars didn't know what was going on, but had no choice except to stop and follow suit, the ubiquitous press close at hand. I stood on the outer perimeter, fascinated by the drums and gyrating bodies. Inch by inch I advanced toward the core, until the tempting rhythm was impossible to ignore. I had to join in, just a little. As I was recognized, the participants fell away and urged me into the center. Finally there was one engrossed dancer and me. He only saw feet moving, never looked up. At the pounding finale, he did a knee slide to the other pair of shoes, arms outstretched "ta-da!" fashion, raised his head, and almost fainted. "Jawnet Lee-egg-a!"

What a windfall! That photo manufactured more good will than anyone could have dreamed. I was glad I liked to dance.

Kelly, Jamie, Ginny, and I arrived in New York in time to celebrate Jamie's third birthday, November 22, 1961, with a big party upstairs at Danny's. The New York diaper darlings enjoyed clowns and magic and indoor fun. My invaluable friends Marilyn Reiss (then with Rogers and Cowan, now has her own firm), the Springers, and Fon helped to organize the details on short notice. Jamie's little arm was fine by then and she could romp with abandon.

We listened in horror to details of the devastating Bel Air fire. The John Thomas Dye School, which Kelly attended, was severely damaged. Dolores and Joe Naar, along with too many others, lost their house totally. How awful! When we went home, I drove to the area and was shaken by the destruction. The girls—Jamie was starting nursery school at this point—went to the temporary location of the school, a church on Wilshire Boulevard. (Children are great, they can adjust to anything.)

I accepted an invitation to fly back to New York to introduce Eleanor Roosevelt at Madison Square Garden in the first week of December, first, because I had admired this great woman for many years and was honored to have been asked, and second, because Tony's ship was due in New York soon after and I could be there to greet him and travel on the train with him back to Los Angeles.

The days prior to Tony's arrival were full and fun. Mrs. Roosevelt was even more wonderful in person, her dignity and strength shone like a beacon, and Madison Square Garden rang out with her message of truth and courage.

Word of my South American tour had filtered back to Washington and New York. Vince Canby of the weekly *Variety,* Ambassador Kennedy, and I spent an afternoon discussing how we could implement the program. Vince wrote a lengthy article about the effect of my trip, and I pledged future efforts. When Lucy and Harry Stone came to the States in early 1962, I gave a dinner party to introduce him to the Hollywood community and allow him to make his plea for their cooperation. I know for sure Kirk Douglas listened; he has traveled all over the world on behalf of our country.

Marilyn introduced me to the Peppermint Lounge and Ye Little Club where Chubby Checker's "twist" was in high gear, a new dance craze that had popped up while I was away. People were working off the inches and pounds with unreserved enthusiasm.

Stan Margulies was in New York to meet Tony and together we had amusing placards and banners made for his welcome. Or at least we thought they were amusing. We could have saved ourselves the trouble. A different person came off that liner, someone distant, removed, polite but not in touch. The journey on the train with him was like being in solitary confinement. I should have just flown back once I saw his disposition, but I thought maybe he needed to unwind, to get stateside again. That was not the case, however.

So you see, the year that should have been, wasn't. The emotional tumor had metastasized. Our sun together was setting on the horizon.

CHAPTER TWENTY-ONE

1961 started great, but didn't end well, and 1962 didn't start well.

My Grandma Morrison died on January 1. I will never forget her or what she brought to me.

And on January 13, Ernie Kovacs's gift of genius was abruptly ended in a car crash. Our friend, a world's entertainer, gone. Boom, just like that.

In my shaky world, the girls were my stabilizing influence. And after the year's hiatus, I went back to work, playing Rosie opposite Frank Sinatra in the movie version of that unsettling novel, *The Manchurian Candidate,* which also starred Laurence Harvey, Angela Lansbury, James Gregory, Henry Silva, and John McGiver. The powerful John Frankenheimer directed and United Artists and my old friend Howard Koch produced. I was so proud of Howard's success. (Now Howard Koch, Jr., is a prosperous producer and Papa is still going strong too.)

This was a dynamite film. I had heard that Frank was known for unconventional work habits and I was apprehensive, especially in view of our friendship. I needn't have been. My experience with him revealed his absolute professionalism. He was a caring, giving actor, willing to rehearse indefinitely, taking direction, contributing ideas to the whole. I knew he had tremendous respect for Frankenheimer. Rosie was one of my most difficult roles, not in length, but in content. The character was plunked down in the middle of the script, with no apparent connection to anyone, transmitting nonsequiturs while sending meaningful rays through her eyes. John and Frank were extremely helpful, and I believe I met the challenge.

Philip Strick in 1973 succinctly wrote about *The Manchurian Can-*

didate, "intelligent, funny, superbly written, beautifully played, and brilliantly directed study of the all-embracing fantasy in everyday social, emotional, and political existence."

I was then set to be yet another Rosie, this time a fiery firecracker señorita in *Bye Bye Birdie.* A Dane in a black wig! I saw the Broadway show when I was in New York on a brief location of *The Manchurian Candidate,* and I thoroughly enjoyed the entire presentation. Dick Van Dyke was signed for the movie to re-create his role. And I was very nervous about trying to play Chita Rivera's Rosie. She was so wonderful.

Onna White, whom I met on that trip, was to choreograph, and she agreed to rehearse with me way before the scheduled start. What a talented, dear woman! She, her assistant Tommy, and a longtime friend, musician Freddie Kargar, and I spent lengthy days on a dreary stage. But their efforts didn't allow it to be tedious. Difficult, because she was dealing with someone who wasn't operating on all emotional cylinders.

For in March had finally come Tony's conclusive words, "I think we should get a divorce. I don't want to be married anymore." I don't think those words came easy for Tony. I'm sure they spewed out after months of deliberating torment. But they were said.

The words weren't easy for the recipient either. Strange, even though you know something is coming, and perhaps even understand and agree to a certain extent, when it becomes an actuality, it's still a shock. You struggle to cling to the existing state of affairs, yet knowing that state is bankrupt. You go through the motions of denial, of pseudoassurances: It will pass, it will be resolved. But of course it doesn't pass, it isn't resolved.

So the great love affair was finished, kaput, over. After ten and a half years this Cinderella and her Prince Charming didn't "live happily ever after." If only we could wrap it all up in a neat package and place the blame on one doorstep. But our house of life had too many doors for that simplicity.

Early poverty affected Tony and me differently. One doorstep basket accounted for. I believe he didn't want to be Bernie Schwartz any longer. I remained too much the plebeian Jeanette Helen Morrison, and was a constant reminder of the beginnings he would have liked to forget. Perhaps Christine Kaufmann provided the timely bridge to that other world; she was European, spoke various languages, and she knew only the new Tony Curtis.

Whatever the rationales, failure is hard to absorb. There is agonizing from all parties. There is guilt which brings anger, recriminations. There is defiance, justifying self. There is a black hole of sadness, for all things shared and lost. There is fear, for tomorrow. There is shame, in having to acknowledge defeat.

Warren and Stan (Tony had left Rogers and Cowan in the past few months and engaged Stan) handled the separation announcement. What a heyday the media had with that news.

My first task was to tell the children. But *how?* I knew I had to have help in presenting this in a way that wouldn't scare or scar them. I contacted Dr. Rocco Motto, then head of Reiss-Davis Clinic, and he saw me immediately.

Some of his pearls of wisdom: "The most important aspect is to stress that this is not their fault—the decision has nothing to do with them. There isn't a child alive who at some time hasn't verbalized or thought, 'I wish Mommy or Daddy would go away,' and if death or divorce does take a parent out of the house, they might feel it's because of that wish."

At one point I started to weep and said, "Oh, I know I can't do this in front of the girls."

"Yes you can! If it happens, it is perfectly natural. They shouldn't get the impression this is a joyful occasion, once they are convinced it isn't their doing. You are a person who experiences pain, who has frailties, and they have to know that. Always admit a mistake—'Mommy goofed'—so they understand they are not the only ones who err."

So much responsibility. I didn't want to botch it. I continued to listen.

"Explain to them that it is an adult determination. 'Mommy and Daddy believe we would be happier not living in the same house. Daddy will always love you and will always be your Daddy. Mommy loves you and will always be your Mommy. Nothing has changed that fact. That is absolute.' Janet, never speak of their father in disparaging tones. They could pick that up. In time there will be questions; answer honestly but prudently, and they will make their own judgments."

I lived by his guidance. Every problem, every question, every alteration—when I remarried, when Tony remarried, when Tony had other children, when he divorced—I followed his counsel. If the girls emerged relatively unscathed, it must be credited to Dr. Motto.

More unfinished business. I made a quick trip to New York to confer with some magazine editors. It seemed unfair to have them caught with articles such as "The Blissful Curtis Family." Also, I thought by being so upfront I might defuse the slimy stories that were sure to surface. I was a little late, for some articles had already appeared under pseudonyms; evidently rumors had been circulating for weeks about Tony's love for Christine Kaufmann and our impending split. I did manage to abort a few, and tried to give them instead an equitable account of the separation.

A bitch of a day! I was exhausted and torn apart. Joe Warren, who had come East with me, Marilyn Reiss, a doctor friend, and the Springers took me out of that suite to dinner at Danny's. I managed for a while, had some drinks, but I couldn't last. The walls with all the photos, even the wedding dinner picture was there, moved in on me, and I just wasn't able to cope. They took me to the hotel, waited while I went in to take a sleeping pill and a shower, and my next waking moment was in a hospital room.

The klutz really did it that time. I had slipped, fallen, I don't know. Severe concussion. Severe repercussions. Bedlam in the tabloids. Suppositions ran rampant. Hell, it was a jungle. Only I didn't have Tarzan anymore. The hospital was besieged by press, friends, the curious, the anxious, the studio.

To stop or at least abate the speculations, everyone thought I should be seen in a happy environment as soon as possible. So Joe arranged a gala dinner at Sardi's when I was released from the hospital. Arthur Loew, Jr., was in town, and Jorge Guinle from Rio, and they and other pals celebrated my "coming out" party. When Joe and I landed in Los Angeles, a bevy of newsmen wanted to know when I was going to marry Jorge, or Arthur, or both.

You plug one hole, and the water leaks somewhere else.

Bye Bye Birdie was in full rehearsal by then, with Maureen Stapleton, Paul Lynde, Ann-Margret, Bobby Rydell, Jesse Pearson, Ed Sullivan, Robert Paige, and those special people, "the gypsies." Fred Kohlman produced, and once again, George Sidney directed.

Columbia had changed since Harry Cohn died in 1958. Miss Burns
had left MGM and had worked with Cohn awhile before his death.
She missed his central force too, that focus toward a goal, whatever
guises he used to achieve it. He was sometimes right, sometimes
wrong, but his singlemindedness had created undiffused motion
pictures.

George had changed as well. I couldn't *exactly* define the difference. It might be accredited to the transference of his Svengali
attitude from me to the new and young Ann-Margret. He saw,
perhaps, an opportunity to mold another budding career. I was
"old hat" after the numerous pictures and tests we had made together. His dismissing behavior wreaked havoc with my already
precarious stability. Worse, it caused a rift in my relationship with
Miss Burns that took years to mend, because I wrongly assumed he
reflected both of their sentiments. Another pillar toppled.

But in its place other support structures grew. Dick and his wife
Margie, Onna, Tommy, Freddie, Paul, Maureen, and I developed a
bond, a union, that helped cushion my rocky road.

A bruise heals. If you touch it, there will be flashes of pain, but
gradually the discoloration and sensitivity fade. I could look at
Tony and me with increased objectivity. I thought of opera singers
performing a dramatic duet in perfect harmony, blending voices
and passions and destinies. Progressively our duet had become two
solos, straying to pursue individual melodies. And there was no
way the conductor could lead us back to the written score.

The settlement was not a factor at that time. We split our assets,
Tony paid support for the children, and I received token alimony, a
dollar a month or a year, something like that. There were no restrictions on visiting rights; Tony had carte blanche. Actually I
hoped he would see the girls more often than he did. I believe he
was still harboring the anti-responsibility, anti-routine, anti-regular-
ity feelings.

The friends were steadfast, especially directly following the separation. Eventually some settled in a specific camp, Tony having
"custody" of certain friends, I of others. Generally, the close chums
maintained a relationship with both, which was as it should have
been. Jackie Gershwin was my required witness in court—God I
hated that experience—and concurrently Tony was staying at their
house for a few days.

Lennie Gershe was my companion until he went to England, and before he left for the summer in the East, Arthur Loew escorted me to some gatherings and functions. He had married Tyrone Power's widow, Debbie, but was by then divorced and free. I guess people surmised we were going to rekindle that old flame. But it was not to be.

I V

Janet Leigh Brandt

(Only I Can Be Myself)

CHAPTER TWENTY-TWO

Jeannie Martin and Mort Viner decided to play matchmakers. They dragged me out of the house one Sunday for a tennis game at a pal's house. We drove up Benedict Canyon, turned on Hutton Drive and then onto a dirt road called Deep Canyon. Electric gates swung open to reveal a rural, peaceful setting, with a small pool house, an Olympic-size swimming pool, and an unmanicured landscape leading up to a hillside tennis court. A tall, sturdy, dark-haired, virile-looking, handsome man came to greet us. I remembered seeing him before, at Jeannie's.

"Hi! I'm Bob Brandt." Those casual words, that simple afternoon were the beginning of a lasting partnership.

He rode me home on his motorcycle, planning to take Kelly and Jamie for a spin. In the flurry of excitement, Tony arrived to see the girls, not thrilled to find this attractive stranger. Bob sensed the tension and excused himself, promising another time to Kelly and Jamie.

He called the next day, and we had a quiet dinner in a remote restaurant, hoping not to attract attention. Each successive evening revealed facts of his life and added his good qualities and dimensions to my growing list. He was my age, almost to the day (moon children, July 6 and 7, I read later, are compatible). He had been raised in Burlingame, on the San Francisco peninsula. He had enlisted in the Marines at seventeen and worked his way through college after the war. He was a stockbroker, previously married, single for about two years, no children. He liked to snow-ski, water-ski, surf, play tennis, and had played football in school.

He was funny, well mannered, very intelligent, warm, sexy, strong, practical, realistic, steady, private, perceiving, and disarmingly naïve, in regard to my profession especially. Gradually he began to embody everything wonderful for me.

Kelly and Jamie had their ride on the big Triumph bike. Squeals! They enjoyed going to "the country" in Deep Canyon. Bob had bought a four-acre estate, retained an acre and a half with the pool house, pool, and court, and sold the two and a half acres and main residence to a family with four girls, two of them close to Kelly's and Jamie's ages. Another household down the street kept a mule across the road. So the children had built-in playmates and playground.

On Kelly's sixth birthday, June 17, I took ten children, with nurses, to Disneyland for a weekend. Bob joined the troops. Jamie spotted a free ride, raised her arms, commanding, "Up! Up!" He carried that smart little devil on his shoulders for two days. ("What I did for love!" was his favorite tease to Jamie for years.)

I had rented a house at the beach for July and August, thinking it would be good for the girls to have a change of scenery. I drove out every day after work to be with them until their bedtime, and then I drove back to spend the evening with Bob. We had some friends in common, and came to share the rest.

At almost thirty-five years of age, you would think I might have overcome my fear of rejection. But that fear was still lurking in the shadows. I wanted Bob's comrades to like me and accept our developing alliance. I only knew (know) one way to approach new acquaintances—plunge in, exposed and vulnerable, ready to embrace them immediately. True, sometimes I am disappointed and hurt as a result of trusting too quickly, but often a lasting connection is made, and for me those make up for the disillusions. Luckily, this time there was a happy outcome. Bob's closest friends—Glenn and Bill Cooper and their five children; Donald Bren; Jack Davis—and others returned my overtures of friendship.

Bob exercised more caution toward potential acquaintances. He was always cordial and pleasant, but slower in expectation. Once credence was earned, however, his loyalty was everlasting. There is no right or wrong in something this intangible. The two of us now, I think, have absorbed some of each philosophy. The end result, however reached, was life relationships from both circles.

Bob was not fond of being in the limelight. Our initial public appearance almost frightened him away. Marge and Dick Van

Dyke, Mort Viner and his date, Bob and I attended the premiere of *Anatomy of a Murder*. I stepped out of the limo first. There were shouts, "There's Janet! Who is she with?" and a horde of cameras and people came running toward the car. Bob was just about to get out when he saw this mass of equipment and blinding lights attacking, and backed into the car. Mort wasn't about to let him escape notice, and gave him a shove in the rear. Bob was propelled into the den of lions. His good looks made everyone think he was an actor, but they were finally convinced he was a businessman.

He much preferred outdoor activities, things I always imagined would be fun but had never had an opportunity to do. Kelly, Jamie, Bob, and I joined all the Coopers on a weekend to start at Lake Mead and shoot the Colorado rapids. That was an adventure. Gary (Bill's nickname) had a specially built river boat. As a matter of fact, he had a specially built anything that had to do with motors—boats, motorcycles, cars, jeeps, airplanes. This was a whole new world for the girls and me, and we ate it up. Scared, for sure, we watched in awe as these daredevils did everything—water-skied, floated the rapids in tubes. Bob was caught in a whirlpool and nearly drowned.

For my birthday Bob gave me a small motorcycle. I didn't do too badly, until months later I ran over my own foot while "kicking" it, and he decided it would be better if I rode tandem with him. At one point, he bought a bike with a sidecar. Jamie sat in my lap in the sidecar and Kelly would ride behind Bob. We would go visiting on a Sunday. "Here come the crazy Brandts!" our friends would say when they heard the roar of the bike engine.

The thrills and spills of motorcycles between Bob and Steve McQueen brought us in frequent contact with Steve's wife, Neile, and their children, Terri and Chad. I really liked that family. Neile was a talented dancer who helped her husband before he hit it big, and whom I grew to love also because of her work in SHARE. Steve was a real man's man, with a rough uncut-diamond exterior, a cuddly puppy-dog inside, and the sexiest, most penetrating pair of eyes. An irreplaceable friend.

I had a cast party at the beach near the completion of *Bye Bye Birdie*. The evening was in full swing, when the date suddenly hit me. August 12. *August 12!* My God in Heaven, what had I done? One year ago my daddy died. AND I WAS ENTERTAINING!

I fled to the sand and water, far away from the festivity, hysterical with guilt and self-loathing. How could I have been so callous? So selfish? How could I have been so immersed in my own life that I neglected to set aside this day? I had betrayed all I held dear.

Bob found me in a soggy heap. Not surprisingly, he was confused. But he recognized the intensity of my distress and just held me and comforted me until the ravaging sobs subsided. Then he compassionately tried to soothe my troubled feelings. I had told him about Daddy, just not the date. And he had met Mom before she went to live with Grandpa Westergaard. So he was aware of the family tragedy that plagued me. He did his best to treat that still tender wound.

The movie was finally finished. As much as I enjoyed exercising my craft, as much as I treasured the people this film had introduced to my life, it had been a trying experience. Maybe it had to do with my personal transitions, maybe it came from a completely external source, or maybe it was both, I didn't know. I was just glad it was over.

Bob and I, Don Bren and Mardi (who became Mrs. Bren in a year) left in Don's single-engined plane for a week in Aspen. It was glorious. No makeup, jeans, old shirts, wandering in the mountains, hiking around the clear streams, and loving each other.

We were two adults, intoxicated on the nectar of sensuality, yet knowledgeable that love was a potpourri of many ingredients. Jeannie joked that she and Mort knew we would hit it off because our respective professions required very early rising, eliminating a problem of one wanting late nights and one not. Silly reasoning? Not necessarily. That could easily become a bone of contention. We were both neat and organized. Not important? Don't be too sure. One tidy person and one slob could eventually produce a disagreement. Any of the everyday mundane duties of living under the same roof could be a disturbing factor. Better to address the perceptible idiosyncrasies at the onset because new ones inevitably would continue to surface.

Finances—attitude toward finances—may just be a leading cause of divorce. It certainly hadn't been a healthy subject in *my* past marriages. Bob and I were inclined toward conservatism. I had deviated somewhat, uncomfortably. Bob coined a phrase that has become a way of life for us—*comfort zone.* But of course. Live within your comfort zone. Not according to anyone else's standards, but yours, what *you* can handle. It applied in all areas.

We had been together every day since June 1. But now the picture was done, the lease at the beach was nearly over, school preparations were at hand, and I told Bob that it was time to return to normal on Summit Drive and that I would be staying there once I moved the girls back to town. We were painting a wooden bench for the tennis court. It was dusk, a warm evening.

Bob said, "I don't want you to be anywhere but with me. Why don't we get married?"

And, as if it were the most natural question in the world, I gave the most natural answer in the world. "Okay!"

The interrogation came later. Was I losing my senses? Did I dare rush into another involvement after only six months? Was the chasm between our environments too wide to bridge? The most important query, what effect would it have on Kelly and Jamie?

An urgent appointment with Dr. Motto. "The decision has to be yours," he said, "what is right for your life, your happiness. Don't put that on the children. Too often parents don't do something 'for the sake of the children,' and then lay that burden on those little shoulders."

My God, it fit, I thought. My mom and dad should have divorced long ago. They might both still be alive (for in reality, Mom had already given up). I knew there had been provocation, and in my mind I imagined the conversation. "We have to think of Jeanette." The times, the economics, the lack of an adviser worked against them. And subsequently, against me.

"And if you are comfortable," the doctor said, "they will be comfortable."

The comfort zone!

"And if this should be your resolve, understand it is reassuring for them to have a father figure in the house. I said 'figure.' You should not, at any time, ask the girls to call your husband Daddy. Daddy is 'Daddy,' or the continuity is disrupted. On the other hand, your husband would become head of the house, and his leadership must be respected. If he is what you have said, he will provide a stability, a basis of dependability, structure, and values. He will merit their love."*

I believed, with all the faith I could call upon, that this was a right move. I knew I loved Bob, was fulfilled in all ways, and I didn't want to be anywhere but with him. We weren't youngsters; why should we wait and waste time just to satisfy conventionality? Why shouldn't we get on with our lives? I didn't care what "they" said, and I knew "they" would: "Rebound . . . Can't last . . ." all that trash. What if we did come from two diverse cosmos? Weren't we mature enough to blend our interests, especially with my 1, 2, 3 priority doctrine? We were aware from our previous attempts that there was no perfect man, no perfect woman, no perfect existence, that compromise was a key to survival. We had entered into marriage before, presumably for life. Wiser now, we could begin our union tackling one day at a time, making every day workable, keeping it in proper perspective, building our years with each successful day.

With luck, we could keep this from becoming a circus. We confided in only a few: Jackie and Jerry; Jeannie and Dean; Mort, Glenn, and Gary; Barbara and Warren; Dr. Lew Morrill; Edie and Lew.

When I was shooting *Bye Bye Birdie,* Blake Edwards had visited the set, and was fascinated by me in the black wig. He was preparing *The Pink Panther* (and a wig ended up serving as the disguise for the lady's escapades) and approached me to do the film. Peter Ustinov was to play the detective (the reasons for the substitute casting of Peter Sellers were not known to me), and also to star were David Niven and R. J. Wagner. The entire production was to be filmed in Europe, over a period of several months. That was not the way to launch a marriage, so I later explained to Blake that a long absence would be detrimental for me personally at that time, and bowed out of the picture.

Next, I had to tell Tony. I didn't want him to read about it, or

---

* Driving the car pool a few years later, I was inconspicuously privy to a gratifying conversation coming from the children in the back seat. "My daddy told me . . . what did your Daddy say?" a child asked.

Kelly and Jamie answered, "We have two daddies."

"Wow! You're lucky."

"Daddy Bob said . . . ." I just smiled to myself and sent up a prayer of thanks.

hear from someone else (a courtesy that was reciprocated when he and Christine were married soon after). Also, because the year was not completed and the final divorce papers not ready, I alerted him that I would be flying to Juarez, Mexico, for a quick decree, which freed him as well. That was an awkward call, obviously. Sad too, but not unbearable. The bruise had healed; new cells had formed.

I left with Joe and our lawyer Marvin Meyers on September 13. Our plan was to strike fast, maybe throw off the preying press. We were in court on the morning of the fourteenth and back in Los Angeles the same night. Naturally that became hot news, and prompted the conjectures of when the next obvious move would occur. "They" didn't know it was set for the following day.

Kelly and Jamie, too young to comprehend in depth, did understand Mommy was happy, Mommy and Bob were going to "get married," and Bob was going to live with us and be our man of the house. They liked the idea; there was nothing subtracted from their world, only something added to it.

A wonderful stroke of accidental timing. Dean was playing an engagement at the Sands in Las Vegas, Nevada. Jeannie was with him, and they gave us our wedding. When we went for the license, the cat was out of the bag, but not in time to muster a full media battalion. Warren assured coverage for everyone from the one authorized photographer.

Jeannie had arranged the details so beautifully, even the nosegays. Their hedged patio in the suite was filled with flowers. Standing candelabras led to a blossoming altar. Not the typical image of a Las Vegas wedding by any means. And in this lovely setting, surrounded by fourteen cherished friends, I became Mrs. Robert Brandt.

Jeannie and Dean hosted a dinner between shows in a private dining room, where other chums appearing in Vegas joined us. The wedding party then proceeded to see Dean's second show. When Bob and I entered, the room burst into applause. Bob was very nervous. We were seated at a long ringside table. Near the end of the performance, Dean wheeled in a huge tiered wedding cake. I stole a glance at my husband, and could see him tucking in his shirt. He had guessed what was coming.

"And ladies and gentlemen, let's welcome the newlyweds, Mr.

and Mrs. Robert Brandt. Come up here, you two." Dean helped me from my chair up onto the stage, and reached back for Bob. What we saw were glasses and bottles tumbling every which way over the table, and horrified expressions from the people they landed on. In his flustered state, Bob had neatly folded the edge of the tablecloth deep into his trousers along with his shirt. The audience, our group, and Dean and I were doubled over. Even Bob, after the paralyzing shock, was in hysterics. I didn't think the band would be able to finish the show. That was the finale anyway. What could top it?

I had married a fellow klutz, and I knew we could make it. How I loved him!

The dawn of my new day did come. I can say that because I am Mrs. Robert Brandt.

And there really was a Hollywood. I can say that because I am also Janet Leigh.

And I always believed there was a Hollywood. I can say that because I am still Jeanette Helen Morrison.

V

Afterword

(1962–1984)

INTERVIEWER: You closed your book with the dawn of a new period. Is that the happy ending for Janet?

JANET: Hold it! I'm alive and kicking and having a ball. So, ending, no. Happy, yes! Bob and I have amplified our "one day at a time" to over twenty-one years and we're still going strong.

INTERVIEWER: Tell me about your marriage. How did you manage to beat the odds and remain together for so long?

JANET: It *ain't* easy. You really have to put effort into any relationship—spouse, children, friend, parent—and even then it doesn't always prove successful. I believe you must establish your order of priorities and abide by it, and accept it—I mean honestly accept it, not just give it lip service. Remember, my inclinations are just that—mine. The 1, 2, 3 theory—1, husband; 2, children; 3, career—is still in effect for me. It's not always a piece of cake, but what is?

When you adhere to your bylaws, there are bound to be missed opportunities in one division or another. If I'd done "that" picture, I might have been a bigger star. If I'd taken "that" position, I might have become—If I'd gone on "that" trip, I might have—

Regretting, second-guessing, is just a waste of time and very non-productive. You make a choice because it is right for you at that time. You acknowledge *your* comfort zone, instate *your* set of values.

Sometimes I feel like a juggler, trying to keep several balls in the air. I attempt to comprehend my husband's business, be a silent partner, a companion, a lover. I am convenient to Kelly's wants, Jamie's wants. My friends know I am there for them. I run a household, Camp Run-a-Brandt, with six animals. I try to keep up with all of my involvements, professional, charitable, athletic. My life is so full I don't know where the hours, the days, the weeks, the months, the years go.

The reward for it all? My husband *talks* to me. My children *talk* to me. My friends *talk* to me. I am needed. I know I made the right choice.

But you can never stop trying.

INTERVIEWER: You mentioned professional involvements. Do you still work?

JANET: Do you know what writing a book entails? I have slaved for over two years. And the amount of specifics that are the publisher's responsibilities—I had no idea. Editing, line editing, copy editing, intricate book designs . . . I'll never be able to walk casually through a bookstore again.

But it is exciting. I can't get over my boldness in experimenting with something so new. I guess we all have a little of the adventurer in us. Why climb that mountain? Because it's there! Same with every challenge.

INTERVIEWER: Yes, well. Actually, I was referring to your acting career.

JANET: Oh. Sure, I continued making pictures after Bob and I were married. Quite a few, as a matter of fact. I've done many movies expressly for television, some really good pieces, some so-so. And numerous guest-star appearances, specials, things like that. My love affair with the performing arts is intact. A scene well done continues to bring great highs.

There has always been a stipulation, however. The job has to harmonize with the family schedule.

Kelly was about twelve, Jamie ten, and we had just returned from eight weeks' location in Florida on *Hello Down There!* Whenever we traveled, the girls' teachers would outline the lessons to be covered during our absence so they didn't lose ground. Usually they returned further along than the class, in addition to having had the educational advantages of the trips themselves, one to Rome, two to Spain, another to South America, and so on. This particular time, the girls came home from their first day back in school, and they weren't happy. It seemed their "best friends" had found new "best friends" while we were gone. So I knew any nomadizing was a thing of the past, unless it took place in the summer months. They had reached the stage and the age where touring was a disruption.

INTERVIEWER: Then theatre for you was out of the question?

JANET: Pretty much so. Certainly not any "six weeks there, then six weeks here" type of engagement. But! Jamie went to Choate–Rosemary Hall in Connecticut her senior year; Kelly was at Skidmore College, in Saratoga Springs, New York; Bob arranged business in the East; and this set of circumstances did open a pathway to Broadway. I accepted the role in Bob Barry's play *Murder Among Friends,* opposite Jack Cassidy. What a thrill. To be a part of the theatre community had long been a hidden desire, another dream come true. And it was all I thought it would be: the anxious first rehearsals, the drab rehearsal halls, the frenetic ceaseless new pages (only now can I truly appreciate the pressure on Bob Barry), the first time seeing the set, the agonizing introduction of an audience and the delight with the instantaneous response, the out-of-town tryouts and the waiting for their reviews, and the unexpected happenings onstage. Then the previews, the opening night in New York, too scared to know your own name, the walk into Sardi's and being completely undone by the warm reception, and the nervous gaiety disguising the inner anguish about the critics. Even the heartaches had a place. I'm glad I didn't miss that experience.

INTERVIEWER: Miss Leigh, Janet, you have weathered—I mean, you have held up—uh, you look quite well.

JANET: Don't be embarrassed about my age, I'm not. Do you mean, "I don't look bad for an old broad?" That was a line from the Barry play.

INTERVIEWER: Well, I guess that is one way to phrase it. To what do you attribute this?

JANET: Thank you, and I don't know for sure. Metabolism helps. I don't gain weight, I struggle to maintain what I have. God blessed me with good bone structure. We are not participants in the drug culture. Alcohol is not a dominant factor in our life, not to say I don't enjoy white wine at night. As I became older, I found I had less tolerance for liquor, and switched to dry white wine for a cocktail.

INTERVIEWER: Do you exercise?

JANET: I don't have a regular exercise schedule at this time. My husband does and we have a lot of gadgets, so I'll get back to a program soon. I play tennis three or four times a week, or I did before I was swallowed up by writing. We spend several weeks skiing in the winter; we have a home in Sun Valley. And we love to fish. We are purists—dry fly, flattened barb, only catch and release.

I guess I am just so active. There are so many options in our life, so many branches have sprung from our roots, so many arms of those branches to embrace. I am content.

INTERVIEWER: "Content" leads me to another subject.

JANET: Is this an inquisition?

INTERVIEWER: Not in the literal definition. Does religion have an influence in your well-being?

JANET: Absolutely! I believe in God. I have implicit faith there is a force emanating through our souls. As I matured, a structure to house my God became less important, a label or denomination was unnecessary, for the Supreme Being is in each of us. On every show someone eventually comes to me and asks what I mutter before a take, am I going over my lines or what? I am just repeating a simple sentence, "Life is the showing forth of the very Self of God." It helps set my head straight. I don't hold with passivity; we must contribute, activate these principles, demonstrate this gift of Energy. And start again when we flounder.

I am aware scientists have many answers to the phenomena of our universe, but there are some areas even analytical brilliance cannot explain. Einstein said, "Genius is God's gift to you. What you do with that genius is your gift to God." Certainly there was a respected physicist, and he related to a God. I need the conception there is a more powerful spirit than just me.

We're talking in dangerous waters here. Every person has their own special private persuasions, and that is how it must be; I can only convey *my* opinions. You know the two taboo subjects to discuss: religion and politics.

INTERVIEWER: I was just going to ask you about politics.

JANET: I knew it! I knew it! What are you trying to do to me?

INTERVIEWER: My intent is to construct a profile of the woman before me. I really can't do that without broaching delicate topics. You did mention a political association in the book.

JANET: Touché. Fair is fair. I continued a visible coalition in the political world for a while. I fulfilled my promise of more trips for the USIS. I was appointed to the National Advisory Council for the Peace Corps, met several times in Washington, D.C., toured campuses. I was a member of the California State Recreation Commission and traveled through the state in its behalf. I campaigned for my chosen candidates. And not many people know I was asked to be an ambassador.

INTERVIEWER: You mean a good-will ambassador?

JANET: No, I mean an ambassador, to Finland. As a courtesy to the one who was assigned to the post, I was cautioned not to speak of it for many years. Jack Valenti, who was in the office with President Johnson when he called, assured me mention is not inappropriate now.

Kelly, Jamie, Bob, and I were in Aspen on a skiing holiday, in March of 1964. We were on the bunny slopes with the girls so they could show off their new skills. Each time I went on the lift, the operator said there was a message for me, and each time I said I'd get it later. On the last run, he handed me a note with shaking hands. "The call came through again. I think you should know, Janet, it is from the President of the United States." I beat a hasty path to the ticket booth, and the lady allowed me in, breaking the mountain's rule of no personal telephone conversations. I dialed the number, one person answered, and the next voice was that of President Johnson.

"Janet, how are you?"

"Fine, sir, thank you."

"What do you value most, Janet, your country or yourself?"

"I never had a reason to sort that out before, Mr. President. I guess—my country of course."

"Good! Because I want you to serve your country by accepting the ambassadorship to Finland."

The manager was knocking on the glass front of the stall motioning me to get out of there, the sweet attendant was attempting to calm him down, the girls were dropping their skis and poles, the car horn was honking, which meant Bob had the car at the entrance, and the President of the United States had just honored one of his citizens.

"Sir, I am overwhelmed by your trust. But truthfully, I know nothing about such a position, I am not qualified."

"Protocol is easily learned. We do that here in briefings, as well as define your mission. The staff at the embassy is well trained and handles the operational requirements. I've been informed of your accomplishments for the USIS, and I am satisfied you have the credentials for the brand of diplomacy I need. Finland is a bridge between East and West, and I feel you could be valuable.

"I understand this is unexpected, you have to contemplate. No rush. Call me in twenty-four hours with your decision, at this number. Say nothing to anyone. And, I'm counting on you."

He hung up. I was jolted back to the realities of Aspen. I apologized to the manager; thanked the woman; grabbed the girls, three pairs of skis, three sets of poles, scattered mittens and caps; and rushed to a waiting Bob who was taking a roasting from the buses and autos he was blocking.

"What were you doing?" he asked, and when I told him he almost went off the road.

That was quite a night. We talked into the wee hours, weighed the pros and cons. No one pressured me about the ultimate verdict; I knew in my heart, from the beginning, the only conclusion. But I knew, too, it was a once-in-a-lifetime milestone, and I wanted to savor this ambrosial morsel for the full twenty-four hours.

It was too soon to put our marriage to this test. The minimum term of office was a year. Bob couldn't leave his business for that period. And he was too strong, too independent, to ever be Mrs. Ambassador's husband. There was the matter of finances as well. A nominal remuneration was offered, and some expenses taken care of, but previously I had been advised that it could be a costly situation. I wasn't convinced it would be a solid move for the children either.

I declined, with no qualms. What I had was a wonderful glow that I had been given this distinctive recognition.

INTERVIEWER: What is your standing now?

JANET: When President Kennedy was assassinated, then Robert Kennedy, Martin Luther King, Jr., each loss was a knife cutting away at any desire of coaction. I don't know, I just sort of lost heart.

And I observed a gradual shifting. My center remained constant, but it seemed a political earthquake had jumbled values, ideals, judgments, priorities. I believe so much in our country, I grieve when I see misuse, or a lack of respect. Maybe I have come to the realization I really don't know everything. I thought I did. We are as informed as laymen can be, we evaluate issues from every angle, we vote, and that is the extent of our participation.

INTERVIEWER: Don't despair, Janet, we're almost finished.

JANET: Thank God!

INTERVIEWER: I have a hunch this subject will not be hard. Your children.

JANET: Why did you wait so long? There is so much to say about my Jamie and my Kelly. I love them with every ounce of my body. I am so proud of them. They are beautiful, inside as well as outside. And I know growing up isn't easy in any generation. I think, perhaps theirs presented more difficulties than mine, so more credit is due. When I was five, I wasn't aware of what a President was. On Jamie's fifth birthday (Kelly was seven and a half), November 22, 1963, they not only knew about President Kennedy, they saw him killed on television. That is learning fast, that is tough. How could I ever assume them to hold the same outlook as I, to place similar significance on thoughts? We came from two different times. Today moves swifter, technology doubles itself incalculably, competition is extraordinary, and they have to deal with it. All I could hope was that I could provide a base, simple fundamental values that would guide their direction, the security of a love and a haven.

I'm sure that being the offspring of two well-known personalities added to their load. This probably didn't become an overt annoyance until they were in adolescence and increased their circle of friends. As toddlers they were fairly insulated. No matter how I tried to keep a normal atmosphere, our environment was not average. I keep saying "I" when obviously I mean "we."

Someone asked me the other day if the girls ever felt rivalry with a "glamorous" mother. Honest to God, that is one worry that never entered my head, but then I'm not them. I don't know. Maybe that is one of the quiet riddles of which I wasn't even aware. Maybe they too have their own "secrets" to cope with. I hope not.

INTERVIEWER: Did you have any advice for them, in their vocation?

JANET: I didn't presume to suggest a profession. That had to be their choice. But work, effort was always stressed.

At fifteen, Jamie gravitated toward show business.

I didn't discourage her being an actress—it's a wonderful occupation—nor did I encourage, because it has to be wanted and motivated. I urged her to study, prepare, major in drama, but give herself the time to be a "kid." Go to dances, be a cheerleader, whatever teenagers did, enjoy! At least until she finished high school; college was a question mark. She accepted that. I think she grasped immediately what I was saying.

They are so different, and each so special. Kelly has a more intellectual approach, with profound emotion. Jamie is more of a hip-shooter, also with deep passion. They are interesting in their modifications. We don't always agree; how could we? But what joy they bring! I glory in our friendship, because friendship has to be earned.

INTERVIEWER: Just one more question. Do you have any comment about the people who were included in the book. Where or how they are today?

JANET: Only this:

Some are more productive than ever, and happy.
Some are more productive than ever, and unhappy.
Some are less productive, and happy.
Some are less productive, and unhappy.
Some are together still.
Some have changed partners.
And some have left us.

INDEX